DATE DUE

Breaking the
Cycle of Poverty

Kumarian Press Library of Management for Development

Selected Titles

Democratizing Development:
The Role of Voluntary Organizations
John Clark

Intermediary NGOs: The Supporting Link
in Grassroots Development
Thomas F. Carroll

Gender Roles in Development Projects:
A Case Book, edited by Catherine
Overholt, Mary B. Anderson, Kathleen
Cloud, and James E. Austin

HRD: International Perspectives on
Development and Learning
edited by Merrick Jones and Pete Mann

Training for Development, 2d Edition
Rolf P. Lynton and Udai Pareek

Opening the Marketplace to Small
Enterprise: Where Magic Ends
and Development Begins
Ton de Wilde and Stijntje Schreurs,
with Arleen Richman

Seeking Solutions: Framework and Cases
for Small Enterprise Development
Programs
Charles K. Mann, Merilee S. Grindle,
and Parker Shipton

Getting to the 21st Century:
Voluntary Action and the Global Agenda
David C. Korten

The Water Sellers: A Cooperative
Venture of the Rural Poor
Geoffrey D. Wood and Richard
Palmer-Jones, with M. A. S. Mandal,
Q. F. Ahmed, and S. C. Dutta

Growing Our Future: Food Security and
the Environment
edited by Katie Smith and Tetsunao
Yamamori

Keepers of the Forest: Land Management
Alternatives in Southeast Asia
edited by Mark Poffenberger

Working Together: Gender Analysis in
Agriculture, Vols. 1 and 2
edited by Hilary Sims Feldstein and
Susan V. Poats

Women's Ventures: Assistance to the
Informal Sector in Latin America
edited by Marguerite Berger
and Mayra Buvinic

Change in an African Village: Kefa Speaks
Else Skjønsberg

Breaking the Cycle of Poverty

The BRAC Strategy

Catherine H. Lovell

KUMARIAN PRESS

Breaking the Cycle of Poverty: The BRAC Strategy

Published 1992 in the United States of America by Kumarian Press, Inc., 630
Oakwood Avenue, Suite 119, West Hartford, Connecticut 06110-1529 USA.

Cover design by Linda Colebrook
Cover photos by BRAC-Shehzad Noorani
Copy edited by Dorothy Brandt
Typeset by Rosanne Pignone
Proofread by Jolene Robinson
Index prepared by Barbara DeGennaro

Printed in the United States of America on recycled acid-free paper by Edwards
Brothers, Inc. Text printed with soy-based ink.

Library of Congress Cataloging-in-Publication Data

Lovell, Catherine H.
    Breaking the cycle of poverty : the BRAC strategy / Catherine H. Lovell.
       p.   cm. — (Kumarian Press library of management for
development)
    Includes bibliographical references and index.
    ISBN 1-56549-005-3 (alk. paper). — ISBN 1-56549-004-5 (pbk. : alk. paper)
    1. Bangladesh Rural Advancement Committee. 2. Rural development—
Bangladesh. I. Title. II. Series.
HN690.6.Z9C6374   1992
307.1'412'095492—dc20   92-5270

96   95   94   93   92   5   4   3   2   1
First printing, 1992

Contents

Figures and Tables

Figures

Tables

Preface

IN SPITE OF a global commitment to alleviating poverty we find few successes on a large scale. Rather than curse the darkness I decided to light a candle—to bring to light the work of one successful nongovernmental organization (NGO) now working with half a million of the poorest people in the villages of Bangladesh. It is my hope that this book will not only inspire other indigenous NGOs in other developing countries, but that it will also inspire other writers to share their insights about other success stories.

From 1984 to 1986, I had the extraordinary privilege of working in a consulting capacity with the Bangladesh Rural Advancement Committee (BRAC). At that time I was on leave from my work as a professor in the Graduate School of Management, University of California, Riverside. Before starting to teach I had had a long history of management work with domestic NGOs in the United States. During two years in Bangladesh I was asked to do many jobs for BRAC, among them to evaluate training activities and to work with a BRAC team to design and execute a management training program; to assist in proposal writing for the Child Survival Program (CSP), and, since assistance to the government in managing its Extended Program on Immunization (EPI) was a large component of the CSP, to work with the training for that program. During those two years I learned much about BRAC from the inside.

After working in development in Indonesia for several years, primarily evaluating development projects, I had a chance to return to Bangladesh and spend another month at BRAC in the fall of 1990. BRAC continued to stand out as a success story, whether measured by results in movement of the poorest villagers out of the direst poverty, by the breadth of program coverage, by the continuously growing scale in numbers of people reached and in movement toward sustainability, by the ability to generate financial support, by an extraordinary dynamism, or by an effective management system. This book is an effort to document and share the successes of BRAC and is one person's analysis of why BRAC has become the success that it is.

The book may raise many questions. Interested readers who want to know more about BRAC or any of its programs may wish to communicate directly with Fazle H. Abed, Executive Director, BRAC, 66 Mohakhali Commercial Area, Dhaka, 12, Bangladesh.

Those who contributed to this book in the most important way are the colleagues with whom I worked at BRAC—from the executive director, to the other managers at headquarters and in the field, to the newest program organizer in the village. It is their work and their spirit observed at first hand that grounds this book.

The help of BRAC staff members in providing reports, research papers, and records; supplying every request for data; and spending hours in explanations was indispensable and I am profoundly grateful. I must, however, accept responsibility for any errors or ommissions.

The research underlying parts of Chapters 4 and 5 was supported by Development Alternatives, Inc., under the Growth and Equity through Micro Enterprise Investment and Institutions (GEMINI) project of the U.S. Agency for International Development (USAID).

A part of Chapter 3, the section on BRAC's health programs, may be found in expanded form in a forthcoming book edited by Jon Rohde, *Scaling Up in Health*, to be published by Oxford University Press.

I want to thank those who helped with editing and advice: Colette Chabbott, (who knows BRAC through her work with USAID in Bangladesh), for reading and commenting on an early draft; Susan Davis, previously with the Ford Foundation in Bangladesh (now with Women's World Banking), for general encouragement, help with information, and review of the final draft; and Coralie Bryant of the World Bank for her incisive editing and helpful suggestions for refocusing parts of the book. I want to give special thanks to Ted Thomas of the Institute of Public Administration, my husband and colleague, who has read and wisely critiqued many of the drafts and without whose help and support I could not have met the publication deadlines.

Introduction

THIS BOOK IS about one organization's success story, success at breaking the cycle of rural poverty on a large scale. BRAC (the Bangladesh Rural Advancement Committee) is a private, nongovernmental, rural development organization founded, managed, and staffed by Bangladeshis. Descriptions and analyses of BRAC's history, strategies, programs, management systems, and resource bases are presented in this book in the hope that they will provide some useful lessons for other NGOs, for donors, for consultants, and for students of development.

BRAC is probably the world's largest indigenous nongovernmental development organization (NGO), and among practitioners of development it is one of the best known and most admired. BRAC's pioneering leadership in advancing new ideas and approaches, its entrepreneurial spirit, the significant role it plays in national development, its management strengths, and the respect it has gained from government, international donors, and other NGOs have made BRAC a pacesetter in development. It is known worldwide among health professionals for its path-breaking, nationwide program to teach oral rehydration for diarrhea to 13 million women in the 68,000 villages of Bangladesh and for its experimentation in primary health care. It is known worldwide among education professionals for its innovative and successful approach to primary education for the poorest rural children, particularly girls. It is also known worldwide among development management specialists as a prototype of the "learning organization" and as an organization that has learned to scale up rapidly and effectively.

Not as well known is that BRAC also operates one of the world's largest nongovernmental financial intermediation programs with the rural poor. BRAC's savings and credit activities, including a self-supporting banking institution, are essential components of an overall rural development program. But these financial intermediation activities in practice build on BRAC's basic institutional intermediation programs, which organize the poorest villagers, help them to become conscientized, and provide training in organization and leadership as well as economic skills. Equally important, institutional intermediation also includes economic subsector interventions and government facilitation programs through which BRAC over two decades has changed the very nature of several economic subsectors and has improved the provision of essential government services to rural villages.

1

By mid-1991, BRAC was staffed by 4,700 regular full-time employees, plus more than 6,000 part-time teachers, and had an annual budget of $20 million. The target of its work since 1977 has been the poorest of the poor who live in rural villages. By the end of 1990, working in nearly 4,000 villages, BRAC had organized over 550,000 poor men and women into more than 7,000 village organizations. The members, 65 percent women, have mobilized approximately $3 million in savings, and in 1990 they received more than $12 million in loans from BRAC's credit programs to finance individual and collective income-generating activities. BRAC is now growing at the rate of 2,000 new village organizations and 100,000 new members each year and has evolved a strategy that graduates these members to sustainable self-reliance. BRAC's strategic plan projects a 30 percent increase in program coverage each year for the next ten years.

Awards to BRAC and International Service

BRAC's work has been recognized as having an important, positive impact. BRAC received the 1990–91 Rotary International Award for Community Development; in 1990, F. H. Abed, BRAC's founder and executive director, received the Brown University Alan Shawn Feinstein World Hunger Award; UNESCO gave BRAC its NOMA Prize for Adult Education in 1986; the Giraffe Project awarded BRAC its Commendation in 1986; the Asafuddowla Memorial Award for Community Development was given to BRAC in 1985; and in 1980 Abed received the Ramon Magsaysay Award for Community Leadership (established in memory of a president of the Philippines as the Asian equivalent of the Nobel Prize).

BRAC is a member of the World Bank Global NGO Committee. Abed is a member of the board of El-Taller Foundation, an international NGO network for development and capacity building based at Rheus, Spain, and is also a member of the International Task Force on Health Research for Development, Geneva, Switzerland. BRAC is a member of Approtech-Asia, Manila, and Salehuddin Ahmed, BRAC's director of programs, is vice president. Ahmed is also a board member of South Asia Partnership, Bangladesh, and an executive committee member of the SAP International Network, which includes not only Bangladesh but also Canada, Sri Lanka, Pakistan, India, and Nepal. Mr. Ahmed is also an advisory board member of the Sri Lanka-Canada Development Fund, Colombo, and a member of the International Center for Diarrhoeal Disease Research, Bangladesh (ICDDR,B) Program Coordination Committee. BRAC's head of the Research and Evaluation Division, Mushtaq

Chowdury, is a member of the British Society for Population Studies, an honorary member of the Centre for Applied Oncological and Biological Research, St. Etienne, France, and a member of the Social Science Research Advisory Council, ICDDR,B, Dhaka. Kaniz Fatema, program coordinator of the Non-Formal Primary Education Program serves as a consultant to UNICEF in New York.

Focus of This Book

I have written this book to share my learning and experience of BRAC with others in the development field. It is based on several sets of data. The first is my personal observations of the workings of BRAC over a period of two and a half years, along with extensive interviews with BRAC headquarters and field staff, villagers, government officials, donors, and leaders of other NGOs. Equally important are the program data gathered by field staff and submitted in weekly, monthly, and annual reports. Additional data came from BRAC Research and Evaluation Division research studies, and Monitoring Department, Personnel Department, and Accounting Department reports.

The book is divided into three parts. Part I, which includes the first five chapters, is labeled "What BRAC Is and What It Does." The first chapter describes the Bangladesh context within which BRAC works, giving special attention to the unique characteristics that both enable and constrain NGO activities in Bangladesh. Chapter 2 provides a brief history of BRAC, outlines its guiding principles, and explains how BRAC arrived at its targeting strategy rather than taking a communitywide approach to rural development. Chapter 3 provides an overview of what BRAC does and how it is organized. It describes the four main programs: (1) the core Rural Development Program, which organizes target villagers, facilitates income-generating projects, provides credit, intervenes in economic subsectors to improve performance, and works with government organizations to link them to village needs; (2) the Rural Credit Project, the new self-sustaining BRAC banking operation; (3) health programs; and (4) primary education. Chapter 3 also describes briefly BRAC'S emergency programs and its various commercial enterprises. Chapter 4 gives attention to the history of BRAC's financial intermediation—credit and savings—activities and explains how these activities evolved to their present state. Chapter 5 describes in some detail the economic subsector interventions and government intermediation efforts that BRAC has found to be essential to enable villagers to move beyond bare subsistence activities.

Part II, "How BRAC Does What It Does," includes Chapters 6, 7, and 8.

Chapter 6 focuses on the management of BRAC and analyzes the management structures and methods that have enabled BRAC to become the large, professional, and effective organization it is today. Chapter 7 describes the management and program support systems that are so essential to BRAC's operating method and efficiency. Chapter 8 documents BRAC's financial sources and donor relationships.

Part III is called "The Future." It includes only Chapter 9, which examines the results of BRAC's programs and summarizes the characteristics that distinguish BRAC from most other development organizations. The chapter also gives a preview of BRAC's program strategies for the 1990s, and discusses issues of sustainability.

BRAC is large, complex, and multifaceted, and because it is continually evolving—learning, adapting, changing, growing—it is difficult at any one moment to capture an accurate picture of the details of all of its activities. Although basic attitudes about development remain the same, specific implementation strategies change frequently. This book presents the status of BRAC's programs and management as they were in the period from the end of 1990 to the middle of 1991.

BRAC, A Learning Organization

A special perspective of this book is an examination of BRAC as a "learning organization." BRAC has been characterized as a learning organization, and its extraordinary success in rural development has been attributed to this basic feature of its operational mode (Korten, 1980). David Korten, the first to apply the term "learning organization," observed that BRAC "learns as it goes" through a responsive, inductive process, and that programs grow out of village experience because BRAC is strongly participative. As a result, he noted, BRAC exhibits an extraordinary fit between beneficiary needs, program outputs, and the competence of the organization. Martha Chen, another close observer of BRAC, in her book describing a half-decade of the development of women's programming in BRAC, provides further rich detail to support Korten's characterization (Chen, 1983).

Although he was writing not about BRAC but about a recently developed general theory of "the learning organization," organizational theorist Peter Senge develops the defining characteristics of a learning organization in terms slightly different from those Korten used. (Senge, 1990). For Senge, "a learning organization is a group of people continually enhancing their capacity to create what they want to create . . . having the desire to bring something into being in the context of the community . . . learning is the capacity for effective action as assessed by a community." For Senge, a learning organization is grounded in five disciplines, defined as bodies of practice based on some underlying theory or understanding of the world that provides a developmental path for acquiring certain skills or competencies. His five attributes necessary to the learning organization are: (1) *building shared vision*—binding people together around a common identity and sense of destiny, the practice of unearthing shared "pictures of the future" that foster genuine commitment; (2) *personal mastery*—the skill of continually clarifying and deepening the personal vision of organizational participants—connecting personal learning with organizational learning; (3) *examining mental models*—the ability to unearth internal pictures of the world, to scrutinize them, and to make them open to the influence of others, changing as necessary the deeply ingrained assumptions, generalizations, or even pictures or images that influence how organizational leaders and staff understand the world and how they take action; (4) *team learning*—the capacity of members of a team to suspend assumptions and enter into a genuine "thinking together" by mastering the practice of dialogue and discussion; and (5) *systems thinking*—the discipline that integrates the others, which makes full patterns clearer and helps organizational leaders to see how to change existing patterns effectively and to understand complex policy and strategy issues.

While the organizational theory literature talks about the importance of the learning organization, almost no examples are provided. Since BRAC has been described by some as one of the few examples of a successful learning organization, one intention of this book is to show how learning organization concepts are operationalized in BRAC—how participants in BRAC, from villagers to top management, base their strategic planning, program planning, implementation strategies, and day-to-day activities on a shared vision arrived at through extensive dialogue grounded in learning from past and current field activities.

Chapters 3, 4, and 5, which describe the evolution of BRAC's programs, illustrate how the learning process approach has affected decisionmaking on program design, implementation, planning, and redesign. These organizational elements operate as mutually reinforcing processes. Chapters 6 and 7, in reviewing staff development and decisionmaking processes, illustrate how the five learning process "disciplines" operate in the minds, hearts, and behavior of BRAC staff and managers.

PART I

What BRAC Is and What It Does

CHAPTER 1

The Context

TO UNDERSTAND BRAC one must understand the context that influences, impels, and enables its work. Population numbers and densities, economic conditions, religious traditions, health status, literacy rates, nutritional habits, land arrangements, political economy, government structures and effectiveness, levels of infrastructural development, numbers of educated unemployed, and other factors are all variables relevant to development and differing from country to country. Development strategies appropriate in one country are not necessarily needed or appropriate in another. Since contextual constraints and possibilities differ widely, particular programs are not necessarily replicable country to country even where needs are similar. Bangladesh is characterized by extensive landlessness, fragmentation of land holdings, vigorous agricultural growth strategies based on the expansion of irrigated area, and the inability of other sectors to absorb significant numbers of underemployed surplus labor in the economy.

The following paragraphs briefly describe the most important contextual variables influencing the work of BRAC and other nongovernmental organizations (NGOs) in Bangladesh. Those variables that have most significantly shaped programs and that provide the environment within which the organizations must work include size, density and growth of the population, percentages and absolute numbers of people who live in rural villages, prevalence of landlessness, extent of hardcore rural poverty, illiteracy, religious preferences, the especially deprived social and economic status of women, the small size of the industrial and business sector, infrastructural deficiencies, resource constraints, strong centralization of government, and dependence on foreign aid.

Demographics and Social and Economic Indicators

Bangladesh is the ninth most populous country in the world, with 112.5 million people in 1989, ranking after China, India, the then Soviet Union,

9

the United States, Indonesia, Brazil, Japan, and Pakistan. Bangladesh is about the size of the state of Wisconsin in the United States or Nicaragua in Central America and ranks among the most densely populated places in the world, with nearly 1,700 people per square mile. Figure 1.1 compares the population density of Bangladesh with that of India, China, Indonesia, and the United States. [1]

Comparisons between Bangladesh and the other most populous developing countries on several other important variables are found in Table 1.1.

As Table 1.1 shows, annual population growth is 2.7, substantially lower than that of two of the other largest countries—Pakistan and Nigeria—but higher than India, Indonesia, and China. Eighty-four percent of the population, or about 80 million people, live in Bangladesh's 68,000 villages, compared with 63 percent for India and less for the other countries shown. Life expectancy at birth is fifty-one years, equal to that of Nigeria, and shorter than that in any of the other comparison countries. The GNP per capita is $170, markedly lower than all the other countries shown in Table 1.1, and lower than all but five other countries in the world. Rural per capita income is much below the national average.

Figure 1.1   Population Density per 1000 Hectares: Bangladesh and Selected Countries

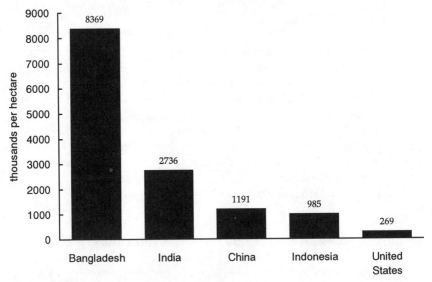

Source: GOB Bureau of Statistics (1989)

Poverty

Estimations of the proportion of the rural population living in absolute poverty range from 60 to 85 percent, and it is certain that at least 27 and possibly 52 percent of the population constitute a hard core of extreme poverty that subsists on a per capita annual income and nutritional intake less than half that of those at the poverty line (Bangladesh Institute of Development Studies, 1990; World Bank, 1987; Osmani, 1990). These percentages mean that at least 67.5 million rural people live in absolute poverty, and of these, 30 to 46 million exist in extreme hard core poverty. The number of people in hard core poverty is larger than the total populations in all but nineteen other countries in the world. Over 60 percent of *all* children below the age of five are moderately or severely malnourished by accepted international standards.

Literacy

Bangladesh ranks 107th among 131 countries in literacy, with a government-measured adult rate of 32 percent, slightly above Pakistan but lower than the rest of the countries in the comparison table. Forty-four percent of primary-age children do not enroll in the government primary schools at all, and of those who do enroll only 20 percent finish the primary grades compared to 49 percent in Pakistan, 80 percent in Indonesia, and 68 percent in China (UNICEF, 1991; Bangladesh Bureau of Educational Information and Statistics, 1987; *UNESCO Statistical Yearbook*, 1989). Nonenrollment and dropout rates for girls are even higher. Eighty-five percent of Bangladeshi women cannot read or write or understand numbers at a functional level (*UNESCO Statistical Yearbook*, 1989). While 84 percent of Bangladesh's population lives in the rural areas, 70 percent of the government's education investment goes to the urban areas, mostly to higher education for an elite few. Bangladesh spends only 2.2 percent of its GNP on education compared with a regional average of 4.4 percent (*UNESCO Statistical Yearbook*, 1989).

Religion

About 80 percent of the population is Muslim, 12 percent Hindu, a few percent Christian, and the rest, primarily hill tribe people, animist. Although Bangladesh is a secular state, the Muslim influence is dominant. BRAC is a secular organization.

Because Hindus are a small minority, there is little evidence of a religious caste system. At least 50 percent of the women, primarily in the

Table 1.1 Selected Social and Economic Indicators for Populous "South" Countries

Indicator	Bangladesh		Indonesia		Nigeria		Pakistan		India		China	
Total population (millions) 1989	112.5		180.8		105		118.8		835.6		1,22.4	
Population growth rate 1980–89	2.7		2.0		3.2		3.7		2.2		1.3	
Percentage rural population	84		70		65		68		73		68	
Population under 16 (millions) 1989	52.5		69.7		52.1		56.5		324.5		327.4	
GNP per capita, US$ 1988	170		440		290		350		340		330	
Percent of population below absolute poverty level 1980–88	urban 86	rural 86	urban 26	rural 44	urban —	rural —	urban 32	rural 29	urban 28	rural 40	urban —	rural 10
Life expectancy at birth 1989	51		61		51		57		59		70	
Under age 5 mortality	184		100		170		162		145		43	
Annual number of under age 5 deaths (thousands) 1989	857		499		864		883		3,780		1,057	
Literacy 1985	male 45	female 19	male 80	female 64	male 55	female 31	male 43	female 18	male 58	female 29	male 80	female 55
Percentage of Grade One enrollment completing primary school	20		80		63		49		—		68	
Secondary school enrollment ratio 1986–88	male 24	female 11	male —	female —	male —	female —	male 26	female 11	male 50	female 27	male 50	female 37

Source: UNICEF, State of the World's Children, 1991

rural middle class of small landholders, are in purdah, meaning that they stay close to their own compounds, visit primarily with female friends, and do not go to the market to purchase food or clothing. Marketing is done by male members of the family. This is true for many urban families as well. Destitute women who now work in food-for-work programs in rural areas are now out of purdah, as are the thousands of young women who staff the urban garment factories. Many urban middle- and upper-class women also now work in government offices, banks, boutiques, business offices, NGO offices, and elsewhere outside the home.

The Muslim and Hindu religions, however, still heavily influence what is acceptable behavior for women. Although NGOs have for a long time employed women in their headquarters offices, BRAC and other NGOs have been gradually enlarging their use of women in field work over the last decade. BRAC's first extensive use of women in the field began in 1979 when large numbers of young women were employed as teachers of oral rehydration therapy to village women. Women were also employed in the field at Jamulpur, a program entirely for women. In the mid-1980s, opportunities for women to work in the field in other programs began to expand rapidly.

Health

After almost two decades of independence, the health status of the Bangladeshi population, especially the most vulnerable groups in the society (pregnant and nursing mothers and children under three), is tragic. Human suffering and wastage continue on an unacceptable scale. Only 30 percent of the population has access to primary health services. The infant mortality rate in rural areas is 180/1,000 live births; almost three out of every five infant deaths occur during the first month of life. As Table 1.1 shows, the under-five mortality rate is 184 per 1,000 compared to 145 for India, 170 for Nigeria, 100 for Indonesia, and 43 for China.

The nutritional status of young children is equally depressing, with 59 percent of children twelve to twenty-four months old being classified as moderately or severely malnourished. An estimated 30,000 children under six years of age become blind each year due to vitamin A deficiency. How many die due to depleted vitamin A stores and resulting reduced ability to fight infection has not been estimated but can be assumed to be significant. Forty-seven percent of pregnant and nursing mothers suffer from iron-deficiency anaemia. Given high levels of infection, high fertility (total fertility rate of 6.5), and short birth intervals, Bangladesh is one of the three countries in the world where women have a shorter life expectancy than men. For every 1,000 live births, six mothers die, again one of the highest maternal mortality rates in the world.

Landlessness and Lack of "Off the Land" Employment

The absolute size of the population crammed into a small space, one-fifth of which is under water normally and one-third during the flood seasons, results in intense competition for resources, especially land. Over half of the rural households, or some 7 million families, are classified as landless (that is, owning less than a quarter of a hectare); 30 percent of the population owns no land at all, not even a small homestead plot. Landlessness can be tragic for a family where jobs are not available off the land to provide income to pay for food.

The main economic activity in Bangladesh is agriculture (46.3 percent of GDP), but the agriculture sector cannot absorb all those needing jobs. Although the green revolution has not spread as spectacularly in Bangladesh as in several other parts of the Third World, technological progress (fertilizers, irrigation, insecticides, and high-yield varieties) has led to robust agricultural growth and created increasing employment opportunities in agriculture during the late 1970s and 1980s. But these opportunities have not kept up with the available labor supply. The average farm size is decreasing—between 1977 and 1987 the average size fell from 3.5 to 2.3 acres (World Bank, 1987). Smaller farms tend to generate more employment but less hired employment, and the small farm owners themselves need to sell part-time labor off the farm to earn enough for their families to subsist.

Improvements in agriculture have been accompanied by low and declining productivity in the nonfarm sectors (Osmani, "Structural Change," 1990). Pressures for nonfarm jobs have resulted in a high degree of work sharing, leading to a precipitous fall in productivity per off-farm worker.

The manufacturing sector, which is concentrated in urban areas, makes up only 9.5 percent of the GDP. Although Bangladesh has a growing garment sector and some very large jute mills, at least half of all manufacturing still takes place in microenterprises, constituting what is usually referred to as the informal sector (World Bank, 1987). These small firms proliferate but seldom grow and prosper, so that little need for wage labor is created. Wage rates in the few rural industries that do exist are lower than the wage rates of unskilled agricultural workers (Osmani, 1990).

Thirty eight percent of the GDP is created in the service sector, transportation, and petty trading. People who are self-employed in services, as in cottage industries, earn a return per unit of family labor that is typically less than the agricultural wage rate (Osmani, "Structural Change," 1990). Both farm and nonfarm wage labor in rural areas of Bangladesh are part-time at best. Most landless families subsist (albeit below the poverty level) by piecing together a combination of seasonal farm labor, cottage industry, services, petty trading, government-donor food-for-work programs, and fishing.

The Especially Deprived Status of Women

Many of the statistics cited above have demonstrated the disadvantaged status of women, but their condition was dramatized further in a recent publication that ranked the relative status of women in ninety-nine nations (Population Crisis Committee, 1988). Of the ninety-nine countries studied, Sweden was ranked first and Bangladesh last on data derived from five areas: health, marriage and children, education, employment, and social equality. The report revealed the following facts regarding the status of women in Bangladesh:

- Although women live longer worldwide than men, the average Bangladeshi woman lives to be forty-nine, two years less than the average man in a culture where from birth males get better care than females.
- One girl in five fails to see her fifth birthday.
- One fifteen-year-old girl out of six will not survive her childbearing years. About one-third of the deaths relate to pregnancy and childbirth. The average Bangladeshi woman bears five to six children but has an average of eleven pregnancies. Contraception is practiced by only one-quarter of Bangladeshi women.
- Two-thirds of school-age girls are not in school, and female university enrollment is less than 2 percent.
- Seven percent of Bangladeshi women work for pay, comprising only 14 percent of the formal labor force.
- In all the nations surveyed, the study found substantially more women than men who were widowed, divorced, or separated. In China there are 182 women in these categories for every 100 men; in Bangladesh the ratio is 927 women to every 100 men.

Resource Constraints and Infrastructural Deficiencies

Bangladesh's basic natural resources are fertile lands for agriculture, numerous fresh- and saltwater bodies for fish production, and cheap and abundant labor. Although the country has some natural gas, it has few other mineral resources. What little economic management is done by the government and private investors is directed toward agricultural improvements. Overall economic growth averaged about 4 percent per year in the 1980s, a respectable accomplishment when compared with low-income countries generally, but far below planned targets and not sufficient to permit progress in tackling the problem of poverty. The economy continues to perform far below its potential (World Bank, 1987). The country also continues to be hit by horrendous natural catastrophes such as floods and cyclones. Flood damage is increasing each year due to the silting of rivers caused by deforestation in Nepal and other neighboring countries.

Social and economic infrastructure in rural areas is still deficient. Although some progress is being made on rural road construction (largely through food-for-work programs), maintenance of roads is poor and deterioration rapid under the floods and usage levels normal for Bangladesh. Electricity and telephones reach only about 15 percent of the villages. Marketing and distribution systems are poorly developed.

Banking services are not within reach of most rural villages. The rural banking system in general is underdeveloped and inefficient in mobilizing financial savings, allocating them to productive uses, and promoting discipline in economic activity (World Bank, 1987). Bank lending to the agricultural and industrial sectors, strongly encouraged by and mostly financed by government in the 1980s, resulted in dangerously low recovery rates. By the mid-1980s, recovery rates had fallen to 10 percent in the industrial sector and to 27 percent in agriculture, indicating mismanagement and corruption and setting a general tone of financial irresponsibility. (These low recovery rates contrast sharply with recovery rates of 98 percent in BRAC and Grameen Bank credit programs for the poor.) Although steps were taken in the later 1980s to improve the situation in government bank lending, recovery rates are still far below acceptable limits, indicating resource misallocation and harsh inequities in the government lending programs (North-South Institute, 1986).

A wide variety of technical services, from veterinarian to managerial, are not available in most Bangladeshi towns and villages. In short, the average rural town and village operates in a vacuum of physical, social, and economic infrastructure.

Government

The government of Bangladesh is strongly centralized, and while big plans are made in Dhaka, the capital city, few or grossly inefficient services are delivered at the periphery. (For details on the condition of health service delivery, for example, see BRAC, *Tale of Two Wings*, 1990; for the condition of education, see World Bank, 1987, and Lovell and Fatema, 1989.)

A major effort at decentralization was begun in 1982 when the country was divided into some 460 *upazilas*. Each *upazila* covers a population of between 200,000 and 300,000 people and is composed of about ten local *unions*, the unit of government closest to the people. *Upazilas* are now run by locally elected chairs and councils and have some autonomy in allocating governmental funds to be spent at local levels. This decentralization represented a rather radical move in the long history of central–local relationships in Bangladesh, which had previously been characterized by carefully centralized control of both leadership and spending allocations (Blair, 1989). However, decentralization has not resulted in improved resource generation for use in rural areas and has so far made little difference in the lives of the rural poor despite the fact that some of the organized rural poor are beginning to participate in *upazila* politics.

While the new decentralized districts have gained some authority to make decisions and spend money, they remain almost totally dependent on the central government as the source of their money; consequently, *upazila* leadership must remain loyal and in general follow orders from the center. Approximately 95 percent of the funds available to most *upazilas* comes in one form or another from the central government. The annual allocation to each *upazila* by the central government amounts to less than $30,000. An additional allocation is made in the form of food aid, which must be distributed to the poorest women or used as food-for-work payments for donor-influenced schemes such as roads, bridges, and culvert projects. Funds from the central government often do not arrive in timely fashion, and the estimated "leakage" between allocation and final outputs results in a loss of about 30 percent of this amount. (This information comes from interviews by the author with central and local government officials and researchers.)

Generation of local government income could provide a basis for at least some local autonomy; however, methods for such local government revenues have not been developed. Although rural land revenue taxes contributed more than half of government revenues in 1900 under the British, the share of land revenue taxes had declined by the 1950s (when Bangladesh was part of Pakistan) to 10–20 percent and by the 1980s to just over 1 percent (Blair, 1989).

The generally low level of domestic resource mobilization by the central government for public purposes has long been recognized as a serious constraint on development in Bangladesh. The ratio of total taxes to

GDP has been consistently less in Bangladesh than in other developing countries (Government of Bangladesh, 1985, p. 57). In recent years, total government revenues have amounted to less than half of overall yearly expenditures, with the balance reflecting the high degree of dependency on foreign aid. All of the annual development budget and a portion of the regular budget are covered by foreign aid.

The government in general is overstaffed, and employees, who are underpaid, are not highly productive. Because of resource constraints, inefficiency, and ineffectiveness, the government is unable to meet basic social needs. The scarcity of resources is exacerbated by a system of bureaucratic state power that is rooted in regulatory functions and inherently obstructive of developmental goals. The political system is dominated by patron-client politics with only a fragile foundation of democratic processes.

In addition to financial constraints, government must deal with geographical and infrastructural problems, difficulties in travel to rural areas, and a preference among its employees for living in the cities because of superior amenities such as schools for their children. These constraints mitigate against effective attention by government officials to rural services and problems.

The Bangladesh government is no different than most other less developed country (LDC) governments in its urban bias, even though public rhetoric may indicate otherwise. (For a discussion of the reasons for and pervasiveness of urban bias in LDCs, see Bryant and White, 1982, ch: 4 and 13.) As a concrete example of the urban bias in Bangladesh, in the period from 1980 to 1985, food aid programs targeted to the rural poor increased from 244,000 to 927,000 metric tons. Yet, according to one report, as much as two-thirds of the food available for public distribution from both foreign assistance and local procurement was allocated to selected urban groups like government employees, the military, police, teachers, employees of large enterprises, and other "priority" groups. Fifty percent of the remainder was directed to rural areas through a rationing system that benefited mostly rural elites and their clients (North-South Institute, 1986, p. 44). Knowledgeable sources also estimated that at least 30 percent of the food grains specifically targeted for the poorer elements of the rural population were in fact captured by government officials and rural elites.

NGOs Working Within This Context

Because even the best-case scenario of projected economic growth will not be sufficient to make serious progress in alleviating poverty in the next several decades, and because of the biases and incapabilities of government to provide basic services to rural villages, most Bangladeshi students of development and almost all foreign donors have decided that special extragovernmental interventions are required to assist the most vulnerable. The help of NGOs is needed to reach the landless and women—to give urgent attention to job creation, education, health, family planning, and nutrition. The importance of the NGO role is recognized by thoughtful Bangladeshi leaders and by foreign donors who urge the GOB to cooperate with NGOs (North-South Institute, 1986; Hossain, 1986; World Bank, 1987). Although government is sometimes less than enthusiastic about and sometimes even obstructive to NGO work, the magnitude of unsolved needs and donor pressures prevent the government in most cases from interfering too heavily in NGO work. Some foreign donors have decided to give a large portion of their total aid to Bangladesh directly to NGOs; about 15 percent of all foreign aid to Bangladesh goes to NGOs.

In practical terms, the context described above means that NGOs have extraordinary challenges and extraordinary opportunities. The resources to finance NGO work are available if their leaders understand how to ask. Unfortunately, all NGOs are not equally effective, and donors must learn through experience which ones merit their continued support.

The challenges are so overwhelming that deciding on a distinctive niche is the key strategic decision for an NGO. The combination of extensive landlessness and lack of off-farm jobs has become a key variable in all decisionmaking by rural development NGOs, causing most of them to include income-generating activities as part of any program.

The network of problems is so interwoven and seemingly indivisible that a single-factor approach may seem inappropriate for all but the smallest, local NGOs in Bangladesh. Even Grameen Bank (not strictly an NGO but a quasi-governmental organization), whose intervention strategy focuses on credit and is considered "single purpose," has found the need to mobilize and educate rural people to change dependency patterns, and has been forced to intervene, even when ill-prepared, into economic sectors and social services (see Grameen Bank, 1986–90). From its beginning, BRAC with its systemic viewpoint, accepted an integrated, multipurpose approach and continues to experiment with how to balance all the needs and integrate responses.

The density of the population in rural Bangladesh and the extent of unemployment and underemployment means that certain types of grassroots organizing strategies are appropriate that would not be appropriate in a country with low-density, scattered villages and low landless rates (for example, in a country like Guinea). In Bangladesh, rural people have time to go to meetings, and large groups can easily be assembled from within a very short radius. The exceptional density also means that a relatively small number of staff members can reach a very large number of villagers. The vast pool of college and university graduates who can't find other work makes it possible for BRAC and other NGOs to easily recruit staff members at the educational levels they require.

The pervasiveness and huge absolute numbers of people in hard-core poverty, and the dearth of basic services, place extraordinary demands on NGOs for programs that can scale up rapidly and effectively.

The extraordinarily deprived position of women in Bangladesh also demands special attention; consequently, most NGOs in Bangladesh place some emphasis on women's programs. Their circumstances and the fact that most have not yet entered the market economy mean that women are especially eager and responsive to development initiatives. Furthermore, according to NGO leaders, including BRAC's, women have not yet been corrupted by negative experiences in the marketplace and are the best savers, the most responsible borrowers, and the most industrious workers.

Physical infrastructural constraints (lack of roads and rural transportation systems; scarcity of telephones, electricity, and living accommodations; and slow travel from cities) makes working in rural areas difficult and means that the NGO has to bear the expense of providing housing, transportation, and other necessities for its field staff. Staff members have to be especially dedicated to be willing to live in remote areas with minimum amenities.

In promoting economic activities, marketing problems are almost always crucial. Because of the dominance of marginal agriculture, combined with landlessness and insufficient jobs, very little buying power has existed in the rural areas. Demands for services and for the products of cottage industries—for example, women's saris—are limited and seasonal, essentially confined to harvest periods, once or twice a year. As a result, marketing strategies for all kinds of economic endeavors are always of major importance.

NGO and Government Programs Directed to the Rural Poor

There are now about 250 continuously operating indigenous NGOs in Bangladesh, with very mixed capabilities. Most of them are very small, working locally in a few villages or urban neighborhoods. Some six or seven are relatively large and work on a broader basis covering many villages. An additional sixty small and large international NGOs work in either urban or rural areas, sometimes in both. Besides NGOs, there is the quasi-governmental Grameen Bank credit program, and there are several government programs, including credit activities, designed specifically for poor villagers. (For further details on membership and credit coverage of the largest government poverty alleviation programs, see Table 4.1 in Chapter 4.)

By the end of 1990, indigenous NGOs, the Grameen Bank, and the governmental programs were doing poverty alleviation work in about 35 percent of the 68,000 villages in the country. The need and scope for expansion remains great. Two quasi-governmental programs, the Grameen Bank and Swarnivar, have stressed credit operations and have been effective at going to scale in that service. BRAC is the largest of the NGOs in number of members, geographical coverage, and amounts of credit issued. It ranks second to Grameen Bank among all the programs in amount of credit issued and total membership.

The government poverty alleviation programs have remained relatively small and ineffective compared with the need. However, the effectiveness of these programs has improved over the last five years, primarily due to their utilization of the unique strengths of selected NGOs in partnership with these government programs. For example, BRAC was responsible for training target group members and extension staff under the government's Second Rural Development Project, administered by the Bangladesh Rural Development Board (BRDB). The Danish Aid Agency (DANIDA) has worked closely with the government's Rural Poor Program in one area of the country. CARE, an international NGO, is responsible, together with the government, for implementing the Food-for-Work Program financed by the U.S. Agency for International Development (USAID). BRAC is now a major player in the government's wheat distribution program to the poorest women in the country (through its income-generating program for destitute women described in Chapter 3).

It is important to point out that the government, in addition to its direct poverty programs, also makes decisions on many policy matters that affect rural development; these include decisions on agricultural policies, fertilizer prices, irrigation subsidies, land use regulations, tax policies, credit and financial institutions, export-import policies, and delivery patterns for social services to rural areas.

The difference between Bangladesh and most other countries in attacking rural problems is that the governmental focus cannot be primarily on agricultural policies, but must recognize and respond to the preponderance of landlessness and the need for off-farm jobs. Bangladesh is almost unique in its configuration of landlessness combined with a paucity of nonagricultural jobs. Few ready-made or previously tried solutions are available.

BRAC, with other indigenous and international NGOs, and with some government agencies, is working to generate and implement new approaches to releasing the poor in Bangladesh from the cycle of poverty in which they have been so entangled. The rest of this book is about that program of generating new solutions and new hope for the poorest of the poor.

CHAPTER 2

Theory of Development and the Targeting Strategy

Brief History of BRAC

BRAC was born in 1972 as a small charitable group helping to reconstruct a small corner of Bangladesh after the terrible upheavals of the country's liberation war, when 10 million refugees started trekking back home. The founder was F. H. Abed, a Bangladeshi executive of a British corporation who gathered around him a small number of equally concerned people who raised money and helped to assemble a small core staff. BRAC initially worked to help resettle refugees in the Sulla area of Sylhet district in northeastern Bangladesh, an area so remote that it could not attract other relief assistance. The small founding core of BRAC attracted a larger group of young, nationalistic youth who were willing to assist with the relief and rehabilitation efforts for those war victims whose homes, livestock, fishing boats, and other means of production had been totally destroyed.

BRAC imported bamboo to build houses, timber to build fishing boats, and twine to weave fishing nets. They also provided tools such as looms, wheels, hammers, saws, and chisels to the craftspeople of the area. They opened and ran medical and community centers.

After a year of relief activities, Abed and his colleagues realized that relief and reconstruction-oriented activities could serve only as stopgap measures, so they began to experiment with more permanent solutions to help the villagers improve their conditions. They launched a program of integrated community development which after a great deal of experience was replaced by an approach targeting only the poorest in the villages.

After several years of learning and many changes in approach, BRAC expanded from northeastern Bangladesh into other parts of the country. (More on BRAC's programming and learning during this period and the years that followed is found in Chapters 3, 4, and 5.)

BRAC's "Theory of Development"

Although adaptation and change have undergirded BRAC's organizational modus operandi, its approach to development, once derived, has maintained certain constants. BRAC has had no written "theory of development" per se, but has always grounded its work in key guiding precepts drawn from its own experience and the experiences of other NGOs worldwide. Extensive conversations with BRAC managers and perusal of the speeches and writings of some of those managers have elicited the following principles and explanations:

- No matter how illiterate or poor a person is, he or she, if given the opportunity, can rise to the occasion and deal with problems.
- A development organization should never become a patron.
- Conscientization is necessary to empowerment.
- Self-reliance is essential.
- Participation and people-centeredness are essential.
- Sustainability is essential.
- There is no one "fix-all" approach.
- Going to scale is essential.
- A market perspective and entrepreneurial spirit are useful.
- The importance of women in development is primary.

BRAC staff members understand that the life and prospects of the rural poor cannot change until villagers are, as conceptualized by Paolo Friere, *conscientized*—that is, until they have learned a methodology and acquired skills through which they can understand their own situations and the reasons why circumstances are as they are. Before they can improve their positions, poor village men and women must acquire a framework that permits them to reject fatalism and enables them instead to analyze their own communities and the structures of economic forces and exploitation that have caused their poverty. Above all, people need to learn how, through their own actions, they control their situations. Only by adopting such a framework and methodology can people become empowered. BRAC's core Rural Development Program organizes the poorest village men and women into action organizations whose purpose is to establish a supportive atmosphere in which real consciousness raising, learning, and economic progress can take place.

A second guiding precept is *self-reliance*. Village poor people, empowered through an understanding of their circumstances and reinforced by the support of others in their groups, can be self-reliant if dependency relationships are not established. Most of what happens to the rural poor in the long run has to depend on their own efforts; for example, savings, even though small, can make investment and credit possible. Learning to look for and maximize every asset available, plus hard work in the right endeavors, can pay off. The young BRAC program organizers (POs), who are the ground-level professional staff working in the villages, believe, however, that achieving self-reliance by villagers does not mean that outside help is not needed. In the initial stages of development, the intervention of POs is needed to help with conscientization, organization, motivation, and (at later stages) technical assistance, training, and credit. Everyone—villagers and staff—have the potential to be creative, but conditions and opportunities have to be established so that creativity can be released.

And, as villagers act to help themselves, outside help may also be needed to prevent retaliatory abuses from those whose patterns of exploitation and dependency have been disturbed, and to assist in identifying and expediting government services and improving infrastructure.

A third guiding principle is *people-centeredness*, or participation. All of the BRAC POs are taught that development must be responsive to the needs of the village poor, not imposed. The leadership defines BRAC as an assisting agency that is only one participant in a community-driven development process. BRAC training of village organization leaders, both male and female, is designed to encourage broadened political participation and to help those leaders gain access to information and to the means by which they can hold officials of their own organizations and those of the government accountable. The BRAC area managers (who manage areas that each comprise 100 organizations of village landless people) and the POs who work under them recognize that BRAC's long-range contribution will be measured in terms of the enhanced capacity of the village people to determine their own futures.

A fourth guiding principle is the need for *sustainability*. BRAC does not want the benefits generated by its village interventions to depend on its continued presence or the availability of donor subsidies. It recognizes that self-reliant village development initiatives are likely to be sustained only as long as they are based on locally supported systems or linked into a supportive national development network backed by effective infrastructural improvements. This means that national systems need to be changed, policies reoriented, and work modes strengthened. BRAC field managers are expected to accept the role of catalysts in helping bring about changes in governmental and private market systems in the areas where they work. The managers in the field engage actively with government agencies to improve rural services, and the head office and regional offices concentrate technical services to overcome constraints and break bottlenecks in relevant economic sectors (more about how BRAC does this is provided in Chapter 5). The BRAC leadership recognizes that where government and the private sector have not or cannot seem to create necessary service institutions, NGOs may need to create new institutions large enough to provide essential local services on a sustained, self-financing basis. The Grameen Bank and BRAC's new bank project are examples of such institutions.

A fifth guiding principle is that there is *no one "fix-all" approach* to rural poverty. The BRAC leadership believes that employment generation—the creation of new off-farm jobs above the bare subsistence level—is key to moving people out of poverty. But it also recognizes that creating jobs that are real and sustainable and can provide more than bare subsistence depends on several factors, including improved skills, availability of technical services, infrastructure development, improvements in economic subsectors, and availability of credit.

A sixth guiding principle of BRAC's work is the concept of *going to scale*, that is, expanding programs as rapidly as possible. Although some of BRAC's methods and strategies may provide models for other development organizations and for government agencies, the BRAC management does not consider the organization's only or even principal job to be one of building and demonstrating development models. Although transfer of experience and systems is considered important, the essential job of BRAC is to reach as many of the rural poor as possible, and as fast as possible, with interventions that can help them change their lives. BRAC's management believes that because it has learned (and continues to learn) how to do rural development, and because it has the structural base and resource capacity to expand rapidly, and because *there is such need*, it has a responsibility and imperative to scale up rapidly. Rapid and very large scaleup may not be appropriate for all NGOs, or for all countries, but in the Bangladesh context of huge population and overriding need, rapid scaleup is essential. Rapid scaleup always entails problems and risks, but the opportunity costs of not scaling up are too great for the rural poor to bear.

A seventh guiding principle is the importance of a *market perspective and an entrepreneurial spirit*. The top management of BRAC has always insisted on a policy of not interfering in normal market operations except to overcome obstacles or to prevent obvious exploitation. Cost recovery is considered essential wherever possible. Credit for villagers has never been subsidized (although attendant training, technical services, and other development activities have been); borrowers pay the full market rates. Village women and men buy the forms on which they apply for loans, their groups pay for minute books and all other supplies, borrowers buy all inputs for economic activities, and so on. On the larger economic schemes (such as deep tubewells), borrowers must pay BRAC's specialists for needed technical services. The market perspective fosters self-reliance and business thinking for both villagers and staff.

The market perspective and entrepreneurial spirit are stressed in BRAC's own internal operations as well. The staff is taught to have a business outlook through a combination of cost centering and cost recovery systems; for example, the training centers are expected to be self-supporting by charging the programs for their services and by making a profit on training supplied to other NGOs, both local and international. They tailor their training programs to meet demand. The computer center, operating three shifts around the clock, sells its services to outside businesses so that it can be self-supporting. In the economic subsector interventions described in Chapter 5, BRAC managers have taken an entrepreneurial approach: in mulberry tree planting, for example, they have thought in millions of trees, not thousands; in deep tubewell installations they have thought in hundreds per year, not tens, and in thousands of shareholders, not hundreds. In poultry operations, they have encouraged villagers to start numerous auxiliary businesses that support and are sustained by the growing poultry sector.

BRAC also operates a number of commercial businesses, all of which have grown out of perceived needs for supporting activities to BRAC programs but which were not available in the existing market. The profits of those businesses now provide about 15 percent of the income of BRAC and are used to support its development activities. The commercial enterprises are described briefly in Chapter 3.

A final guiding principle of BRAC is the *importance of women* in the development process. Like in most other development agencies, BRAC's leadership has learned that women are particularly affected by poverty. And poor women in rural areas have the least power. Traditionally, women in Bangladesh villages have few rights, little choice about the course of their lives, and almost no opportunities to change their situations. Women work nearly twice as many hours each day as men and they are often pregnant or lactating. They have little or no access to people or positions of influence; for the most part they are illiterate; they eat last and eat least. They are often deserted when husbands cannot find income in the villages and move away to pursue work.

From research studies conducted throughout the world, and from their own experience, BRAC's health managers have learned that women are the key to primary health care, nutrition, and family planning. The field managers of the credit programs have found that women are better savers than men and more responsible borrowers. BRAC staff members at all levels have come to believe that social and economic development cannot take place without a changed role for women. BRAC's field workers are instructed never to organize a men's group in a village unless they have first organized a women's group. A guiding rule is that women must have equal or preferential treatment in literacy programs, health programs, education programs, loan opportunities, and income-generating activities.

BRAC's Targeting Strategy—
Focus on the Poorest of the Poor

After its first year of operation in northeastern Bangladesh, BRAC began to evolve from a relief organization to a development organization. For the first four years as a development organization it followed an integrated, communitywide development approach. Experience gained in those four years, however, plus extensive input from researchers, persuaded the leadership to change to a targeting approach, to focus on the poorest in the villages rather than on the village as a whole.

During the initial four years, although BRAC workers organized co-operatives for the poorest in the villages as instruments for economic support, they also organized social services villagewide and talked about building "human infrastructure" villagewide. As Martha Chen, who has written in depth about this period of BRAC's history, explains, "Village Development Committees, representing the interests of all the subgroups in a village, were to be constituted to debate solutions for the village as a whole" (Chen, 1983, p. 8). At that point, according to Chen, BRAC conceived the development process to lie in:

- extending an integrated package of essential services to remote villages;
- providing education and training as needed;
- fostering village-wide cooperation in solving village problems;
- forming credit cooperatives to support the poor. (Chen 1983, p. 8)

During those first years, BRAC asked educated young people from the villages to volunteer to teach literacy classes and to work in health and family planning. BRAC experimented with village community centers, health insurance schemes, and other activities that combined all the subgroups in a village in community activities. (Examples of these experiences are given in the discussion on health in Chapter 3.) Unfortunately, most of the experiments did not work. The richer and poorer villagers felt that they had contributed and benefited unequally. The young elite men and women who were initially volunteering to help provide services sometimes became what Bangladeshis call "touts" (those who align themselves with the government or other elite groups and become corrupt). Because communitywide spirit did not develop, hopes for villagewide cooperation were not realized.

While these learning experiences were taking place in BRAC's village programs, a group of BRAC researchers, using participatory research methods, was studying the viewpoints of poor villagers in a sample of the villages. (BRAC's early participatory research studies were published in a series called *Peasant Perceptions*. The first volume on famine, credit needs, and sanitation, was published by BRAC in 1984. The following analysis of what the researchers found about village structures is taken largely from that first volume.)

These early studies exposed certain essential characteristics of the rural social structure that BRAC leaders had not taken into account in the organization's early work. The studies revealed the cultural complex of attitudes, beliefs, modes of interpersonal relationships, and behavioral norms that play a part in determining the nature of economic transactions in rural areas; and these findings helped to explain BRAC's failures in their early communitywide efforts. The studies identified three features of village social structure that form the dominant themes necessary for understanding the economic and social relations between different sets of villagers: discontinuity, dependency, and disadvantagedness.

Discontinuity was identified when the researchers found that several households in a village tend to form associative groupings. The researchers called these factions. Although the factions are not obvious to a casual observer, or even formally recognized within the community itself, they do play an extremely important role in regulating interhousehold cooperation and alliance. The degree of cooperation and interaction is high among households that are members of the same faction. The faction itself usually has an internal hierarchy in which the positions of dominance are occupied by those members who are the wealthiest, have the greatest influence on local affairs, and have control over a large proportion of the village resources such as land, credit opportunities, local business, external resources, and employment opportunities. Factions usually evolve as a result of the leading members gathering support for themselves by holding out the promise of economic assistance to those who join with them. It is individual wealthier households that lead each faction and have the greatest interest in ensuring its survival. The poorer households, although forming the bulk of the faction members at any given time, tend to associate with a faction only to the extent that they gain some security and protection from it.

The feeling of solidarity or common cause that was found within a faction was in contrast to the lack of solidarity and cooperation that exists between factions—the aspect of the factional groupings the researchers referred to as discontinuity. The discontinuities tended to generate conflict while inhibiting cooperation. The factional structure has the effect of carving up the total number of households in the village into a number of units (typically, not more than four or five in a village). These divisions tend to block out the possibility of larger-scale cooperation in economic affairs and social relations and tend to promote and perpetuate interfactional conflict. The discontinuity inhibits the free flow of reliable information, resulting in suspicion and a lack of confidence in all information and thus hindering the development of economic cooperation among individual households. Conflicts arise chiefly because of the direct rivalry between leading members of different factions who are trying to gain ascendancy and control over locally available resources.

The second major feature of the socioeconomic structure of the village was labeled *dependency*. Dependency characterizes the nature of the relationship that exists between the poorest members of the community and the richer households and is related to the structure of factionalism. The amount of exploitable resources available in a village is limited and distributed very unequally across the range of households. Such resources include tangible assets that are economically productive, chiefly land, as well as intangible assets such as political influence over other villagers or cooperative relations with officials of the local governmental administrative system.

The unequal distribution of resources results in conditions in which the wealthier landowners can have far-reaching influence over the actions of the landless or marginal farmers and can withhold or give economic assistance as they choose. To earn a subsistence income, the poorest households must depend on the landowners for access to resources such as wages for labor or credit for petty trading, or credit for marriage ceremonies. In order to subsist, the landless have to maintain good relations with landowners by contributing services and also by giving political support when required. Through this system of patronage the wealthy household can have an enormous influence over almost every aspect of the poor villager's life. Given the ever-present possibilities for conflict inherent in local factionalism, the poor villager can ill afford to antagonize all the powerful people in his village. He has to seek the security of a powerful backer in order to deal with any difficulty he might confront, whether in the nature of a conflict with another villager or in the nature of an economic or subsistence need. This asymmetrical relationship, or dependency, is a deeply embedded characteristic of village social structure in Bangladesh.

With the above conditions of factionalism and dependency the norm in villages, it was almost inevitable that the system of relationships should turn exploitative. Such exploitation is particularly rampant in a system with a weak judiciary and a weak and often corrupt government structure. The exploitation is carried out in the unequal exchanges identified by the researchers in almost every aspect of the economic sphere—for example, in the very low wages paid for labor and the very high interest rates charged for credit. The exploitative relationship was so institutionalized that those involved were not necessarily conscious of it.

A fundamental result of this state of affairs, where poorer villagers were totally dependent on the richer landholders, was the inability of the poor villagers to improve their condition because they could not accumulate wealth. This condition was identified by the researchers as their third theme, which they called *disadvantagedness*. The disadvantagedness theme suggested that rural poverty is not just a random condition but is a result of the processes described that confer a built-in disadvantage to a particular set of poor households while conferring a corresponding operational advantage to the wealthier households. The processes include not only the ones that control economic activity but also those social and cognitive processes that ascribe value, prestige, credibility, authority, and freedom of choice and association. Thus, the poorer households not only confront their predicament with a very small material resource base at their disposal, but they also must operate under constraints and disadvantages that the wealthy households do not face in anything like the same proportions.

Reassessment of the Communitywide Approach

The above analysis by the researchers helped explain to BRAC leaders why their programs based on a communitywide development approach had been less than effective in the field. In late 1977, as a result of failures in the field and these research findings, each of which had helped inform the other, BRAC leaders began a reassessment of approaches. After much discussion among field workers, researchers, and leaders, both the leaders and the field workers became convinced that they had not addressed the major structural constraints to the elimination of poverty in the villages. As Martha Chen explained:

BRAC's internal analysis and collective field experience had shown:

- that there is a very fundamental relationship between the rural power structure and the distribution of resources;
- that programs designed for the whole community deliver most of their benefits to the richer and tend to by-pass the very poor;
- that programs designed for the poor must address the rural power

structure, which keeps not only power but also resources in the hands of a few; and
• that in order to address the rural power structure, the capacities of and institutions for the poor (and powerless) must be developed. (Chen, 1983, p. 11)

In light of BRAC's reanalysis and new set of basic assumptions about the institutions of poverty and what kinds of development might be needed to bring about changes in these institutions, BRAC's board and management adopted the new targeting strategy. Under the new strategy, development efforts were to be directed to the poorest group in the villages so that they could break out of the dependency relationships. The poorest would be organized into solidarity groups so that mutual help among members of a group, combined with opportunities that BRAC could provide, would gradually break the hierarchical dependency relationships that existed in the village.

Since 1977, when the targeting strategy was adopted, almost all BRAC activities have been provided to and through the village organizations made up entirely of target households. (An exception has been made in some health programs, where activities such as oral rehydration training, immunization, and midwife training serve the community as a whole.) Educational activities, management and skills training, technical services, credit, and intermediation with government agencies are all provided with the participation of or management by the village organizations made up of the poorest of the villagers. BRAC's field workers use the village organization meetings, their special discussion sessions, and joint social and productive activities to foster and strengthen solidarity among the poor to help them break the exploitative, factional relationships that previously existed. (The methods BRAC uses to enter and organize in a village are described in Chapter 3.)

Defining the Target Group

Over the years since 1977, BRAC has struggled with the definition of "poorest" as the criteria for who is eligible to become a member of a BRAC village organization. In the beginning, the definition was rather general: the landless, fishermen, and women. Soon the definition was further refined to

those households who sell their manual labor to others for survival, irrespective of occupation, provided they do not have political patrons among the non-target people, and provided they cannot still exercise status considerations.

The definition was further refined several times and today the target group is defined as

> those households that own less than 0.50 decimals of land, own no implements of production, and in which the principal worker has had to sell at least 100 days of labor over the past year in order to subsist. Additionally, at least 50 percent of each village organization must be comprised of people who own *no* land.

BRAC's targeting strategy has also increasingly given special emphasis to women, recognizing that women face problems by reason of their gender as well as by reason of their poverty. Poor men and women are organized into separate groups. As mentioned previously, a men's group is never organized in a village before a women's group is formed. The separate groups of poor women allow the women to address their own problems as women with limited autonomy and power, as well as to address their own special economic and social problems. The separation of male and female groups is also compatible with the dominant Muslim culture. As the groups in a village mature, and the members have become conscientized and solidarity has grown, program organizers help link the separate male and female groups in joint economic activities and social actions. Examples, which include joint ownership of brick fields, deep tubewells, and other income-earning assets by men's and women's groups, are described in Chapters 4 and 5.

In 1977, when the targeting strategy was adopted, BRAC changed its concept of the role of its field staff from motivators to professional program organizers (POs), and dropped the use of village volunteers (except in certain limited capacities such as members of health committees or parents' committees). The job of the paid POs (now always young university graduates) became that of professional staff, organizing and developing the village groups to the point where they can plan and implement their own social and economic activities. The PO's job is also to provide technical services and credit. The PO is now the entry position in BRAC, and all managers are promoted from among PO ranks.

Targeting BRAC programs to the poorest in the villages, including conscientization, organizing into solidarity and mutual support groups, and providing technical and financial services to widen opportunities, remains BRAC's core approach today.

CHAPTER 3

An Overview of BRAC's Programs

BRAC's DEVELOPMENT EFFORTS are conducted in four main categories: (1) the Rural Development Program (RDP), the largest and central program of BRAC, which organizes the poorest of the poor into men's and women's groups at the village level as instruments for conscientization and empowerment, for income-generating activities facilitated by credit, and for implementation of various social programs; (2) the Rural Credit Project (RCP), BRAC's new self-sustaining bank, to which village groups graduate for banking services after four years under RDP; (3) health programs, which focus on women and children and emphasize preventive health and improving services of the government rural health system; and (4) the Non-Formal Primary Education (NFPE) program, a major primary education program designed for the poorest children who have never attended school. Some parts of the health and primary education programs are integrated with RDP, others run parallel.

To support these four main village programs, BRAC now has large program support systems, some located at headquarters in Dhaka, others located at various field sites throughout the country. By 1991, the support systems consisted of six training and resource centers, a management development program, a large research and evaluation division, a monitoring department, a logistics department, a computer center, accounting and audit departments, a personnel department, a materials development unit, a publications department, and a series of related commercial enterprises.

The headquarters office of BRAC, with its staff of 200, is located in Dhaka, in its own six-story building (plus two floors rented in a building nearby). The remainder of the over 4,000 full-time staff members reside in area field offices (which include living accommodations and are located in village areas), in BRAC's residential training and resource centers located in various parts of the country, or in temporary field camps.

An additional 6,000 primary school teachers live in their own villages near where they work.

This chapter provides an overview of the history and current status of BRAC's four main programs and briefly describes BRAC's commercial enterprises. Chapters 4 and 5 give more detail on the financial and economic activities of two of the programs—the core RDP and the RCP (the new BRAC banking operation). It is hoped that these three chapters will make more relevant the discussion in Chapters 6 and 7 of BRAC's management methods and program support systems. Knowledge of what BRAC does should make more meaningful the analysis of how it manages to do all that it does and why effective management has been identified as the key to BRAC's success.

The Organizational Structure

The basic structure of BRAC remains fairly constant, yet the details of the structure of programs are always experimental, with changes often made after trial in the field. Although program structuring is flexible, some general principles always govern organizing decisions: structure must enable accountability, minimize hierarchy, encourage and enable participation, decentralize decisionmaking, maximize feedback opportunities, and maximize flexibility.

Flat Structure

Figure 3.1, an organogram, shows the overall BRAC structure as it looked at the end of 1990. It must be characterized as a flat structure, since there are very few intermediate levels between top management and field implementation. All program coordinators, the designation used for the head of a major program, and about half of the heads of the program support systems, report directly to the executive director. Four of the program support systems—training, management development, construction, and logistics—report through the director of support systems. Organograms of BRAC's four main programs are provided as those programs are discussed in subsequent sections.

In designing its programs, BRAC follows a *needs-led* approach, which requires in the initial stage that the particular constraints and opportunities in a given situation be identified so that an appropriate response can be tailored. A needs-led approach is different from the *methodology-led* approach, which confines the organization to doing what it already knows how to do efficiently and effectively. Methodology-led ap-

Figure 3.1 Organogram of the BRAC Structure

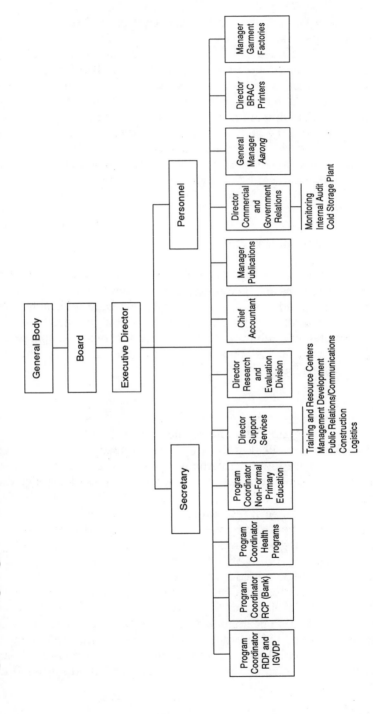

Source: BRAC organizational records, March 1991

proaches are generally thought to produce moderate levels of impact at relatively low cost, whereas needs-led approaches may produce larger impacts but at a higher price, particularly in the initial stages. BRAC follows the needs-led strategy in the design stages of new programs and for alterations of existing programs. New programs test various methods and attempt to find those that prove to be effective and that can be replicated cost effectively. These methods are then scaled up to large programs or integrated with existing programs.

The Rural Development Program (RDP)

The Rural Development Program is the largest of the BRAC programs and is the core of all its work. Figure 3.2 shows how RDP is organized. As the organogram shows, there is only one level, regional managers, between the program coordinator and area offices. RDP is headed by a program coordinator, under whom (as of the end of 1990) were eight regional managers, two of whom had offices at headquarters in Dhaka and the rest in the field. The program coordinator is also assisted by headquarters specialists in five economic subsectors—agriculture, irrigation, fisheries, sericulture, and livestock and poultry—and by secretarial and statistical reporting assistants.

The field activities are organized under regional managers, each of whom oversees ten area offices, each of which is headed by an area office manager. The area offices, which are the field management units, have deliberately been kept small. Each area office covers forty to fifty villages, with 100 village organizations and 6,000 to 7,000 village members. Each area office has three general program organizers (POs), young entry-level university graduates who do the basic village organizing and maintain relations with the groups. Each of these general POs is assisted by three *gram sheboks* (GSs), young villagers with at least a tenth-grade education. The area offices are also sometimes assigned other specialized POs depending on which of BRAC's other programs are being conducted in the area. Most area offices have two or more NFPE POs who oversee the nonformal primary education schools in the villages in their areas. Some of the area offices also have health POs who work with the villagers specifically on health matters, and paralegal women or men to assist the village members in learning about and defending their legal rights. (Later sections in this chapter describe the primary education, health, and paralegal programs.)

The members of the area office staff live together, eat together when they are not in the villages at meal time, have regular meetings, and

Figure 3.2 Organogram of the Rural Development Progam (RDP), November 1990

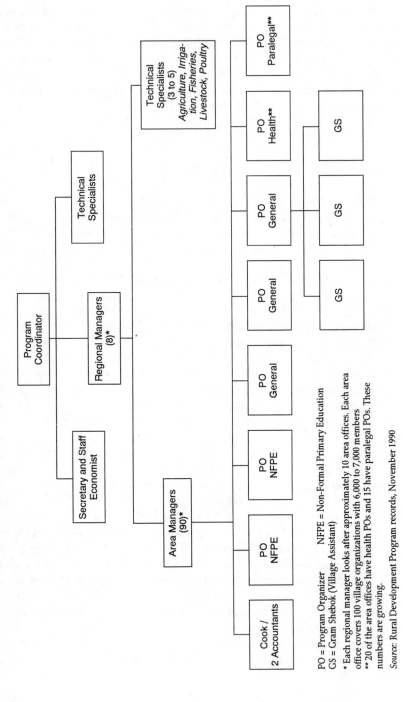

PO = Program Organizer   NFPE = Non-Formal Primary Education
GS = Gram Shebok (Village Assistant)

* Each regional manager looks after approximately 10 area offices. Each area office covers 100 village organizations with 6,000 to 7,000 members
** 20 of the area offices have health POs and 15 have paralegal POs. These numbers are growing.

Source: Rural Development Program records, November 1990

spend many hours in dialogue about village problems and BRAC responses. These area offices are given the freedom to make operational decisions, within a given framework they themselves help to determine, so that every staff member, regardless of his or her seniority, must take part in decisionmaking processes. It is this small field unit that continuously faces new challenges and must adapt to changing circumstances.

The area offices share the services of the regional office specialists in poultry and livestock, fisheries, tubewell management, agriculture, and sericulture. These specialists are available as consultants to the area offices and individual borrowers and are also available to do special training of staff or villagers as required. (Chapter 5 discusses in detail the economic subsector development work of RDP and the role of the specialists in that work.)

The Village Work of RDP

The organizing and other village work of RDP follows a pattern developed through trial and error during the 1970s, and it was then scaled up in the 1980s. A BRAC RDP employee, the PO, enters a village. His or her (about 10 percent of the POs are now women) first task is to conduct an initial house-to-house survey to identify the households of the target group. The PO then discusses with the women and men in these households their concerns and how these concerns might be addressed through organization. After a couple of months of individual and small-group discussions, separate men's and women's organizations are formed, the women's group first; a male group is never formed without a women's group having been formed in the same village. Each member begins a savings program, setting aside in a bank savings account a few taka (Tk) each month. (In 1990, about Tk38 was the equivalent of one U.S. dollar.)

The first joint activity for each village group is a basic requirement for a "functional education" course for all members. It is taught by a BRAC functional education trainer. These trainers are chosen from villagers with at least a high school education. They are given special training at BRAC's training and resource centers on how to teach the course, and they and the participants are provided with special learning materials that provide the structure for the course. The method used is participatory, in which people are encouraged to discuss, reflect on, and analyze their own problems. Typically, the required portion of the course is thirty lessons focused on basic conscientization and awareness building. An additional thirty lessons stressing literacy and numeracy are also available; this portion is taken by about 50 percent of the members. In earlier stages of BRAC's work, the full sixty lessons were required for all, but by the mid-1980s, in many branches, fewer than half of the members were actually completing the full course, and the "compulsory" rule was observed more in the breach than in the practice. Experience showed that the literacy portions of the classes were not necessarily useful over time because the villagers had no way of keeping up their reading skills and within a few years lost what they had learned. Experience had also demonstrated how difficult it was for many older people to complete sixty lessons, averaging three hours each, because of time constraints, illness, or lack of immediate motivation.

The courses follow a special adult-oriented curriculum, created and recreated by BRAC's materials developers based on field experience with village groups (the basic methodology was drawn from the work of Paolo Freire in Latin America). The fundamental aim of the class is to develop villagers' political consciousness and awareness of their own environment and possibilities. For most poor villagers, the class sessions are the first time they have sat together to discuss and analyze their environment, to examine dependency relations, and to analyze the constraints and possibilities in their lives. This participatory learning experience builds a sense of group solidarity, encourages lateral rather than hierarchical dependency, and develops a belief in the efficacy of collective action.

During the functional education courses, villagers with particular commitment or ability are identified by the group members and by the BRAC PO, and these members are then invited to go to one of BRAC's training centers where they receive training in leadership and group participation techniques, and where they participate in further consciousness-raising activities.

The groups gradually take on a range of activities, such as small income-generating activities using their own accumulated savings as capital. As confidence and solidarity grow, they undertake more difficult activities, such as demanding that local government give laborers their proper payment under food-for-work programs or petitioning government for the use of unused government-owned land or ponds. In some cases, village groups are able to bargain for improved wages or tenancy arrangements with landowners.

When the village organization (VO) has established solidarity, smaller groups of five to seven persons are formed and credit is introduced. (A detailed description of the RDP credit program is given in Chapter 4.) The credit program is usually introduced about three to six months after a VO is formed, which gives the members time to complete their functional education class, to establish solidarity, to gain a sense of their own efficacy, and to establish a savings discipline.

Making both organizational and technical training available to VO members is a major responsibility of RDP. Training is conducted in one or another of BRAC's six residential training centers, or in RDP branch offices or other field locations. Training is given by BRAC's training and resource center (TARC) trainers or by the RDP sectoral specialists. In 1990, over 150,000 participant days of training were given to VO members. Training to upgrade the members' skills in the various kinds of income-generating activities they wish to undertake—such as poultry raising, fish culture, sericulture, livestock rearing, tubewell management, or textile production—is made available, along with leadership, communication, group, and management skills.

After the groups are formed, functional education classes are completed, and credit operations are introduced, the VOs continue to be served by the POs and their village-level assistants, the GSs.

Each VO holds several monthly meetings. First there is a meeting for all members held early in the morning before working hours to discuss income-generating projects, collecting loan repayments and compulsory savings deposits, and other business matters. This meeting, usually short, is conducted by the VO leaders and is attended by the GS assigned to the group. The GS does the loan and savings collecting work. A second meeting of the whole VO is held each month (in the evening for men and the afternoon for women) to discuss social issues such as health (including sanitation), nutrition, and family planning; dowry problems; legal rights; children's education; and other social topics of special concern. These meetings are attended by POs as well as the GSs. The POs have all received a special ten-day training class on how to lead or participate constructively in such social issue discussions. Additional early-morning meetings of the small five member groups are held occasionally as needed to concentrate on loan approvals for members of the groups, income-generating opportunities, other credit matters, or problems of the members of their group. These are chaired by the secretaries of each small group and are sometimes, but not always, attended by the GS. Also, an important management meeting for the governing body of each VO is held each month. The governing body is made up of the secretaries of the small five-member groups.

In some villages the richer and more powerful villagers, and sometimes government bureaucrats, attempt to interfere in the activities of the landless organizations. Gradually the groups begin to resist this interference. Where it is particularly virulent, the help of RDP POs or even area or regional RDP managers is sometimes needed. The interference takes several forms: one form is rumor campaigns, another focuses on the religious consequences of women members participating in group activities and leaving the constraints of purdah (the Muslim sequestering of women), and still others question the motivations and credibility of BRAC. Interference also takes the form of ridicule, or in some cases threats or actual violence, particularly where the groups are becoming successful in demanding or defending their rights. In a recent small example, an elderly mullah publicly slapped the face of one of the BRAC NFPE teachers when she was on the village street and berated her for her public activities. In most cases the VOs are able to overcome the interference themselves, although the fact that the area managers, the POs, and the GSs are behind them and can step in when it is essential is important.

In 1975, BRAC had expanded its activities from its first Sulla project to an all-women's project covering some thirty villages in Jamalpur, in northern Bangladesh, a particularly poor area where after liberation many women had been reduced to begging in the streets. This area has served as a laboratory for activities addressed specifically to the needs of women. (For a carefully detailed account of this project, see Chen, 1983.)

In 1976, BRAC set up another laboratory area about an hour north of Dhaka in Manikganj, where new approaches would be tested in 180 villages. Here, the first poultry, sericulture, and livestock interventions were tried and developed; here, also, the first government facilitation programs were undertaken. Manikganj has also been the testing ground for various health interventions and for the development of the paralegal program. Manikganj, now covering more than 250 villages, remains BRAC's key laboratory area for trying and learning from various kinds of development initiatives. Most RDP activities have been tried there first. Both the Manikganj and Jamalpur projects are now integrated into the RDP but still serve as important laboratories.

By the end of 1990, RDP encompassed ninety area offices and had organized close to 7,000 village organizations with 450,000 members, 65 percent of them women. RDP is now organizing 2,000 new VOs and 100,000 new members each year. (More information about RDP's activities is given in Chapters 4 and 5.)

The Haor (Flood Plains) Development Program

In cooperation with the government, RDP is now conducting a special program in four flood plain areas in northeastern Bangladesh, the area where BRAC started its first work in 1972. These flood plain areas are under water several months of every year. During those periods, communication among villages and between villages and towns must take place by boat; crop lands are under water, and life is extremely difficult. BRAC began its initial organizing in the flood plain area in 1972 and formed 171 village organizations with about 7,000 members. In 1982, after ten years' experience, BRAC helped the village groups set up their own "landless secretariat" managed by the landless groups themselves. BRAC has now reorganized this flood plain program into the Haor Development Program (HDP) operating in similar fashion to the RDP.

In 1989, the government's Bangladesh Water Development Board (BWDB), with the assistance of funds from the Swedish International Development Agency, started a major project in the Haor area to build earthwork embankments to protect against the worst flooding. The board's preliminary studies, along with the donor appraisal, revealed that unless a parallel integrated development program with socioeconomic and health components was included along with the food-for-work embankment construction work, development objectives could not be achieved. Because of BRAC's track record at organizing in the villages, the BWDB asked BRAC to resume target group development activities in the area by again working with the landless groups formed earlier and by organizing new groups and ensuring the participation of the group members in the works program. In short, they requested BRAC to enlarge its RDP program in the area. BRAC accepted.

In the first year of this program, 1989, RDP established four area offices in the embankment project areas and organized some 300 village organizations. The VO members are participating in construction of the dams and are also pressing for their full share of ongoing maintenance work. VO members, aided by credit available from RDP, are also undertaking activities in social forestry, horticulture, livestock and poultry, and fisheries. Education and health activities have also been introduced by BRAC.

The Income Generation for Vulnerable Group Development Program

A large program run by RDP in cooperation with the government is a major program to improve the income-earning potential of destitute women. In the mid-1980s, BRAC was asked by the government to think about cooperating with the World Food Program (WFP), the Bangladesh government's Ministry of Relief and Rehabilitation (MRR), and the Ministry of Livestock and Fisheries in a special program. The purpose of the program, which is called Income Generation for Vulnerable Group Development (IGVGD), is to provide organization, work training, and other systems supports to women who are on government relief (the relief is provided in the form of a wheat ration) so that at the end of two years the women can be off the program and will have a skill and a sustainable income at least equal to the wheat ration they receive while getting relief.

The WFP provides thousands of tons of wheat aid to Bangladesh each year. Some of the wheat is monetized, but a large amount of it is distributed by the government through the local *union* councils (a subunit of the *upazila* covering about 10,000 people) to women designated by them as the most needy. Nearly 90 percent of the poorest and most disadvantaged women are deserted, divorced, or widowed, and many have children to support. Each woman designated by her *union* council to get aid under the program receives a ration of 31.25 kilograms of wheat per month for a two-year period.

When BRAC was first asked to cooperate in this effort, RDP tested several possible approaches in its Manikganj laboratory area. Handicrafts, particularly textiles, were tried, and livestock rearing, sericulture, and poultry raising were also tested. Poultry raising became the program believed to be the most likely to succeed. In the other approaches, more extensive training was required, capital costs were higher, marketing problems were not easily solvable in some parts of the country, and at that time input supply problems had not been solved either.

The Manikganj area had by the late 1980s solved the key problems in improving poultry raising: cooperation with the government had been worked out, sources of high yield variety (HYV) chicks were stabilized, and the incomes of women raising the new HYV and vaccinated chickens were vastly improved. The RDP managers felt that this program was ready to be spread throughout the country. (The history of the RDP poultry program is described in some detail in Chapter 5.) The MRR agreed with RDP's decision to concentrate on household poultry raising, and an agreement was reached in 1988 to start the IGVGD program.

Working under the general guidance of joint *upazila* committees composed of representatives of Directorate of Livestock (DOL), MRR, WFP and BRAC, RDP organizes the women into support groups, introduces them to their own income-earning potential, provides motivational training, and starts them on a regular savings program. RDP next introduces them to household poultry raising as a business and trains them in HYV poultry-rearing techniques, vaccination requirements, and other disease prevention techniques. BRAC makes loans to the women so they can go into the poultry business.

Most of the women become what BRAC calls key rearers, who have a minimum of one HYV cock and ten chickens. Others become what are called chick rearers who buy day-old improved variety chicks and raise them to an age when they can be sold to other village women. Some of the women are trained by RDP as vaccinators, who support themselves by vaccinating the chicks in several nearby villages (all chicks have to be vaccinated in the first five days of life); still others are trained and set up as chicken feed merchants or as egg sellers. The Directorate of Livestock sells HYV chicks to the key rearer chick units and provides syringes and vaccines to the women selected and trained to become vaccinators.

BRAC works with only about three-fourths of the total number of women nominated by their *union* councils to hold Vulnerable Group Development Cards, which entitle them to the wheat ration. Some of the women are too elderly or are incapable of benefiting from the poultry program and often require a different type of long-term relief. Others are not nominated for the BRAC program by the *union* councils for various other reasons. At the beginning of the cooperative effort, recognizing that there is always some "leakage" in such programs, BRAC suggested that the councils make their own designations of the cardholders who should be included in the RDP program. BRAC does not question the exclusions.

Despite some start-up problems endemic to such a four-way cooperative effort, the program appears to be making a significant contribution to the self-respect and economic condition of these women. Home-based poultry raising is suitable for the target group because poultry is a traditional occupation, is low cost, requires few skills, can be highly productive and profitable, can be incorporated into a woman's household work schedule, and requires no special facilities (except for the very inexpensive chick-rearing units required by the women who are chick rearers).

The methodology for organizing and training the various levels (key rearers, chick rearers, vaccinators, feed merchants, and egg sellers) has been well tested and is easily replicable on a widespread basis. BRAC's IGVGD program is an example of a successful program for reaching the most disadvantaged group in the country by assisting them to organize, save, borrow, and move to self-reliance.

During 1990, RDP worked with some 80,000 relief recipients and supplied about $500,000 in credit to them. The loan realization rate has been over 98 percent. The IGVGD program, operating in 1990 in 294 *unions* in thirty-two *upazilas* and expanded in 1991, is considered a success story of a joint effort between two government agencies, an NGO (BRAC), and an international agency.

The Paralegal Program

Another program that operates as part of RDP is the paralegal program. Most village people in Bangladesh, and particularly women, have little idea of those laws that directly affect their daily lives, and they are usually unable to protect themselves against unfair or discriminatory practices by police or government agencies, or illegal acts by other villagers. Laws on child marriage, divorce, dowry, inheritance, land, and other rights are neither well known nor respected. The attitudes of the poorest villagers are essentially negative and distrusting toward the law enforcement system, including the local *salish* (informal village courts usually dominated by elites), the police, and the formal court system. Domestic conflicts, disputes over land, and acts of violence are a way of life in rural Bangladesh, where poorer villagers have little recourse to justice (see BRAC, *Peasant Perceptions: Law,* 1990).

Ever since the VOs were first organized by BRAC, members who felt that they had been unfairly accused of various crimes (theft, and even rape and murder), or who were in sharecropping or wage altercations with landowners, had turned to BRAC for help. VO members who were in trouble with the law or in conflict with other villagers came to the POs or area managers asking for help. The area office managers or POs often responded by getting involved as conciliators or by intervening with the police. In some cases, BRAC actually hired lawyers to defend the members. As the number of VO members increased, so did the number of pleas for help.

After extensive discussion in the area offices, and eventually headquarters, about this increasing problem, the BRAC program managers, together with the executive director, decided in 1986 to respond to the needs of its members by developing a paralegal services program as a part of the RDP. A prominent woman lawyer in Dhaka joined BRAC to lead in forming the program.

As with other new BRAC programs, this program was tested and refined in the Manikganj laboratory area for nearly a year. Whether or not village people could be trained to become effective paralegals was the primary test. Basic materials were developed and an initial group of sixty village organization members were given legal awareness training. The training was focused on family law, inheritance, land law, and certain limited aspects of criminal procedure and constitutional law—primarily safeguards against unlawful arrest and detention—and fundamental rights. Those who successfully completed the rather intensive course were eligible to become BRAC paralegal village workers. Those who were willing were hired and assigned to BRAC's RDP area offices. Their job is to provide paralegal classes for members of village groups and to assist villagers to defend their rights.

To help defray the costs of the paralegal workers, villagers pay a few taka each for the classes they attend. At the end of 1990, ten out of the ninety RDP area offices were participating in the paralegal program, and another 100 villagers were in training as paralegals and had completed most of their course work. The program is being spread to the other RDP area offices as fast as the paralegals complete their training and become available.

The Ayesha Abed Foundation

The Ayesha Abed Foundation is an independent, separately financed organization that is not a formal part of BRAC. But because it works so closely with RDP, a brief description of it is included here. It was established on the death of Ayesha Abed, the first wife of F. H. Abed, the founder and executive director of BRAC. Ayesha Abed had been an active participant in BRAC since its founding, and in 1983, relatives and friends established the foundation as a sister organization to BRAC. It has always cooperated closely with the RDP. Its board of trustees is separate from BRAC, but its executive trustee, F. H. Abed, is also the executive director of BRAC. Its annual budget is about $600,000. The foundation's activities are directed entirely to women. Its goal is to provide capital, facilities, and training to assist women to enhance the income-generating potential of their traditional textile-related skills and to acquire more marketable skills in that field.

The foundation has established two large centers and some seventy subcenters, where women work in textile-related activities. Two more centers were to be opened in 1991, with a goal of establishing forty-two more subcenters. According to the external auditors, the centers are now self-sustaining, although their original plant and equipment were supplied by the foundation. The main centers supply machinery and equipment, work space, training, quality control, and marketing assistance in various aspects of cotton and silk textile production to affiliated women's associations in return for a fee of 5 percent of the sale of products. The women's association members are all members of RDP village organizations.

The women's associations attached to each center manage the affairs of the centers. They elect officers, who generally manage production operations and provide supervision of the women working at the centers and subcenters. Loans are obtained by the women from the foundation or from RDP or RCP to purchase raw materials, to be made into thread using the foundation's spinning and reeling machinery and then woven into cloth. Loans are also used to buy block-printing and silk-screening implements, dyes, thread, buttons, and other findings for finished garments.

As a quality control measure, all of the association members must work at the main centers or subcenters rather than in their homes. Some of the women work for wages, others on a piecework basis, depending on the type of product. During a training period, wages begin at Tk 15 (about 43 cents) a day. After training, wages vary between 22 and 50 Tk per day, depending on the skill of the women and the type of work being done. Training, when required, usually takes place on the job, but some is done in formal sessions.

Each of the big centers has reeling, twisting, weaving, dying, tailoring, block-printing, and embroidery divisions. Most of the subcenters have no equipment but act as places where the women obtain materials and work under careful supervision to fulfill advance orders. BRAC's *Aarong* shops (described in a later section) buy almost all of the production of the foundation centers (although each center has a small retail outlet where products are available to customers locally). In addition to assisting with designs, *Aarong*, through its purchasing methods, encourages the development of efficient business procedures such as meeting production schedules and implementing effective quality control measures.

Without the centers, the women would not have access to required machinery and materials, would not have ways of upgrading their skills, and would not be connected to marketing outlets. The centers also buy the silk cocoons or silk thread from many of the several thousand women members of VOs employed in the silk production home industry.

In 1990, nearly 7,000 women (a few of them part-time) were employed at the centers. Not only are thousands of women guaranteed steady employment in the centers and subcenters, but the women leaders who manage the various aspects of the foundation's extensive activities have learned management skills and are steadily teaching others. Important side effects of the operation of these centers have been postponement of the marriage age for younger women and, for those already married, more attention to birth spacing and smaller family size.

The Rural Credit Project (RCP)

In 1989, BRAC began its own bank, now operating as the Rural Credit Project. The bank is designed as a self-sustaining, self-financing entity that provides banking services to members of mature VOs who "graduate" to the bank. This new program represents a major step by BRAC toward self-financing sustainability of its long-term credit activities.

Figure 3.3 is an organogram of RCP. RCP is organized similarly to RDP, except that the field units are called branches instead of area offices, and each branch has only three POs and nine GSs. The bank branches do not oversee the educational, paralegal, health, and other general activities as do RDP area offices, since their principal job is banking activities. After a minimum of four years of development by RDP, mature VOs are "graduated" from RDP to the bank. Mature VOs are those that have reached an adequate level of social development and in

Figure 3.3 Organogram of the Rural Credit Project (RCP)

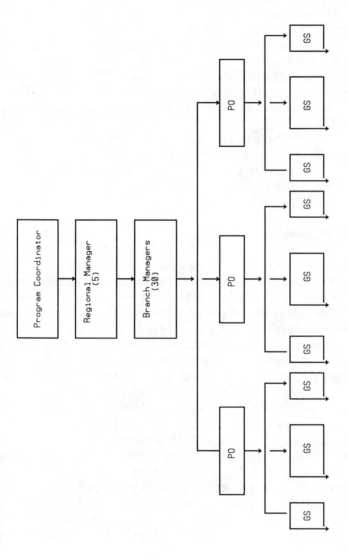

PO = Program Organizer
GS = Gram Shebok (Village Assistant)

Source: BRAC RCP project records

which the members' savings and loan activities under RDP are sufficient to cover ongoing operating costs of credit and savings activities. At that point the bank buys the RDP's investment in its area offices, which includes the VO members' outstanding loans, net of savings, the physical infrastructure of the area offices, and the staff complement. The former RDP area offices become branches of the bank. The advantage to the bank branch of the buy-out system is that it starts with a built-in clientele experienced in savings and borrowing activities and discipline. Although donor money supports the original acquisition of the branches, after the buy-out, bank operations must cover all operating costs of savings and credit activities.

Ten area offices were graduated to RCP branches in 1990, its first year, and twenty more were bought out in the first half of 1991. (RCP is discussed in more detail in Chapter 4, which concentrates on BRAC's financial intermediation efforts.)

Education Programs

BRAC conducts a large primary education program. In 1991, BRAC's Non-Formal Primary Education (NFPE) program was running more than 6,200 schools, by 1992, there were to be 12,000 schools, and by the end of the decade NFPE hopes to be providing primary education to the poorest children in most villages in the country.

The program was started in 1985, in response to demands from the landless parents who had had the opportunity to take part in the functional education programs. The parents kept asking the POs and the area managers why BRAC didn't give some literacy classes for their children as well. After careful examination of the problems in the public primary schools, and the nonenrollment and dropout rates of the poorest children, BRAC decided to experiment with primary education. The poorest children in the villages were obviously not being reached by the government school system.

BRAC assembled a small staff of educators, assisted by a consultant from Dhaka University School of Education. Their first goal was to set up twenty-two experimental village schools to see if a cost-effective way could be found to reach those poor children in the villages who were being bypassed by the formal primary school system. After two years of experimentation with materials and various forms of teacher selection and training, the NFPE group developed a method that became so successful that it could be replicated in thousands of village schools. The program has since received worldwide attention. (For a detailed description of the primary education program see Lovell and Fatema, 1989.)

Figure 3.4 is an organogram of the primary education program as it was structured in mid-1991. It shows the small headquarters staff that manages the entire program, including the government schools facilitation program (discussed in a later section); handles materials development and statistical monitoring; and liaises with BRAC's training centers on teacher training. The field structure is three-tiered: regional managers supervise the field organizers, who in turn supervise the POs, who directly supervise the teachers and relate to parent groups. Since most of the schools are located in RDP-organized villages, the POs reside at RDP area offices and are reportable on a daily basis to the RDP area office managers (see Figure 3.2). The NFPE field organizers and RDP area office managers must work closely together because they both have supervisory functions over the POs. In cases where schools are located outside of RDP areas, the NFPE has set up its own residential camps for its POs, who report directly to the field organizers.

The BRAC schools are operating successfully in a context where 44 percent of primary school–age students (and nearly 100 percent of the landless children) do not enroll in government schools at all; and of those who do enroll, nearly 50 percent leave school before they complete the third grade.

Those eligible for the BRAC classes are the children of the poorest in the villages—those parents who are eligible for membership in the BRAC VOs. Most of the schools are now located in villages where BRAC has organized village organizations of landless groups, but the method was tested and proved equally effective in many non-BRAC areas.

BRAC has developed two primary school models directed at two different age groups. The Non-Formal Primary Education program is a three-year class for children of the target group who are eight to ten years old, who have never attended school, or who dropped out in the first grade. Every three years a new class is started and continues with the same teacher until the course is completed. Since one of the primary objectives is to have the schools close to the children's homes, students are drawn from the same village or cluster of villages. If new classes were started every year for one age cohort, the schools would have to be much farther apart and would lose their village character and oversight.

The second model, Primary Education for Older Children (PEOC), is a two-year program for children eleven to fourteen years old who meet the same criteria. The classes are comprised in the same way, with a new class starting every two years.

The goal of both programs is to have 70 percent girls in the schools, and the achievement has been 65.70 percent girls for the younger children and 73.43 percent for the older children. The schools, including books and other materials, are free.

Figure 3.4 Organogram of the Non-Formal Primary Education Program (NFPE) 1991

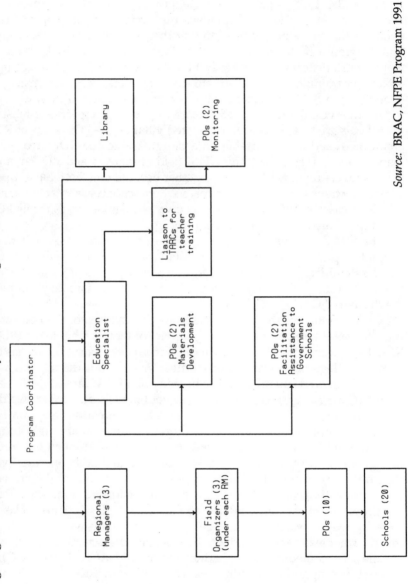

Source: BRAC, NFPE Program 1991

The children follow a carefully designed curriculum developed and tested by the NFPE program. The objective of the curriculum is to help the children achieve basic literacy, numeracy, and social awareness. The curriculum is divided into three subject areas: language—Bangla, which is the official language of Bangladesh, and some English to make the curriculum compatible with the government schools; arithmetic; and social studies, which emphasizes health (including nutrition, hygiene, sanitation, safety, and first aid) ecosystems, community, country, the world, and basic science. The older children cover in one and a half years what the younger children cover in three years, so additional courses to fill out their two years were developed especially for them.

Parents hold regular monthly meetings and take a great deal of responsibility for attendance, setting of class times, decisions about vacation schedules, and so on. Parent involvement is considered one of the keys to the success of the program.

Teachers for the schools are chosen from among the more educated in a village, those who have completed nine or more years of school. They are given twelve days of teacher training in groups of twenty to twenty-five in one of BRAC's residential training centers. There they are taught basic concepts of learning theory and given practice teaching. After they start teaching in the village they must, one day each month, attend continuing teacher training sessions with teachers from nearby villages and their supervising PO. All teachers also attend a six-day refresher course at the end of the first year. A strong teacher supervision system is in place with one supervising PO for each fifteen teachers. Women make up 75 percent of the teachers, in contrast to the government schools, where 86 percent of the primary teachers are men. The teachers are paid a small monthly stipend, currently Tk 350 per month (about $10) the first year, Tk 375 the second year, and Tk 400 the third year.

All books and other learning materials are designed and supplied by BRAC. Teachers follow a very structured curriculum using learning materials that have been prepared in simple modular form with teaching notes. One teacher takes the same children through all three grades, and class size is strictly limited to thirty children. Classes meet for two and a half hours each day for the first and second grades and three hours for the third. The particular time that classes are held in each village is decided in meetings with parents. Classes are held six days a week for an average of 268 days a year (compared to the government schools, which are scheduled for only 220 days a year). Vacations and holiday schedules are decided by the parents.

The school buildings are simple structures, with a minimum of 240 square feet (22.30 square meters), rented from some group or individual in the community, or constructed by landless groups, who sometimes have taken loans to buy the materials and who receive a regular low rent payment from BRAC.

The success of the schools has been extraordinary, and some of the results have been totally spectacular. Careful records of performance have been kept. Daily attendance rates have surpassed 95 percent in both the NFPE and the PEOC schools. But even more remarkable has been the low drop-out rates over the full two- or three-year curriculum: less than 1 percent in both types of schools—.44 percent in the older children's schools and .30 percent for the younger children. And 95 percent of the graduates have passed examinations allowing them to enter at least the fourth grade in the formal system. BRAC expected good attendance rates and high completion rates, but no one predicted such outstanding results.

Also unexpected is the high percentage of the students, from both the younger and older groups, who are going on to the government schools. Table 3.1 provides statistics on the performance of 642 schools covering 19,260 students who have completed either the two- or three-year program. (Since the first twenty-two schools were started only in 1986, the first useful statistics are only now becoming available from the larger numbers of students who started in 1987 and 1988 and finished in 1990 and 1991.)

In addition to the almost nonexistent dropout rates and the very high attendance rates, Table 3.1 shows an unexpected and remarkable finding: 87 percent of the older children and nearly 99 percent of the younger children have been admitted to the government schools at the fourth-grade level or above. Among the younger children with three years of the NFPE classes, 2,437 students (74.85 percent) qualified for Class Four, but a surprising 815 children (25.03 percent) qualified for Class Five. Even more surprising was the level of classes into which the older children were admitted after passing requisite government exams. After only two years of BRAC schooling, 4,538 children (32.59 percent) qualified for Class Four, 9,164 students (65.80 percent) for Class Five, and 224 (1.61 percent) for Class Six.

Continuance into the public schools, except by an occasional student, was unexpected when the schools were first designed. Most educationists, along with most BRAC staff, including those running the NFPE program, believed that many different kinds of pressures would prevent the children from continuing. They believed that the parents would think their children had enough education or that they would be needed at home. Especially the older children from the two-year program, mostly girls, were not at all expected to continue, since they were approaching marriage age and could be used for various work at home.

Table 3.1 Attendance, Dropout, and Continuation Rates, NFPE Program

Older Children, Ages 11–14
Course Duration: Two Years
Session: 1988–1990

No. of Schools	Initial Enrollment			Dropout		Children Completed Course						Children Admitted into Government Primary Schools						Class Level into Which the Children Are Admitted					
	Boys	Girls	Total			Boys		Girls		Total		Boys		Girls		Total		Class 4		Class 5		Class 6	
	No. %	No. %	Total	No.	%	No.	%	No.	%	No.	%	No.	%	No.	%	No.	%	No.	%	No.	%	No.	%
532	4241 26.57	11719 73.43	15960	71	0.44	4241	100	11648	99.39	15889	99.56	3994	94.18	9932	85.27	13426	87.65	4538	32.59	9164	65.80	224	1.61

Younger Children, Ages 8–10
Course Duration: Three Years
Session: 1987–1990

No. of Schools	Initial Enrollment			Dropout		Children Completed Course						Children Admitted into Government Primary Schools						Class Level into Which the Children Are Admitted					
	Boys	Girls	Total			Boys		Girls		Total		Boys		Girls		Total		Class 4		Class 5		Class 6	
	No. %	No. %	Total	No.	%	No.	%	No.	%	No.	%	No.	%	No.	%	No.	%	No.	%	No.	%	No.	%
110	1132 34.30	2168 65.70	3300	10	0.30	1132	100	2158	99.54	3290	99.70	1116	98.59	2140	99.17	3256	98.97	2437	74.85	815	25.03	4	0.12

Source: BRAC, Non-Formal Primary Education Program records

Since the program is so new, research has not yet been able to show how many of the children admitted to Class Four and above will continue, and for how long. BRAC's research division is conducting a long-term study of the program. Researchers are following a random sample of the students to provide information on what happens in later years to these children after they enter the government schools—how long they stay and how their basic primary education and school continuation affect their income-generating potential and various social dimensions such as marriage age, health, child spacing, and family size in later years.

In the past, observers of primary education throughout the developing world have said that the poorest children did not go to school because their parents needed them to help at home. Also, it was believed that parents did not value education for their children enough to make sacrifices. The BRAC experience definitely suggests otherwise. It suggests that there are variables more important than poverty and tradition that influence parents' and children's decisions about school enrollment and attendance. Once the children and their parents have experienced relevant curricula, dedicated and well-supervised teachers with reasonable class size in low-cost or free schools that are close to home and provide a climate where success is expected, their attitude toward education is apparently changed. Having experienced success in the BRAC schools, children and their parents have come to value education and are willing to sacrifice in order to continue.

Because of the remarkable success with the primary education program, and because the program has been able to mesh with the public schools so remarkably, BRAC's top management has identified the program as worthy of very rapid scaleup and is now pursuing major funding for that purpose. Their decision has been undergirded by increasing numbers of studies that document the high returns on investment in education for developing countries. Findings from the studies suggest that increasing the average amount of education of the labor force by one year raises GDP by 9 percent. This holds for the first three years of education; that is, three years of education as compared with none raises GDP by 27 percent (World Bank, 1991, p. 43). The return from an additional year of schooling then diminishes to about 4 percent a year—or a total of 12 percent for the next three years.

Government Facilitation Assistance Program
on Education

In 1988, BRAC entered into an agreement with the government to experiment with ways of improving the existing formal primary education system in four *upazilas*. The Facilitation Assistance Program on Education (FAPE) was set up by BRAC's Non-Formal Primary Education program and the government in twenty-two primary school districts, from which 165 schools were selected for the program. The program goals have been to

- improve enrollment rates;
- reduce dropout rates of students;
- increase daily attendance rates for teachers and students; and
- ensure community participation.

In order to accomplish these goals, school management committees have been activated by the NFPE POs working with the schools and have been encouraged to meet regularly; BRAC has organized training courses for assistant *upazila* education officers, headmasters, and teachers; and workshops have been set up for management committee members. Also, regular meetings have been organized to increase parents' awareness about the need for their children's education and to encourage their active participation in affairs of the schools. NFPE POs visit the schools, the children, and the parents regularly.

The results of the two-year intervention are mixed. Some 500 children of the poorest families who would not otherwise have enrolled are now in the government schools, attendance rates of both teachers and students have improved, the community has demonstrated commitment by raising subscriptions for the schools and helping with minor repairs, and the management committees are more regular in their meetings. However, some of the problems endemic to the public schools have not been solved during the first two years of this experiment. Class sizes remain exceptionally large, some of the curriculum remains irrelevant to village needs, teachers are still poorly supervised and undermotivated, books and other supplies are often not available, homework requiring the assistance of literate parents or paid tutors is still the norm, and special "charges" continue to be levied.

Although the facilitation program has made some progress, the experience has demonstrated how difficult it is to change only a part of a system without making major changes in the whole. Dropout rates still average about 30 percent (compared to less than 2 percent in BRAC schools), only a small improvement over the slightly more than 35 percent that was the pre-FAPE norm. Daily attendance rates average about 65 percent (compared to more than 95 percent in BRAC schools), but represent an improvement over the 40 percent prior to the FAPE intervention. Donors, the government, and BRAC are currently evaluating various alternatives to continuing the program as now constituted or attempting other intervention strategies.

BRAC's Health Programs

BRAC entered the health field early in its history and has continued with health programs in one form or another since that time. From its experience with health programs over two decades, BRAC has learned that for lasting impact on the health and nutritional status of a village, the community must develop a health consciousness, look after some of its own health needs, increase its income-generating capacities, and develop an ability to utilize and make demands upon the existing health infrastructure.

Over two decades, BRAC's health programs shifted from its early efforts to "deliver" health care services to an emphasis on enabling people to address their own health concerns. BRAC now also emphasizes collaboration with the government health system for improving delivery in the public health system itself. (For fuller descriptions and evaluations of BRAC's health programs, see Chowdhury, Waughan, and Abed, 1988; Chowdhury, 1990; Chowdhury, Mahmood, and Abed, 1991; Streefland and Chowdhury, 1990; Briscoe, 1978; Ghosh et al., 1990.) The following paragraphs give only a brief overview of BRAC's principal health initiatives in the past and the current status of its health programming.

BRAC's early experiences in the health field almost parallel those of health programs in other developing countries in the same period. BRAC, as did others, moved from an emphasis on curative services to increased emphasis on preventive measures, with primary health care moving to the forefront.

The first health program of BRAC, begun in 1972, was essentially curative. As earlier explained, BRAC's first project at Sulla was a community-wide development program—it was not targeted to the poorest in the villages. Health was one component. When BRAC workers entered the area, just after the war of liberation, they found disease rampant. As a result, BRAC established four clinics with attending doctors, in which it was soon found that ten to fifteen diseases accounted for 95 percent of health problems.

By the end of its first year, BRAC decided to train locally recruited paramedics (based on the Chinese barefoot doctor model then becoming known worldwide). A list of "essential drugs" that could be administered by the paramedics was prepared, with the aim of breaking doctor dependency. The paramedics, after several months of training, were able to treat simple illnesses and refer more complicated cases to the clinics.

They were to charge a small fee for their treatment. Based on the observed needs of the villagers, family planning was stressed.

In order to make this health program self-sustaining, BRAC experimented with a prepaid health insurance system in which households paid with five kilograms of paddy per person, per year. Under this insurance program, paramedics cared for patients at the first level and BRAC doctors took over at a higher level. The insurance program operated for about a year, during which time problems emerged that caused the plan to be abandoned. The beneficiaries were found to be primarily the well-to-do villagers. The poorer villagers did not join the scheme; the possibility of future illness seemed less important than what the equivalent of the five kilos of paddy could purchase today.

Further experimentation followed wherein the paramedics worked for a group of villages charging set fees for specific services, such as supplying key drugs. However, some of the paramedics began to expand their range of treatment and drugs as though they were qualified doctors. Some started their own practices, adding to the number of "quack doctors" already operating in many of the villages. Finally, BRAC decided to retain only the best of the paramedics and added them to its own staff. These early efforts to establish a self-sustaining curative system failed.

However, the efforts in Sulla were successful in other ways. In 1975, because of BRAC's efforts, the Sulla area had the highest contraception prevalence rate in the country, with about 20 percent of the couples using contraceptives. It also had the highest continuation rate in the country, with more than 50 percent continuing after eighteen months, largely because the clinics were able to take care of side effects from contraceptive use. Through its family planning experience at Sulla, BRAC was able to identify the main constraints to further increasing the contraceptive prevalence rate—status of women, lack of income, illiteracy.

Similarly, the Sulla project became a field base for testing "homemade" oral rehydration solutions to prevent death from dehydration caused by the diarrheal diseases rampant in the area. This experimentation, undertaken in cooperation with the International Center for Diarrheal Disease Research, Bangladesh (ICDDR,B), helped develop a home-based method for treating diarrhea that was later to become important to the entire country. Although in other parts of the world small packets of rehydration salts were beginning to be widely distributed or sold, infrastructural constraints made distribution of the packets to most Bangladeshi villages all but impossible.

In 1977, BRAC switched to its target group approach, concentrating its work with the landless poorest segment of the villagers rather than with the community as a whole. This change in target changed the emphasis in health programming. Another curative model was attempted at Sulla and in the Manikganj "laboratory" area, where by this time BRAC had organized some 200 village organizations. Under this new health plan, one woman in each village was chosen from among the poorest families to be a health worker. Unlike the paramedics who were earlier selected and employed by BRAC, these women were selected by their respective village organizations. The women were accountable to their own groups for their activities and would not leave their villages to become "quacks." They were given simple health and family planning training and supplied with a few basic drugs, which they dispensed to other villagers. To enhance their interest in this job, the women were allowed to charge a small fee for every patient seen and to sell medicines at a small markup. Also, BRAC supplied credit to these women so that they could undertake small income-generating activities. Several hundred of these women have now been trained and continue to work in Sulla and the Manikganj areas, two of BRAC's most integrated project areas.

In the beginning, the women also supplied contraceptives, but later that year the government restricted NGOs in the distribution of contraceptives. At that point BRAC started its first important efforts to cooperate with the government health system by training these women health workers to encourage villagers to go to the government clinics for contraceptive services and for treatment of diseases they could not handle.

During this period, BRAC health workers in the field had become aware of and wanted to tackle the tetanus problem, one of the biggest killers of mothers and their newborn infants. They recognized, however, that the government was not prepared to supply sufficient tetanus vaccines, and even if vaccines could be found, the problems of maintaining an adequate cold chain precluded the distribution and use of the vaccine. BRAC's health managers learned that unless the health infrastructure could back it up, a single NGO should not take on certain kinds of health efforts.

The Nationwide Oral Rehydration Therapy Program

Based on its initial health programming experiences, BRAC turned its attention even more actively to things that the villagers could do themselves to improve their own health status. During this period, BRAC was following and learning from research, events, and policies at the international level. The International Year of the Child in 1979 provided an impetus to BRAC's health programmers to think about programs focused primarily on children that would significantly contribute to their survival.

Diarrhea claimed more young lives than any other condition. BRAC's experiments at Sulla with oral rehydration therapy (ORT) for diarrhea had been successful at saving children's lives, and other field testing of

ORT by ICDDR,B had proved its potential. Also, the work with ORT among the Bangladeshi refugees in the Calcutta area during the 1971 war of liberation had shown what ORT could do in epidemic situations.

All those experiences influenced BRAC's decision to embark on a nationwide ORT program. It tested its approach in the early months of 1979 by undertaking a program to teach oral rehydration to 30,000 families at Sulla, which became the proving ground for effective teaching methods. The health workers running that test program found that it was feasible to teach village women how to make a simple solution of a pinch of salt and a fistful of unrefined sugar (locally called *gur*) mixed in a half liter of water to produce a solution with most of the qualities of the scientific ORT powder being distributed in packets.

In early 1980, BRAC launched its nationwide effort to teach oral rehydration therapy to every one of 13 million village households in the country. This major undertaking was a curative program, but it was a "cure" that village families could do for themselves. BRAC set up a new structure to run the program, called the Oral Therapy Extension Program (OTEP). Backed by a management team made up of people who had gained experience running health programs at Sulla and Manikganj, a well-developed management information system, and an evaluation division, teams of trained female workers were fielded to go house-to-house to teach the women how to make the solution properly and how to give it to their children.

The teaching method and materials were carefully structured and were based on an intelligent use of local belief systems. The female ORT teachers, themselves recruited from the villages in the same regions of the country where they were teaching, worked under an incentive salary plan in which they were paid according to the quality of their teaching. OTEP monitoring teams followed a fortnight later and interviewed a randomly sampled 5 percent of the village women to find out how well they had understood and learned the messages. Samples of solutions mixed by the village women were taken to laboratories for testing on a regular basis. If the village women had not learned how to properly mix the solution and could not remember the essential messages about diarrhea, the teachers were paid less. Supervision of the teachers as they moved from village to village was strict but supportive. (For a more detailed discussion of this program and details on the management system, see Chowdhury, Waughan, and Abed, 1988.)

In November 1990, a decade later, BRAC's OTEP field workers completed teaching the therapy to the final one of 13 million village households in the country. During the ten years, BRAC had supplemented the face-to-face village teaching with radio and television advertising, posters, billboards, and other forms of mass communication.

OTEP has been considered a quantitative as well as qualitative success. ORT in now an accepted part of the treatment of diarrhea throughout the country. Most recent evaluations have shown a high retention of knowledge about ORT (80 percent) and the effective skills necessary to mix and administer it.

The mammoth OTEP undertaking provided several important lessons for BRAC, for donors, and for development professionals. First, it dispelled the perception that NGOs were capable of only small, localized activities of little consequence nationally. Second, it disproved notions that health programs must necessarily lose quality if they go to large scale. It taught BRAC managers and field staff to think nationally and inspired confidence to "go to scale" on other programs. OTEP was responsible for increasing the size of BRAC. In the first half of the 1980s, the number of BRAC staff grew fivefold; over two-thirds of the new staff members were part of OTEP. Also, the size and dynamic of the program required BRAC to develop in major ways its support programs—logistics, training, research, materials development—as well as its management capacities.

BRAC's Child Survival Program

In 1986, in conjunction with the last four years of ORT teaching, covering the last third of the country, BRAC launched another major rural health initiative: the four-year Child Survival Program (CSP). It focused on the preventive health measures of immunization and vitamin A capsule distribution (priorities of the government and bilateral and international donors). This focus was added to the ORT teaching. In this program, BRAC health staff did not itself do the immunization or distribute the vitamin A capsules, but instead worked with the government to improve its capabilities to perform and sustain these services.

In BRAC's CSP, encompassing 155 *upazilas* with 28,853 villages, a third of the country, BRAC health field staff assisted the government's district, *upazila* and *union* health officials to strengthen their management and improve their technical capabilities to provide mass immunization services and to improve their biannual vitamin A capsule distribution program. BRAC played two main roles. BRAC's health workers and trainers served as consultants and trainers to the government's rural health managers through a management development program and with on-site help setting up rural immunization systems. BRAC trainers helped train the government's field-level workers in immunization techniques and in systems for setting up immunization days, rosters, and so on. BRAC's health workers also mobilized village communities to cooperate with the immunization drive and organized them to demand sustained immunization services after the first round of vaccinations was completed.

By 1990, at the end of four years, BRAC's Child Survival Program, which had helped the government immunization program to reach some 4.5 million households and 30 million people, was deemed successful. In the section of the country where BRAC's CSP assisted the government, the government was able to achieve universal child immunization (UCI). As Figure 3.5 indicates, immunization levels in the BRAC-assisted Rajshahi division were considerably higher than in the other sections of the country where the government's program was assisted by CARE (Khulna), or where the government managed the program on its own.

In spite of its initial success, however, sustainability of the government's immunization program remained questionable. As a result, the government health ministry asked BRAC health workers to continue to assist with ongoing management development and with creating community demand in a large number of *upazilas*. Cooperation under what BRAC calls its government facilitation program is continuing for another three years in the some sixty *upazilas* that had the lowest immunization coverage rates.

Primary Health Care Program. A subproject of the Child Survival Program was a significant, multicomponent Primary Health Care Project (PHCP) conducted in fifteen of the 155 *upazilas* covered by the CSP. About 3 million people live in the fifteen *upazilas* where the broader health care effort was conducted. This program added to the CSP interventions (ORT, immunization, and vitamin A capsule distribution) health and nutrition education linked to growth monitoring, traditional birth attendant training, clean water and sanitation development, and family planning. Like CSP as a whole, the program had an explicit goal of strengthening the capabilities of the government health care delivery system. In these fifteen *upazilas*, the goal was to help the health system to upgrade its capacity to supply to the villagers a range of health services that would go beyond immunization and vitamin A capsule distribution. This ambitious program had mixed results. It reinforced BRAC's earlier learning that more sustained work had to be done to develop village community and government capabilities if effective and sustainable health services were to become a reality.

On the positive side, the PHCP had tested an innovative tuberculosis treatment scheme originally pioneered in BRAC's Manikganj laboratory-area villages and found the method to be very successful. Nearly 80 percent of those participating in the TB treatment program completed the year-long course of treatment, some four times higher than in other areas

Figure 3.5 Bangladesh Immunization Coverage, February 1991†

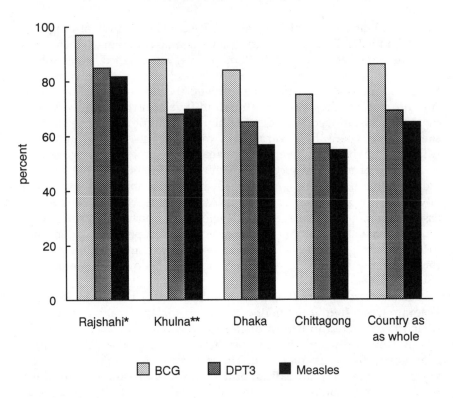

*BRAC-assisted area
**CARE-assisted area
†For children 12–17 months.
Survey independently supervised
by WHO, UNICEF, and SIDA.

Source: World Health Organization

of Bangladesh. In another successful case, involving seventy-five villages with a combined population of approximately 65,000, where family planning interventions were undertaken, a contraceptive prevalence rate of 51 percent using modern methods was achieved (compared with a national average of an estimated 23 percent). In the PHCP, BRAC also was able to improve the regularity and performance of the government's satellite clinics in the targeted *upazilas*. Mothers' clubs of the poorest women were organized, and well-attended monthly meetings proved to be a useful means of increasing the villagers' awareness of health and nutrition issues. Attempts to activate villagewide health committees in the target areas, however, were not as successful.

The activities begun by the PHCP and evaluated as successful are being continued either by BRAC's Rural Development Program area offices or under a restructured health program described in the next section.

The Women's Health and Development Program

In late 1990, BRAC introduced a restructured and renamed health program that is to be more closely integrated with BRAC's basic RDP and with the NFPE program. The new $8.6 million (for the first three years) program is being carried out in ten *upazilas* during the first two years and in fifteen *upazilas* the third year; it will cover a population of approximately 2.4 million people in 1,500 villages. Named the Women's Health and Development Program (WHDP), the new program brings together various village-based initiatives and government health system improvements with a primary goal of reducing maternal and infant mortality by 25 percent. Additional goals are treatment and cure of a large percentage of the tuberculosis cases using the methods tested earlier, plus an initial experiment with the cure of other respiratory diseases, particularly pneumonia, in children.

The WHDP plan calls for integration of health programming with BRAC's ongoing RDP during a six-year phase-over period. The program's long-term strategy combines literacy for young women, health education, credit and income generation, plus preventive, promotive, and a small amount of curative health care. The overarching goal is a health system that will be sustainable without BRAC.

The structure of WHDP is shown in Figure 3.6. Under the program manager there is a nutrition adviser and medical consultant and four regional managers (RMs). Three of the RMs oversee the managers of the ten WHDP *upazilas*. One RM oversees four *upazilas*, the other two oversee three each. The fourth RM is responsible for the facilitation work with the government to support the management component of the government's Extended Program on Immunization (EPI). The organogram shows the composition of the *upazila* and area teams.

The first component in each village is the selection of thirty adolescent girls, eleven to sixteen years old, who will complete BRAC's twenty-four-month primary education program for older children. The course will include special attention to health issues. The parents of each young woman sign a contract agreeing that the girl will not marry until she reaches the legal marriage age of eighteen. Once trained the thirty young women serve as a village health cadre with each member being responsible for seven to ten households close to her home. Working initially under health program POs, the young women's job is to help the neighboring households with sanitation, nutrition, immunization, the proper use of ORT, and the use of trained birth attendants (TBAs); they also identify and refer special health problems to government satellite clinics or larger health complexes. The young women also help at the government's health posts, which BRAC is attempting to revitalize. Village health workers are also being trained for every village (based on the Sulla and Manikganj model discussed above). Their job is to provide general health care and basic medicines for simple illnesses. They also help in the TB program, in which they are trained to collect sputum for laboratory testing and to administer the appropriate medicine. The women have a set of basic drugs available and can assist in the treatment of diarrhea, dysentery, worms, skin infections, and other simple diseases.

Other components of WHDP include the training of TBAs so that there will be at least one well-trained TBA for each village. Prenatal care and identification of high-risk mothers, care of the newborn, family planning, vitamin A supplementation, and immunization are also included in the program. Mothers' clubs and village health committees are being organized to link the community with the public health structure for immunization, vitamin A capsules, and interventions in high-risk pregnancies and acute respiratory infections. The village health committees also maintain contraceptive depots until this function is taken over by the government. Membership in the two committees are primarily women and the landless. The activities of the village committees are being carried out in close collaboration with the health staff at the government's *union* health post, the service closest to the village. Part of the job of WHDP is to continue to upgrade the services of these health posts.

An important part of WHDP will also be a continuing program of training in health management for the government's rural health administrators and continued work in the field with rural health administrators to improve their management systems, with special attention to achieving their EPI goals. The Management Development Program of BRAC provides the management training and field follow-up as it did under the Child Survival Program.

Health Resource Center. A portion of WHDP resources is to be invested in starting the new Health Resource Center (HRC). The purpose of the HRC is to build an improved capacity within BRAC and other organizations to deliver higher quality health services in the rural areas. The executive director of BRAC recently said that he has never been satisfied that BRAC has found the right mix of health interventions that are

Figure 3.6 Organogram of Women's Health and Development Program (WHDP)

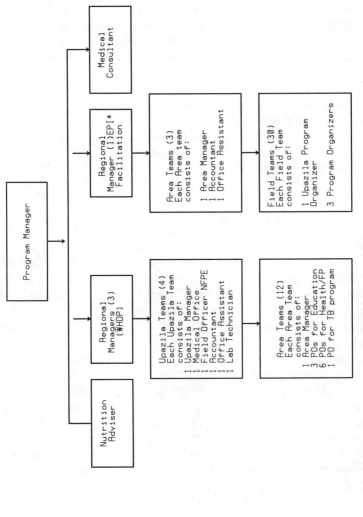

Program Manager

Nutrition Adviser

Medical Consultant

Regional Managers (3) (WHDP)

Regional Manager (1)EPI* Facilitation

Upazila Teams (4)
Each Upazila Team consists of:
1 Upazila Manager
1 Medical Officer
1 Field Officer NFPE
1 Accountant
1 Office Assistant
1 Lab Technician

Area Teams (3)
Each Area team consists of:
1 Area Manager
1 Accountant
1 Office Assistant

Area Teams (12)
Each Area Team consists of:
1 Area Manger
3 POs for Education
6 POs for Health/FP
1 PO for TB program

Field Teams (30)
Each Field Team consists of:
1 Upazila Program Organizer
3 Program Organizers

*Extended Program on Immunization assistance to Goverment of Bangladesh

Source: BRAC WHDP records, 1991

effective and can be sustained after BRAC withdraws from an area. One of the main purposes of the HRC is to find effective and sustainable health interventions.

A small initial HRC staff will conduct monitoring, evaluation, and research activities on health issues as well as begin to provide training in the health field. It is designed to assist not only BRAC's health programming but also that of other organizations in Bangladesh, and eventually, as it grows, it hopes to establish links with other regional health research and training facilities. The HRC is to be a part of BRAC for its first three years, beyond which it is expected to become an autonomous, self-supporting institution.

HRC will also establish and continuously update a library or clearinghouse for health studies open to health researchers. The HRC goal is to upgrade health research in order to discover the best combinations of health interventions that can reach the poorest of the poor and that are appropriate for the village context. The overall aim is to provide scientific backing on health issues to villagers and the government health system.

Two Decades of Learning on Health Programming

BRAC is moving toward integrating its health programs with the core RDP rather than operating parallel efforts. Health education is an important part of the curriculum of BRAC's large nonformal primary education program. Health issues are also an important part of the adult functional education-awareness course which every BRAC village organization member must complete. Furthermore, health issues such as nutrition, sanitation, immunization, oral rehydration, breast feeding, supplementary feeding, and family planning are discussed regularly at the monthly issue meetings of some 7,000 village groups. Women's development remains a key focus of all BRAC's development activities; health workers in the field have learned that progress cannot be made on health issues without the full involvement and leadership of women. Experience in the various health programs has proved that once empowered, the poorest women can become leaders in health improvements.

BRAC continues to search for the right combination of health interventions appropriate to the village context and with the capability to move both the villagers and the government health system toward higher and sustainable levels of prevention and care. It is hoped that research and ideas generated by the new Health Resource Center will help contribute to more effective health intervention strategies.

Emergency Programs

Because BRAC is a large NGO, with an efficient and flexible management capacity, it is often called upon by donors and the government to receive and deliver relief assistance to victims of emergencies such as extreme floods, cyclones, or drought. For example, during the floods of 1987 and 1988, BRAC OTEP and RDP staff with area offices and field camps near the affected areas were diverted from their regular work to reinforce the need for ORT during the diarrheal epidemics that followed, ran emergency feeding stations to provide cooked food to stranded villagers, supplied housing, and distributed clothes, medicine, and other emergency supplies. As soon as the flood waters had receded, RDP field offices nearest the affected areas started postflood rehabilitation programs, including house repairing and reconstruction, housing loans, asset loans, and free poultry houses. During the severe drought in 1989, RDP area managers cooperated with the Food-for-Work Program on employment schemes for the members of BRAC's village organizations.

BRAC also operated an extensive emergency relief program following the devastating 1991 cyclone that hit the eastern coast of the Bay of Bengal about midnight on April 29. Early on the morning of April 30, the executive director called together all top managers at headquarters to set priorities and prepare BRAC's assistance plan. An RDP regional manager was sent immediately to the affected area to make contact with BRAC health workers already on the spot and to begin to assess the local situation. In the meantime, thirty teams of BRAC health workers (some 120 POs) who were stationed in the affected area helping the government with its immunization efforts started their own relief efforts without waiting for instructions from headquarters. Although many of those staff had lost all their possessions, they formed the core of BRAC's initial cyclone relief effort of getting drinkable water and food to survivors. On May 2, a high-level team from the BRAC head office, including the executive director and top program managers, visited the cyclone-torn areas, discussed problems with the workers already on the spot, and made contact with other relief agencies and the government. The formal relief efforts started on May 4 following the design of a program proposal worth Tk 26.8 million and the deployment of a larger team of BRAC staff drawn from other parts of the country to join those 120 health POs already on the spot. The effort was led by a field administrator sent from the head office, the director of support services.

The first stage, which lasted about a week, was devoted to delivering relief materials—food, fresh water, medicines, and clothing. At the second stage, BRAC chose seven of the worst-hit *upazilas* where other organizations were not already working. In those *upazilas* BRAC's emergency staff conducted a more intensive relief and rehabilitation effort, which included providing temporary shelter, draining and disinfecting ponds, and supplying clothing and medical services. In the third stage, BRAC introduced a three-month cash-for-work program, providing short-term employment and income-generating activities such as house repair, land leveling, homestead cleaning and development, feeder road repair, desalinization and cleaning of ponds, making and repairing of fishnets, tubewell repair and installation of new tubewells, installation of sanitary latrines in primary and secondary schools, tree planting for reforestation, and extension of a vulnerable-group feeding program that fed 14,500 families for three months. In order to check misuse or misappropriation of funds, monitoring staff visited the field regularly. A special method for monitoring the cash-for-work projects was designed and followed.

Altogether, BRAC fielded nearly 400 staff and volunteers to work in the area, spent about $1 million for materials and cash-for-work, and distributed hundreds of thousands of dollars worth of food and medicines made available to BRAC by various bilateral and international donors and individual contributors. Because BRAC is known as an honest, accountable organization, it received more offers of cash donations, food, medicines, and other materials than it could use. (For a full documentation of its relief effort and accounting for donations, see BRAC, *Cyclone Relief*, 1991.) Approximately 31,000 households were assisted in the survival relief stage and 25,000 in the relief and rehabilitation stages.

For long-term work in the cyclone-prone area, BRAC has introduced its RDP into one of the hardest-hit offshore *upazilas*, with a population of about 300,000 inhabitants. Along with other aspects of development work, RDP plans to introduce a network of effective cyclone shelters.

BRAC's Commercial Operations

BRAC has four commercial operations: the *Aarong* shops, BRAC Printers, a cold storage facility, and garment factories. About 15 percent of BRAC's budget is now supported by the profits from these activities. All of the commercial companies are planned as adjunct operations designed to enhance BRAC's development efforts.

The Aarong Shops

Aarong, meaning village market, is the name of a BRAC company that currently operates six high-quality and profitable retail shops located in three cities of Bangladesh as well as a growing export business. The first *Aarong* shop was originally organized in 1978, together with the Mennonite Central Committee (MCC), as a much-needed marketing outlet for textile and handicraft products produced by BRAC and other NGO-organized women's groups and local artisans. After the first shop was well established, MCC withdrew and BRAC became the owner of the shop and concept. (For details on the formation of the *Aarong* shops, see Lovell, 1989.)

In order to expand demand for village-produced products and improve the production of artisans, *Aarong* operates a design center that develops new designs and innovates with traditional designs. In addition to its design services, it provides product development services, training for artisans, and the testing of new products for diversification.

One success of *Aarong* has been in stimulating the use of traditional Bangladeshi designs. An unanticipated but significant consequence of the design center and the six Aarong outlets has been the resurgence of Bangladeshi-produced saris using unique Bangladeshi designs and domestically produced silks and cotton. Aarong is also the main outlet for *nakshi kantha* (traditional embroidery) products, as well as for many other types of textile and handicraft products. In 1990, about 30 percent of *Aarong*'s products were produced by BRAC VO members and Ayesha Abed Foundation producers, with the remaining coming from village artisans all over the country, primarily women. *Aarong*'s six shops are located in Dhaka, Chittagong, and Sylhet. Turnover in 1990 was close to $2 million, and over 200 full-time people are employed in its shops and service divisions.

BRAC Printers

BRAC Printers is a highly profitable, high-quality commercial enterprise that provides printing services to businesses, government, and other NGOs. It also produces all of BRAC's own materials, including proposals, reports, books for all of the schools, BRAC's children's magazine, all the forms for the credit program, and training materials. The company employs on average forty people. It uses the latest printing technology, including a color separation scanner, computerized typesetting, and offset printing machines.

Cold Storage Facility

BRAC also owns and operates a cold storage facility, which was built originally to help very small tenant farmers store potatoes beyond harvest time so they could get a better price. At that time, BRAC was encouraging village groups to grow potatoes as an alternative crop to rice. The plant has a capacity to store 4,250 tons of potatoes, or other produce.

Garment Factories

BRAC's most recent commercial acquisitions are three garment factories. The factories are already commercially viable, but after acquiring more experience in the garment industry, BRAC plans to connect the garment production to the Bangladesh handloom industry, with a goal of eventually using only Bangladeshi-produced materials. At present, most garment factories in Bangladesh serve only as "tailor shops," which turn imported materials into finished products. Garment factories, the fastest-growing industry in Bangladesh in numbers and capacity, are now providing hundreds of thousands of low-paid jobs, especially for women, but they are so far making only a small contribution to the development of related industries. The garment industry has proved that Bangladeshi workers can compete with the rest of the world, but so far only very cheap labor is the value-added component of the final product, since cloth, thread, buttons, zippers, and other findings are almost entirely imported. BRAC hopes to change that pattern by connecting its garment industries to local products.

Conclusion

This overview of BRAC's programs provides only a glimpse of the complex and varied nature of BRAC's current work. It has described how BRAC has grown and how the management has defined its programs through a needs-led approach, how it has branched out, and then branched out farther, in response to dominant needs as expressed in the field.

Activities have been started or developed because of the need for vertical integration. For example, the *Aarong* shops were required in order to provide markets for home industry such as traditional embroidery, leather goods, carving, block printing, and markets for the silk produced by the growing sericulture industry—and to provide leadership in designs and improved quality.

Activities have been developed also because of the dynamic requirement of horizontal integration. The addition of a new element to support others in the RDP village work provides examples. Income-generating projects could not stand alone without credit programs; credit programs could not be successful without the discipline of saving; income-generating skills are required, so training must be provided; sick people cannot conduct successful income-generating projects so health measures are called for; as the previously powerless gain power they want to understand their legal rights, therefore the paralegal program is introduced; and so on.

None of the programs undertaken by BRAC has its own internal logic divorced from the broader needs picture. The design and implementation strategies of each of the programs can be understood only when viewed in relation to the whole complex of interlocking needs of the village poor, and to the other programs that have been designed in response.

CHAPTER 4

Financial Intermediation Activities

THE WORK OF BRAC's Rural Development Program (RDP) and its new bank, the Rural Credit Project (RCP), were discussed in the previous chapter. Further attention is given in this chapter to both programs because financial intermediation activities—credit and savings—are such an important part of the total work. BRAC now operates one of the largest savings and credit programs in the world directed to the rural poor. The present stage in these financial intermediation activities has been reached through trial and error over more than ten years of learning.

Although BRAC started its first experiments with credit in the early 1970s, it began to include credit as a regular part of its development strategy only in 1979. Today credit is a major component of development activities.

The most recent stage in BRAC's financial intermediation activities started at the beginning of 1990, when a full-fledged, self-supporting banking operation was introduced. By the end of 1990, BRAC's landless organizations had, over a ten-year period, mobilized more than $3 million in their own savings, and had received, cumulatively, nearly $20 million in loans from BRAC to finance individual and collective activities. During 1990 alone, BRAC's two credit programs made loans to 150,000 villagers, two-thirds of them women, disbursing close to $12 million that year in loans ranging from $35 to $150. Ninety percent of these loans were used for small individual income-generating schemes, but the remaining 10 percent were collective loans in which borrowers combined to fund larger projects (such as deep tubewells) owned on a share basis by the borrowers and managed by managers they selected.

Savings activity is introduced by the RDP immediately after a village organization (VO) is established. Credit is introduced within three to six months when most group members have completed their initial conscientization training and have demonstrated responsible savings activity.

As we have seen in earlier chapters, the management of BRAC has always been dedicated to "going to scale," but decided to scale up even more extensively beginning in 1989. Through both RDP and the new bank project, RCP, BRAC has planned further rapid growth in its credit operations for the period 1990 to 1993, when credit is expected to more than triple.

Table 4.1, compares BRAC with the other principal credit programs for the poor in Bangladesh. Grameen Bank, a quasi-governmental organization, and BRAC are the largest. Since its credit program began in 1979, BRAC has loaned about 12 percent as much money as the Grameen Bank has since its inception in 1983; however, most of BRAC's growth in credit operations has taken place since 1988. In 1990, BRAC loaned just over $12 million, or about 19 percent as much as Grameen, which loaned about $64 million. BRAC has nearly two-thirds as many members as Grameen; at the end of 1990, BRAC had just over 550,000 members and Grameen nearly 870,000.

Despite the big scaleup in its credit operations, BRAC's managers and field workers are today more convinced than ever that credit, while essential, is not enough by itself to make any sustainable change in the lives of rural people. In light of the experience with income-generating projects being done by villagers, combined with close observation of other credit programs, the BRAC management team has concluded that to bring about effective change to the rural poor, rural development requires not only financial intermediation but institutional intermediation as well. This is especially true in the infrastructure-starved and government-deficient context of Bangladesh. For income-generating projects to be effective, economic subsector constraints, bottlenecks, or failures must be identified and broken, government services must be improved and connected to users, technological improvements must be introduced, and the village borrowers must be offered chances and support in new or improved kinds of economic activities. This chapter describes briefly the history of BRAC's credit operations, and Chapter 5 describes the institutional interventions considered crucial as complements to credit.

The history of BRAC's credit operations can be divided into three stages: 1979–84, 1985–88, and 1989–90.

Early Programs—Stage One: 1979–84

In 1979 and 1980, BRAC established two new core village development programs—the Rural Credit and Training Program (RCTP) in late 1979 ,

Table 4.1 Comparison of Coverage of Selected Programs for the Poor

Organizations	Total membership	Women's membership	Cumulative credit disbursement through Dec. 1990 (in taka*)	Credit disbursement during Jan.–Dec. 1990 (in taka)
NGO Programs				
BRAC	550,449	381,662	903,852,372	443,116,355
Proshika	349,035	160,861	159,656,023	57,329,406
Caritas	130,861	68,047	7,595,000	1,082,227
Quasi-Governmental Programs				
Grameen Bank	869,538	791,606	7,590,663,000	2,262,563,000
Government Programs				
BRDB** Women's Cooperatives	—	136,138	173,000,000	91,000,000
BRDB Rural Cooperatives	—	244,568	272,000,000	99,000,000
Ministry of Women's Affairs	—	39,680	1,883,200	202,500

*Taka approximate exchange rate: 35 to 1 U.S. dollar
**Bangladesh Rural Development Board

Source: Interviews and organizational records

and the Outreach Program in early 1980. The two programs were operated simultaneously in different groups of *upazilas* under separate program heads and structures, so that their results could be compared. The two programs used a similar approach to the organization of the landless (described in Chapter 3). The difference between Outreach and RCTP was primarily the addition of credit as a major component in RCTP. Both programs placed a heavy emphasis on savings and provided both motivation and convenient methods to support the savings activity.

The Outreach Program—Development without Credit

The Outreach Program was designed to test the limits of what the landless poor could accomplish using only their own resources or local resources that could be tapped through existing channels. An underlying premise was that Outreach should not give any economic assistance to the groups, thus forcing the members to focus on ways in which they might mobilize existing resources, including their own savings.

The program combined functional education, training, savings, problem-solving meetings, and logistics support to obtain inputs from government agencies such as seeds, tree saplings, vaccines for chickens or other livestock, fish seedlings or fry for fish-raising projects, and health services.

By the end of 1985, the Outreach Program staff working out of eighteen centers in eleven *upazilas* had organized some 45,000 villagers into just over 800 organizations in 462 villages. Savings by group members amounted to $75,000 over the five-year period.

Rural Credit and Training Program

Though BRAC management and field staff continued to believe strongly in the importance of self-reliance, they also developed a growing awareness of the importance of credit for the poor. The RCTP conducted the same activities as Outreach but in addition provided credit opportunities to the village organization members.

The philosophy on which this program was based was stated in the initial 1979 proposal prepared for donors: "If lending is made to the groups who have reached an institutionally developed stage, under close supervision ensuring their personal stake in the scheme, and if such lending is followed by borrowers training, technical assistance and the provision of marketing facilities, the neglected poor can be transformed into effective tools of development" (BRAC, *Rural Credit*, 1979).

RCTP managers originally assumed that after six months of functional education and consciousness-raising activities, group solidarity would be sufficient to support a credit program. After a short time, the waiting period was changed to one year because BRAC field staff believed that the expectation of credit drove out real concern for group solidarity.

Initial Loan Rules. Under RCTP all loans were made to the village organizations, which in turn made loans to the individual members. Some loans were taken by the VO itself for group undertakings. VO funds were kept in the nearest commercial bank and all banking was done by the management committees of the VOs. Individuals members did not have their own bank books nor did they have any direct dealings with the bank.

No loan was made for consumption purposes, or to a borrower to buy land from another member who owned less land. At this stage, loan repayments started with the receipt of income from the project being financed by the loan. There was supposed to be continuous and intensive monitoring of the borrowers by POs or village management committee members during the life of the loan (although this was sometimes not achieved). Priority was given to loans that had a strong development component and to projects with visible economic and social profitability potential.

To be eligible for loans a VO had to

- have more than fifty members and include at least 50 percent of the target households in the village;
- hold regular weekly meetings attended by at least 50 percent of the members and two-thirds of those willing to borrow;
- ensure that its members made regular weekly savings deposits;
- have savings equivalent to 10 percent of the loan and set these aside in a fixed interest bank account;
- have an elected management committee;
- have completed the functional education course;
- have set aside an amount equal to 20 percent of the loan amount in a fixed interest bank account to safeguard the group savings;
- approve individual or shared projects for which loans were to be given through a recorded resolution taken after discussion in the VO; loans were also approved by the BRAC program organizer and area manager and in the case of larger loans by the RCTP manager or executive director in the Dhaka head office;
- prepare a formal loan proposal against which a check to the group would be issued. (BRAC, *Annual Report of RCTP*, 1980)

Interest Rates, Terms, and Recovery Rate. RCTP started out with a complex interest rate and fee structure. It charged varying interest rates depending on the type of activity to be aided by the loan. Collective activities were given top priority and charged 18 percent interest (which included a 3 percent service charge). An exception was collective agricultural activities for which loans were given at only 15 percent, including the service charge, because they have long gestation periods and low profit margins. Individual loans for manual paddy husking (done almost entirely by women) were also charged 18 percent, plus the 3 percent service charge. Aside from paddy husking, individual loans up to Tk 500 (about $15) carried 21 percent interest, and above Tk 500, 24 percent interest plus service charges. The prevailing interest rates in the formal credit sector ranged from 12 to 36 percent during this time period, the early 1980s.

The loans were repayable at the end of the scheme and were categorized as (1) short-term, repayable within one year; (2) medium-term, up to three years; and (3) long-term, more than three years. Since the loan was given to the VO, not to the individual, it was the VO that was responsible to RCTP for repayment.

In the first three years of RCTP, only about $50,000 was loaned; in the second three years, as the program grew and more VOs were established, loans disbursed totaled $1,750,000. The accumulated savings of members during the first three years was $56,000, and during the second three years, when there were many more members, $300,000.

During the RCTP period, the on-time loan recovery rate averaged about 87.3 percent. The RCTP staff was determined to take a business approach to loan repayment but had to face the question of whether it should and could insist on repayment if an undertaking failed. This is an especially important question because Bangladesh is vulnerable to so many natural catastrophes (such as floods) that destroy fields, livestock, houses, and implements, and raise food costs. An absolutely strict policy of on-time recovery placed the borrowers in great difficulty and could force them back into the hands of the usurious money lender or cause them to sell their meager assets. However, RCTP managers recognized the problems connected with leniency and also recognized that rolling over a loan did not itself increase the borrower's capacity to repay. Writing off loans or rolling them over were clearly not policy options in most cases.

After experimentation with different methods, the RCTP management adopted a new policy for hardship cases in which the repayment periods for the original loans were rescheduled (extended) and an additional loan was offered for a new and hopefully more profitable income-generating project.

Loans during the initial stages of RCTP were made primarily for traditional activities, with heavy emphasis on agriculture, primarily sharecropping. In addition to crop cultivation, loans were given for release of mortgaged land; agricultural implement purchase; pisciculture; fishing implements; purchase of rural transport such as rickshaws, country boats, horse carts, and bullock carts; weaving; pottery making; carpentry; tailoring; net making; food processing; block printing; small trading; cow or goat rearing; poultry keeping; and paddy husking.

Merger of the Two Programs—Stage Two in Credit Activities: 1986

RCTP and Outreach had tested two different approaches. The Research and Evaluation Division of BRAC had been asked to follow and evaluate the results of the two programs. By 1984, BRAC top management, having examined the research findings, decided that the two programs were not really alternatives and neither alone should be selected for further expansion. Under Outreach the village groups had been expected to develop enough savings to be able to make loans to their own members. Evaluation showed, however, that the VOs were unable to generate enough internal savings from their members to support a loan program adequate to meet member needs; and generally the groups had been unable to obtain credit from established banking sources. The research findings concluded that further progress of the group members depended on making credit an integral part of development activities. The researchers found, however, that the emphasis in Outreach on encouraging villagers to focus on ways in which they might mobilize existing local resources was also valuable and should not be lost.

In 1986, the two programs were merged into one Rural Development Program. By that year, the two programs, Outreach and RCTP combined, had established thirty-eight area offices and had organized 1,800 VOs in 900 villages. The Manikganj area, with about 230 VOs and 12,000 members at that time, remained a separately administered pilot area for testing new activities before integration into RDP. The Sulla project with 171 VOs and 7,000 members and the Jamalpur Women's Project with 38 VOs and 1,860 members also retained their separate identities. All three programs included some credit activities.

RDP, the new program, broadened its organizational targets and expanded its credit operations and made several important changes in credit procedures. It also intensified and expanded its institutional inter-mediation activities, to be discussed in detail in Chapter 5.

Early Changes in Interest Rates and Loan Terms under RDP

At first, the RDP leadership made only small changes in the interest rates and loans terms as practiced under RCTP. However, many of the area managers and program organizers (POs) working directly with credit in the villages began to express their opinions that the interest and fee structure was too complicated and the fee differentials were not really accomplishing their purposes. After extensive dialogue in the field and at the head office, the first step was taken to simplify the interest and fee structure so that all loans bore the same interest and charges—18 percent annual interest, plus a group management allowance of 3 percent, plus a group tax of 5 percent.

At this stage, loans were still issued to the VO management commit-tees, which in turn loaned the money for individual or group projects to their members. The VOs continued to keep their accounts in commercial banks.

Experiments with Large Collective Projects

By the mid 1980s, VOs had begun to undertake a number of large projects with RCTP loans. Some sixty-five shallow tubewell schemes had been installed, and experimentation had begun with landless groups owning and operating deep tubewells to supply irrigation water to farm-ers. Three large brick fields had been organized and were functioning profitably. In the largest of these, 30 VOs had joined together as owners. In another area, 56 men's and women's VOs joined together to lease and operate a marketplace in which they sublet spaces to vendors. The elected management committees of the VOs selected management com-mittees for these enterprises.

Housing Loan Program

In 1987, a small rural housing loan program was added to RDP opera-tions financed by a grant of about $1 million. At the beginning, loans were given in three categories: Tk 4,500 ($136), Tk 3,500 ($106), and Tk 2,500 ($75). A larger category of Tk 6,000 was added after the second year. In the first year, some 3,600 housing loans for a total of Tk 13,855,000 (about $407,000) were disbursed. By October 1990, Tk 47,948,000 ($1,410,500) had been loaned.

All housing loans must be repaid in three years, and weekly installments are Tk 22 minimum. The borrower must have saved the equivalent of the monthly payment for six consecutive months before a housing loan is issued.

In the beginning of the program, the interest rate for housing loans to women was 5 percent plus a 3 percent service charge, and for men 7.5 percent plus the 3 percent service charge. But that rate was later equalized to 8 percent for all borrowers, with no service charge. The equalization of the rate is a second example of what became the push for simplification of loan requirements throughout the history of the credit program.

Although the demand for housing loans is great, RDP has not engaged extensively in this loan activity. At present, the housing loan is not being promoted in the newer RDP area offices. RDP managers have decided that income-generating activities must take first priority in a situation of limited resources. Also, until people are better off financially, accumulating the savings required for a housing loan and paying off the loan is very difficult, so most members cannot take the housing loans.

Problems with Village Organizations Emerge

By late 1988, cumulative learning from field experience caused yet another reevaluation by RDP managers of the project's credit program implementation. Problems with the structure and management of the village organizations and with some of the credit management methods became clear.

The first problem was that of accountability by group leaders to members. In some VOs the management committee members were not being changed often enough and in some cases had become so entrenched that they were no longer sufficiently accountable to members for their activities. In some VOs they had become corrupt. Misuse of member funds by VO management committees was discovered by POs and the field accountants. For example, rather than immediately depositing member savings in the bank, some VO management committees had been utilizing member savings to pay off loans made to the VO, or to other borrowers, in order to make the VO or other borrowers eligible for new loans. Also, it was found that some members were never approved for loans by the VO, while other members received many loans. In a few cases, unfortunately in some of the largest of the collective projects (one of the brick factories and the market lease), group leaders and a few BRAC staff members (one an area manager) were collaborating with VO management committees in major corruption with loans and profits. At the urging of BRAC management, those staff members have been prosecuted.

In order to avoid such accountability problems, several major changes were made. The first important change moved the savings and bank account deposits to BRAC itself, replacing the former system whereby the VOs placed their funds in commercial banks. RDP assumed all the banking functions. Also, and equally important, loans are now made to individuals directly rather than through the VOs. Members receive their loans directly from the RDP area offices and keep track of their own savings and loan obligations. Each member maintains his or her own savings and loan books. The VO management committees have access only to the VO group funds, and these are also banked with BRAC.

In another significant change, all members of VOs are now subdivided for credit purposes into small groups of five to seven members. Each group has an elected secretary. The subgroup operates as a peer control group overseeing loan approval, utilization, and repayment. Loans are rotated among the members of the small group. No more than three loans can be taken by a group at a time, and no one in the small group can take a second loan until each person in the group has had a first loan (if they wish and have met the eligibility requirements). Although the small group now does the supervision of individual loans, all loans must be approved by a two-thirds vote of the VO members.

The composition of the VO management committees was restructured. Under the new system, the secretaries of the small groups make up the management committees of the VOs on a rotating basis. Half of the secretaries serve as the management committee one year, the other half the next year, and so on; under this form of rotating leadership, every two years the small groups are reorganized and new secretaries are elected so that the leadership is genuinely rotated on a regular basis.

Finally, the waiting period for a first loan was dropped from six months to three months for women. Men must wait six months for their first loan.

A second problem involved the functional education requirement. Since the beginning of RCTP in 1979, one of the prerequisites for a VO to become a recognized group to whom loans could be made was that most of its members had to have completed the required sixty-lesson functional education course. By the mid-1980s, in many branches fewer than half of the members were actually completing the full sixty-lesson course. For many people, particularly older people, the course was too long. Reevaluation in the field led to the reduction from sixty to thirty lessons for the required section, although learners can still take the full sixty lessons if they wish; about 50 percent opt to do so.

Completion of the thirty-lesson course is now enforced as a prerequisite for credit. During the course, each member now also learns seventeen points that pledge her or him to certain kinds of social behavior. These seventeen promises are repeated by all members at the beginning of all meetings. They are also printed on the back of each member's savings and loan books. Following is the list of those promises, which the VOs are continually reviewing for possible revision:

1. We shall not do malpractice and injustice.
2. We shall work hard and bring prosperity to our family.
3. We shall send our children to school.
4. We shall adopt family planning and keep our family size small.
5. We shall try to be clean and keep our house tidy.
6. We shall always drink pure water.
7. We shall not keep our food uncovered and will wash our hands and face before we take our meal.
8. We shall construct latrines and shall not leave our stool where it doesn't belong.
9. We shall cultivate vegetables and trees in and around our house.
10. We shall try to help others under all circumstances.
11. We shall fight against polygamy and injustices to our wives and all women.
12. We shall be loyal to the Organization and abide by its rules and regulations.
13. We shall not sign anything without having a good understanding of what it means (we will look carefully before we act).
14. We shall attend weekly meetings regularly and on time.
15. We shall always abide by the decisions of the weekly group meetings.
16. We shall regularly deposit our weekly savings.
17. If we receive a loan we will repay it on time.

A third problem was a loan recovery rate that was less than satisfactory. Although a great deal of attention had been given to loan recovery, the on-time rates still hovered in many branches at only 92 to 95 percent when the goal was 98 percent. Under the old rules, repayment did not begin until the investment financed by the loan began to pay off and a variety of repayment schedules were in use.

In 1989, steps were taken to improve recovery rates. The repayment system was changed by RDP to require repayment on all loans to begin immediately after receipt of the loan, and all repayment schedules were changed to weekly. If a villager takes a longer-term loan for a project on which returns are not expected for some time, a second income-generating activity could be undertaken with an expected short-term payoff to help with the required weekly loan payments. The weekly payments for all loans are very small.

Also, a common set of requirements for loan eligibility was established. The minimum savings requirement for loan eligibility was stabilized at 5 percent of the requested loan for the first loan, 10 percent for the second, and an increasing 5 percent for each additional loan. All members must save at least Tk 2 per week, though many members save more than the minimum, particularly as they begin to earn extra income from the investment of loans in individual or collective activities. No one can receive a loan who is indebted to another organization or has a poor repayment record on earlier loans. The borrower must have a record of fifteen weeks regular saving and also have saved at least Tk 50 (about $3.00) during the six months prior to a loan.

In 1989, RDP managers again simplified interest rates, and an additional compulsory savings and insurance scheme related to loans was introduced. Under the new rules *all* loans (except the housing loans) carry a 16 percent annual interest rate. At the time of distribution of the loan, 10 percent of the total loan is withheld. Half, 5 percent, is deposited in the individual's savings fund, 4 percent in the VO fund, and 1 percent in an insurance fund that pays up to Tk 5,000 (about $140) to the borrower's family in case of the borrower's death.

At the same time as loan interest rates were simplified, a rate of 9 percent interest payment on individual savings was established. Savings can be withdrawn only when a member has been saving for four years or more, or leaves a VO.

Under the new small-group structure and weekly repayment system, loan recovery has been advanced to the 98 percent desired target level.

A fourth problem that had become evident, especially to the POs, was inadequate attendance at meetings. Some VOs had slipped to 50 percent attendance at meetings. To help solve the problem, the RDP program coordinator and regional and area managers, after extensive discussion with the POs, decided to reorganize meeting schedules and make more specific the purposes of the different kinds of meetings required. They believed that this clarification would make meetings more purposeful and attractive.

Under the revised system the VOs hold short weekly meetings in the morning before working hours at which all savings are submitted and repayment of loans takes place. Loans are disbursed by BRAC on a preset day each week at the area offices, not at these morning meetings. A second, monthly meeting of the full VO, in the afternoons for women's VOs and in the evenings for men's VOs, now deal with common issues such as group projects and social problems—health, children's education, family planning, sanitation, the status of women, nutrition, and so on.

The small member groups, each consisting of five to seven members, meet as they feel it necessary on their own schedules. The management committee, made up of the elected secretaries of the small groups, meets monthly.

To be eligible for a loan, a potential borrower must have attended meetings regularly, and this requirement is being enforced.

Reflections on the Four Problems

The introduction of the new systems and rules to address the four problems identified above was intended not only to improve accountability, remove opportunities for corruption, and provide for more individual responsibility and individual learning, but also to sustain a strong support group situation. Reflecting on the decade of experience and the necessity for this latest round of changes, the RDP coordinator, a twenty-year veteran with BRAC, said that he and others had started with the belief that villagers, when properly organized, could do everything. He and other BRAC leaders had learned, however, that too much financial responsibility had been given, too fast, to the VOs without enough real development of the members and without enough controls on the leadership. They had learned the hard way, he said, what the motivational consequences would be of each of the financial management systems they had tried. In spite of their ideals, experience had taught them the extent to which the Bangladesh context of corruption and exploitation, within which the poor people's groups must operate, would affect the groups' leaders' actions. New systems to make such corruption more difficult had been required.

The RDP Program Coordinator and his Area Office Managers also recognized that some of their norms for staff and VO leader training and supervision, and the norms for VO membership eligibility and loan eligibility, had been diluted in the process of rapid expansion. The pressure to organize more groups, and to make more loans, caused the staff members to overlook some of the important institution-building activities required to properly develop the VOs. They had actually disregarded some of their own rules while pushing forward. In extensive discussions between management and field staff, a consensus was reached that the norms must be more realistic and enforced more thoroughly. RDP managers recognized the need for better control systems, and realized that they needed to catch up on services that may have been slighted—such as leadership training and accountability systems in the VOs.

RDP managers also decided that retraining some of their own field staff was necessary. A great deal of emphasis had been placed by the top RDP program managers on the credit operations; branch managers had been evaluated primarily on the amount of money loaned and the recovery rates. Insufficient attention had been given to other variables such as social development in groups, fair loan coverage, loan usage, adequate participation in VO meetings, and other developmental aspects.

Stage Two had clearly brought significant change to the credit and savings program. Stage Three was entered with new rules and norms in place.

Stage Three—The Bank Project: 1989–91

In 1989, BRAC entered a new stage in its financial intermediation activities. RDP was greatly expanded and a new bank project, called the Rural Credit Project, was introduced.

By the late 1980s, BRAC managers were exploring ways to make the credit operations self-sustaining without losing the institutional intermediation activities they thought were so important for the development of the villagers. In 1989, the management team developed a plan that promised to accomplish both purposes. The plan called for a sequenced two-stage program in which RDP in the first stage would continue to do what it had done in the past, but with even more rapid expansion: organize the poorest villagers, offer functional education and conscientization, provide training in leadership and group skills as well as technical skills, facilitate economic subsector improvements, and introduce primary education and health care programs in cooperation with the Non-Formal Primary Education and Women's Health and Development programs. Credit and savings services would also be continued and expanded. In the second stage, however, RDP's mature VOs, those at least four years old, would be graduated to a significantly different program, the Rural Credit Project, and would receive banking services from this new bank.

In early 1989, the executive director of BRAC discussed the idea with the Netherlands Organization for International Development Cooperation (NOVIB) the long-term principal supporter of RCTP and RDP. The amount of money required for the new, two-stage program was beyond NOVIB's capabilities, but NOVIB suggested the formation of a consortium similar to one in which they had participated for the financing of Sarvodaya in Sri Lanka. Together, NOVIB and Abed, the executive director, gathered together a group of donors to discuss the proposal. As a result of the dialogue, a consortium of nine donors was formed. Its members agreed to provide sufficient money, $50 million, for a major expansion of RDP and the addition of the new bank project to begin in 1990 and continue through 1992. The consortium is now expected to continue funding for this program at that or a higher level after 1992.

The original nine members of the consortium were: the Aga Khan Foundation (AKF), the Canadian International Development Agency (CIDA), the Danish International Development Agency (DANIDA), Evangelische Zentralstelle für Entwicklungshilfe (EZE of Germany), Ford Foundation (FF), NOVIB, the Royal Norwegian Embassy Development Cooperation (NORAD), the British Overseas Development Administration (ODA), and the Swedish International Development Agency (SIDA). The government of Japan has also been invited to join the consortium and is expected to do so since it has now made a small initial grant.

In late 1988, RDP had introduced changes that had transformed its savings and credit activities into ones that were almost indistinguishable from those of a bank. RDP has maintained those activities, which has helped make the transition of the mature village organizations to the bank project relatively smooth.

The RCP establishes its branches by buying from RDP its "mature" area offices and their developed village organizations. An area office is considered mature when it is at least four years old and the 100 VOs under it are socially developed and have reached a level of savings and loan activity in which the outstanding loans made to the VO members are sufficiently large that the income generated at the present 16 percent interest rate will cover the ongoing operating costs. At the point of transition, RCP buys the RDP's investment in the area offices being transferred, including the VO members' outstanding loans, net of savings, the physical infrastructure of the area office, and the staff complement. Each area office covers 100 VOs, with sixty to seventy members in each, or a total of 6,000 to 7,000 members.

The costs of the initial RDP developmental period of four or more years, during which villagers are organized and infrastructure developed, have been borne largely by donor grant funds. The costs of ongoing bank operations are paid for by RCP's own savings and loan operations and investments, although the buy-out costs of purchasing the area offices during the first three years in which the bank is getting established are covered by donor grants.

On the basis of RDP's experience it is conservatively assumed that 55–60 percent of the members of a VO will be regular borrowers, with increases in the average loan size occurring as members gain experience in using credit. It has been shown that for the average borrower at the end of the fourth year under RDP, loan size rose from the first average of Tk 1,300 (about $37.00) to Tk 3,100 (about $89).

Experience of the First Eighteen Months of RCP

The Rural Credit Project has been operating since the beginning of 1990 as a bank in all but formal name. On the advice of senior officials in the Bangladesh Bank, the country's central bank, and after careful consideration of various alternative structural options, the BRAC board has approved a two-step process in formalizing the structure of a BRAC bank. The "bank" is initially beginning as a "project" of BRAC called the Rural Credit Project. After two to three years of operating experience it will be organized into a formal bank in any one of several ways.

One option is to request a special charter from the government to establish a separate legal entity similar to Grameen Bank. This option has potential problems; for example, the government would participate and therefore have partial control. Another option is to organize as a relatively independent cooperative bank. More options are being explored. Plans for the borrowers to become shareholders have been delayed while precise ownership and structural decisions are in abeyance. The only significant difference between the RCP as now being operated and a registered bank is in the ownership and management structures. A formalized BRAC bank, no matter which structure is adopted, would require a new board of directors. The Rural Credit Project is currently controlled by BRAC's existing board.

In late 1989, RCP bought out its first ten RDP area offices, which became RCP's first ten branches. In the first half of 1991, RCP bought out twenty more area offices, and twenty additional area offices were planned for 1992. At the end of 1992, the bank will have fifty branches, or a total of some 5,000 VOs and a potential borrower pool of 250 to 275 thousand villagers.

As Figure 3.3 shows, each RCP branch has a staffing level of one manager, three program organizers and ten *gram shebok* (GS) village assistants. Just as under RDP, the POs and GSs meet with the VOs and small five-to-seven-member borrower groups, give advice on economic schemes, help prepare and process loan applications, collect loan installments and savings, and solve special credit problems. Also, about 20 percent of the POs' time is spent on nonfinancial services to VOs, including leading discussions on social issues at village organization meetings. Their assistants, the *gram sheboks*, regularly meet with the small borrower groups, collect weekly loan repayments and savings deposits, and help with other activities.

During 1990, its first year of operation, BRAC was not yet functioning as fully as anticipated because of a delay in the transfer of some of the donor funds to BRAC. BRAC was able to loan some of its own funds to RCP so that the delay did not greatly reduce the amount of money available for loans. However, the delay did prevent investment of bank money, other than in member loans, and therefore earnings from such investment were nil. In the early years of the bank project, its profitability expectations were heavily dependent on income from external investments.

Not enough experience has yet been gained to thoroughly evaluate the bank project. However, the first Annual Donor Review (BRAC *Annual Review*, 1990) found that in its first year, RCP was on target for profit, although it achieved this target in a somewhat different manner than forecast. There were fewer borrowers than projected (about 64,000 rather than the 79,000 projected), but average loan size at Tk 4,017 (about $115) was larger than expected, and more borrowers took middle- and long-terms loans than anticipated. Had RCP received the investment funds from donor sources on time, it would have earned interest income from resulting investments equal to an amount sufficient to record a very respectable profit. The donors are now expected to make up for the lost interest income and then make sure that future funds are transferred as scheduled.

The members' funds position was below forecast because anticipated savings transferred from the area offices of RDP were lower than anticipated. In some cases, particularly in the very old groups (in the first buyouts some of the VOs being transferred were as old as nine years), the individual members were not actually saving as faithfully as they had indicated; in others, the VOs had invested savings funds in income-generating schemes and therefore the cash was not available to transfer to the bank at the moment of buy-out, but would be transferred later when available. Also, the compulsory savings that accompany loans were below projections due to the reduced number of loans disbursed. The review team anticipated that the trend will correct itself shortly since the new area offices of RDP are exceeding savings targets.

Although a formal review for 1991 is not yet available, managers of RCP and accountants have reported that the performance of RCP was exceeding targets for that year.

The on-time recovery rate for loans under RCP during its first year and a half of operation was 98 percent. To be consistent with the definition of on-time recovery used by the Grameen Bank, on-time recovery is defined by both RDP and RCP as the loan and interest paid in full within one year of the due date.

The savings rates in RCP have been good. By the end of the first year, total individual savings were 43 percent higher than when the members were transferred from RDP to RCP. Savings on deposit had increased by 96 percent over the year (men's groups by 87 percent and women's groups by 102 percent).

Patterns of Sectoral Lending

The pattern of sectoral lending under RCP has been similar to the pattern under RDP, although some sectors have increased and some have decreased. Figure 4.1 compares cumulative lending under RDP through December 1989 with the combined lending of RDP and RCP from January 1990 through June 1991. The figure shows an increase of 8 percent in lending for livestock and poultry, and a 6 percent increase for lending in rural trading during that period. It also shows lending in irrigation up 2 percent and rural transport up nearly 4 percent. The most notable reductions in lending were in agriculture, down from 12 percent to 2 percent, and in food processing (primarily women's paddy husking), which was down from 15 percent to 6 percent.

These changes confirm the effect of RDP's economic subsector interventions described in the Chapter 5. Both women and men borrowers are gradually moving away from the more traditional and marginal occupations to different and hopefully more profitable ones.

Concerns about RCP

Two issues about RCP's operations are paramount and will be watched carefully by BRAC managers, donors, and external observers.

The first issue is profitability. Can the bank operations actually be profitable enough to cover operating costs once a buy-out of savers and borrowers is achieved? Can the bank project become independent of donor money? The experience of the first year and a half indicates that it will be possible.

The second issue is whether or not financial intermediation services will be sufficient to really help the village poor climb out of social and economic poverty without extensive institutional intermediation, even after the fourth year. A major, longtime European donor to BRAC did not join the donor consortium because its representatives are convinced that financial intermediation without continuation of other aid is insufficient in the Bangladesh context, even after several years of developmental activities. Actually, under the original plan for RCP, BRAC management first proposed that area offices should be transferred to the bank project

Figure 4.1 Distribution of Credit Disbursements by Sector

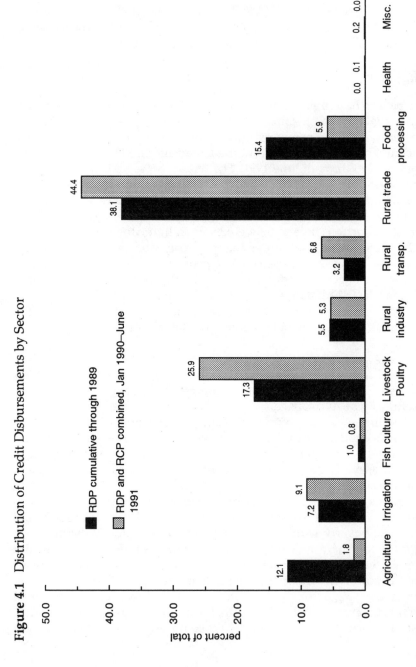

■ RDP cumulative through 1989

▨ RDP and RCP combined, Jan 1990–June 1991

Source: BRAC RED, 1991

at the end of three years. The donor consortium appraisal mission and RDP managers interacting together, however, became convinced that at least four years of development was needed before the bank's financial intermediation, without attendant subsidized developmental activities, could really achieve its development purposes. Although the bank might achieve its profitability goals, it might not achieve its real development goals.

Besides extending the RDP development period from three years to four years, the donors and RDP managers agreed that additional institution-building support by RDP should be continued after the RDP area offices and their VOs are bought out by RCP. As one result of these concerns, arrangements have been made so that during the first two years after transfer to the RCP, BRAC's training centers will make available two trainers for each ten RCP branches to assist with special social training needs and village organization institutional issues. These trainers are responsible for promoting and monitoring the progress of the VO committees; assessing their needs for training, workshops, or other inputs; assisting in the management of large collective economic schemes; and generally monitoring the progress of institution building and social change. Several of the donors urged BRAC to include the services of these trainers in the RDP budget and make them available to the bank branches because they were concerned that the burden of strictly banking activities would overwhelm the POs working for the bank branches. As a consequence, insufficient attention might be given to the continuing institutional development of the village organizations.

Another safeguard against insufficient attention to institution building is the expectation that the bank branch POs will spend roughly 20–25 percent of their time on institution building by attending the monthly social issues meetings of the VOs and otherwise dealing with VO member problems. To further safeguard the commitment to institution building, all field staff recruited to the bank project must have spent a minimum of one year under an RDP area office before they can be transferred to the bank project.

In addition to the above safeguards, a special monitoring division was established outside the bank budget to monitor a set of development indicators as well as financial indicators in the village on a regular basis. (More information on BRAC's monitoring activities is provided in Chapters 6 and 7.)

Careful monitoring of the experience under RCP, and in-depth research over several years, will provide evidence of how the various problems are solved and how the services needed by the members of the village organizations are obtained. The VOs and individual borrowers under the bank branches may still wish to avail themselves of RDP services such as training, assistance in relations with government to obtain needed inputs, or assistance with technical aspects of income-generating projects. Ways are being found for borrowers to pay BRAC for such services. Already, borrowers in fourth-year RDP area offices are beginning to pay for the special training or specialist consultations required to make their investment projects successful.

First Eighteen Months RDP's of Scaled-up Program: 1990–91

The scaled-up RDP, which provides extensive credit operations for the VOs in their first four years of operation, is a continuation of RDP but a greatly expanded program. In 1991, RDP with ninety areas offices was to lend about $10 million. RCP with its thirty branches was to lend about $7 million. In addition to its financial intermediation activities, RDP actively pursues its institutional intermediation roles of organizing and developing new groups, intervening in economic subsectors to reduce constraints, and facilitating with government to improve services. (These last two institutional intermediation activities are discussed more fully in Chapter 5.)

This latest stage in RDP's credit operations started with the new rules and regulations for credit in place. The transition to strict enforcement of these new rules, designed to enhance accountability and internal democracy in the village organizations, turned out to be more problematic than expected. When rules were tightened, some members left or were asked to leave the VOs, and a number of older VOs were closed or restructured. Altogether about 10,000 members were lost (some of them only temporarily). The cleanup and restructuring process described earlier in this chapter was completed at the end of 1990.

Over the years, some of the members of the VOs (almost entirely male) who did not strictly meet the membership criteria, enticed by the credit opportunities, had found their way into VO membership and sometimes onto the management committees. These people, technically landless, were what Bangladeshis call *touts*, that is, those who make their living by exploiting others rather than by selling their labor. Under the revised structures, membership is limited not only to those who own less than .5 acres of land but also to those who must sell at least 100 days of labor per year in order to subsist. As another safeguard, at least 50 percent of each group must have no land at all.

The new method, in which all loans are made directly to individuals rather than to the VOs, with individuals handling their own savings books and loan books, has reduced the possible roles for *touts*.

The restructuring and cleaning up of the VOs had some other troubling side effects. A temporary bottleneck in lending was created because of the restructuring process and because those who had not completed the obligatory thirty-lesson awareness training were required to take it before they could obtain a loan. Coverage of the backlog of people needing such training took almost a year.

In spite of these problems, RDP pursued its 1990 expansion goals both in numbers of new groups organized and in amounts of credit supplied. It achieved its 1990 goal of forming twenty new area offices, which organized the landless in 1,300 new villages into some 1,900 new male and female VOs with 108,500 new members. Also achieved was issuance of $12 million of credit in 1990 with a recovery rate of 98 percent. RDP managers expect to be able to turn over to the bank a healthy group of twenty mature area offices each year.

Conclusion

BRAC's decade-long experience with major credit programs for the poor provides several lessons. *First,* keep the programs simple. In its first credit activities, BRAC attempted to use variable interest and fee rates as incentives for certain kinds of investment behavior; for example, group activities received more favorable rates than individual activities, and certain kinds of investments (those considered superior developmentally) received more favorable rates than others. Area managers and POs handling loans in the villages came more and more to realize that for effectiveness and efficiency of operation the interest and fee structure should be kept uniform. If priority is to be given to certain clients (for example, women), the team learned that it is better to do it by means other than interest rate structures. As a case in point, women may now begin to borrow after three months' membership; men must wait six months.

A *second* lesson learned was that individual responsibility for loans and loan repayment must be maximized. The original two-tier method of loaning money to the VOs, which in turn loaned the money to its members, was too complex and opened possibilities for favoritism and corruption. The system of having each individual borrower handling his or her own loan with individual savings and credit books, provides more accountability, increases individual responsibility, and results in a higher repayment rate.

The *third* lesson was the value of simplification and immediacy of repayment schedules. In the initial credit operations, loan repayment scheduling was tied to the nature of the scheme and to the point at which it began to make money. In most cases, repayment did not start until income was generated from the scheme. That system required heavy monitoring to make sure that loans were invested as promised at the time of borrowing and required more loaner (BRAC) involvement than is feasible or cost-effective. Under the current system used in both RDP and RCP, repayment is made in small, weekly installments and begins the week after the loan is received. This simple and immediate repayment schedule motivates the borrower to move ahead rapidly with his or her investment. The small, but regular, weekly installment amounts makes repayment relatively painless but ties the loan immediately to a disciplined repayment process. The result of this system has been improved loan recovery rates and more cost-effective credit provision operations.

A *fourth* lesson learned was that credit operations alone were not enough to wean villagers from the traditional money lenders who loan money at very high rates (often 100 to 300 percent). Although dependence on these sources has diminished, BRAC's field workers report that it has not fully ended. First, BRAC's credit programs reach only the target group, the poorest of the villagers. Many other villagers, not members of BRAC groups, still resort to the traditional sources. Recent research, in fact, shows that the patron-client relationship and exploitative mechanisms of money lenders have intensified for nonmembers of BRAC or Grameen (Bhattacharya, 1990). Also, even BRAC VO members have turned to the money lenders under certain circumstances, particularly medical emergencies or special occasions such as marriages when larger sums of money are needed. In recognition of this problem, both RDP and RCP have introduced consumption loans funded from the savings of the group members.

Finally, as a result of RDP's institutional intermediation efforts (discussed in the Chapter 5) and individual learning on the part of borrowers, there have been significant changes in the composition of the loan portfolio over the decade since the inception of BRAC's major credit activities. These changes are (1) movement from loans for very small-scale traditional activities toward newer, more profitable investments; and (2) movement toward asset-based and longer-term loans.

CHAPTER 5

Institutional Intermediation

MANY REFERENCES HAVE been made in the previous chapters to BRAC's institutional intermediation work. In this context, institutional intermediation means the work of organizing and conscientizing the poorest in the villages. It means forming village organizations (VOs) and helping the members learn methodologies and skills for understanding their own situations. It means helping village men and women acquire a framework that permits them to reject fatalism and enables them to analyze their own communities and the structures of economic forces and exploitation that have caused their poverty. VO members are also encouraged and helped to survey and take advantage of all assets that might be available to them through government programs (such as unused government lands or ponds or food-for-work programs). Also, with the help of BRAC's health program, members undertake sanitation and health improvement activities so that extensive illness does not interfere with income-generating work.

Another essential part of BRAC's institutional intermediation work is extensive intervention in selected economic subsectors which is accomplished by identifying constraints and obstacles and finding ways to overcome them. BRAC has been determined to help its village organization members avoid "the low-level equilibrium trap" in which borrowers continue to invest in traditional activities that are only marginally profitable (Rahman, 1988). In discussing "credit only" programs, such as those of Grameen Bank, Rahman says that the rate of return from the activities pursued by Grameen Bank borrowers is not very high (Rahman, 1988, p. 226). As he points out, one has to evaluate the rate of return, keeping in view what alternative income-earning opportunities these poor, particularly poor women, would have had before joining the bank. BRAC also recognizes that these borrowers are better off than they were before, but believes that they could make even more progress if the opportunities in the economic subsectors in which they are investing could be improved. Avoiding or overcoming the low-level equilibrium trap provides one important part of the rationale for why BRAC leadership decided not to conduct "credit only" programs and why the Rural Development Program (RDP) invests staff time and money in a range of economic subsector interventions designed to enhance profitability possibilities for the village borrowers.

BRAC's institutional intermediation in selected economic subsectors has taken many forms, depending on the sector. Most improvements have required initiatives to stimulate relevant government ministries to supply required services or other inputs. It has also been necessary to develop new sources of input or output services, sometimes in relationship with international and local nongovernmental organizations (NGOs), sometimes through BRAC-developed businesses and often through businesses developed by BRAC village organizations or individual members.

In 1985, BRAC (with Ford Foundation funding and the loan of one small enterprise expert) established a small unit called the Rural Enterprise Program (REP) to examine and test new ideas for rural enterprises and to develop and test ways to improve performance in existing rural industry. External consultants—specialists in fields such as fishing, sericulture, textiles, irrigation, and soap making—joined local experts to examine subsector operations, suggest projects, and evaluate field tests. REP continues to operate with eleven staff members, and although it has made no major breakthroughs in introducing new industries, its work has contributed to improvements in the economic subsectors where BRAC has decided to concentrate. This chapter focuses on the institutional intermediation work in the economic subsectors selected thus far by BRAC for intervention. The interventions began in the early and mid-1980s and have concentrated to date primarily on five subsectors: poultry, livestock, sericulture, fisheries, and irrigation. The interventions are having substantial payoffs in the 1990s. In each of these sectors RDP managers and sector specialists started intervening in a modest way, learned from field experience what the bottlenecks were, and then experimented with ways of overcoming them. When an intervention worked well in one RDP area, it was spread to other areas.

Poultry

Efforts to improve the quality and quantity of homestead poultry raising has had major payoffs. Obstacles such as the unavailability of high yield variety (HYV) chicks, unavailability of vaccines and trained vaccinators, and lack of trained chick raisers and distributors were recognized early as the main constraints to improvements in this subsector. Once the constraints were recognized, experiments were begun to find ways to overcome them.

RDP staffers entered the poultry subsector in a very small way in the late 1970s in its Manikganj experimental area. They began by training some 400 women members how to improve household chicken raising. The training was accompanied by a modest HYV cock replacement program. In 1978, BRAC's principal training and resource center (TARC), not far from Manikganj, added a small poultry farm in order to experiment with the supply of HYV hens and cocks to village women. No reliable private sources for improved variety stock existed, and since the government had only one hatchery near any of the BRAC village areas, it could make available only a limited supply of HYV fertile eggs or chicks. The TARC poultry farm first supplied fertile eggs to the rearers, but problems of breakage, incubation, and loss were high.

During this period, the managers and a newly hired poultry specialist at the Manikganj experimental area set a goal of having ten to twenty chicken rearers among the landless families in every one of its 200 villages, each rearer with a minimum of one high yield variety cock and ten hens. A serious problem soon became evident when there was an insufficient supply of HYV chicks to meet the enlarged demand. The Manikganj management undertook to solve the problem by training the better rearers to establish small chick-rearing units. Loans were made to these women, called chick rearers, to purchase or build the necessary facilities, primarily small bamboo structures in which the day old chicks could be raised to an age when they could be sold to the other village women who wanted to become key rearers. Loans also assisted the chick rearers to purchase larger numbers of day-old chicks.

A few of these chick rearers were able to obtain HYV chicks directly from the government hatcheries, but most are too far away from the hatchers. As the program spread to other areas, RDP set up a trucking system in which, seven days a week, four trucks pick up day-old HYV chicks from the government hatcheries and deliver them to various RDP area offices. The village chick rearers know which days the chicks will arrive at their closest area office and are there to pick up the number they want to buy. To pay for the trucking costs, the RDP truckers buy the chicks for Tk 7 each from the government hatcheries and sell them to the chick rearers for Tk 8 each. In mid-1991, 150,000 chicks a month were being delivered by the trucks, but the number was expected to reach 200,000 per month by the end of the year. Plans are being discussed to turn over the trucking operation to village organizations, which will set up a shareholding system using credit to buy the trucks, hire the drivers, maintain the trucks, and buy the first chicks.

As the chick rearing increased, a second problem soon became apparent. An unacceptable number of young chicks were dying from poultry diseases. Chicks need to be vaccinated within seven days of hatching. Without the early vaccinations and other medicines within the first month of life, only one in ten birds survives to adult life. In order to solve this problem, the Manikganj manager and his poultry expert, jointly with the area office of the Directorate of Livestock and Poultry, developed a vaccination program for the 200 villages in the Manikganj area. The VOs in each village were asked to nominate one woman to be trained as a vaccinator; after BRAC trained the vaccinators for five days, the government supplied each graduate with free syringes and vaccines. Vaccines are controlled by the government and not available on the open market. The women are encouraged to buy additional medicines to treat certain poultry diseases they have learned about in their training. The medicines are produced by local pharmaceutical firms, and the women buy them from the government, on the open market, or at cost plus 5 percent from the closest RDP area offices if private stores or government offices are not accessible. These trained women vaccinators, known as "poultry workers," are paid by the rearers a few taka to vaccinate each of their chicks and to supply medicines as needed. It was found that one poultry worker is needed for every 1,000 chickens.

The program was expanded beginning in the mid-1980s from the Manikganj experimental area to all the BRAC RDP areas. By mid-1991 there were more than 11,000 chick rearers who had supplied nearly 750,000 HYV chicks to 132,000 key rearers in 3,500 villages. Serving these rearers were nearly 9,000 poultry workers who had administered more than 12,600,000 doses of vaccine to chicks and mature birds and had supplied necessary medicines.

The poultry workers (vaccinators) and the chick rearers receive five days' training from RDP; key rearers (those who raise the chickens in their homesteads) get one day of training. A poultry worker earns about Tk 150 to 250 ($4.30 to $7.00) per month; a chick rearer who has twenty-two hens and three cocks and rears the small chicks to saleable age makes about Tk 500 per month; and a key rearer with one cock and ten hens about Tk 110. For most of the women, household poultry raising or vaccination work is part-time employment compatible with home duties.

As the poultry-raising activities grew and spread to other RDP areas, further problems appeared. Although the household chickens fend for themselves and eat from what they can forage in their environment, the

HYV chick-rearing units, which sell the chicks to the household rearers, require prepared, properly formulated chicken feed for the very small chicks. None was available on the market. To break this bottleneck RDP began to train and make loans to people to become feed makers and suppliers. The training included such management aspects as how to locate and purchase the ingredients, how to mix proper proportions and measures, and how to do a market survey so that feed, which once mixed has a short shelf life, would not spoil before being sold. By mid-1990, ninety-five women and men were operating successfully as feed merchants and the numbers were growing rapidly.

An additional problem appeared and is also being overcome. Because egg production is becoming so widespread, egg marketing systems had to be developed. In 1989, RDP began encouraging some of the village organization members to become egg sellers and issued trading loans to facilitate the business. By 1990, there were eighty-eight "upgraded egg sellers," each buying eggs from fifteen to twenty villages and selling them in the larger urban markets. The number of upgraded egg sellers is growing rapidly now that a collection system to facilitate the work has been devised. The egg seller (most of the egg sellers are male) is now linked to the village poultry worker, who in addition to her vaccination duties buys the eggs door-to-door from the producers in her village and makes them available on preset collection days to the egg trader. The trader must pay her a 10 percent markup above the price she pays to the rearers. The set price was introduced by RDP and the VOs after experience showed that the egg sellers would often attempt to take advantage of the female poultry worker to obtain a lower price.

Because of its successful track record in the poultry sector, RDP, in collaboration with the World Food Program, the Ministry of Relief and Rehabilitation of the government, and the Directorate of Livestock and Poultry, is now running a major program for destitute women called Income Generation for Vulnerable Group Development (IGVGD). As described in Chapter 3, the purpose of the program is to provide training and other systemic supports to the women, so at the end of two years they will be off the relief program and have an income at least equal to their relief ration—31.25 kilograms of wheat per month.

The IGVGD program is essentially the same as the poultry program described above, with BRAC organizing the women and supplying motivation, training, systems development, and credit support, and with the Directorate of Livestock and Poultry supplying the initial HYV chicks and vaccines. In spite of some supply bottlenecks in the government ministry, over 80,000 of the destitute women were trained during 1990 for the various jobs in the poultry sector, from household rearer to feed merchant. About $668,000 in credit was supplied to set the women up in business. Even among these previously destitute women, loan realization rates have been over 98 percent.

Benefits Versus Investment Costs in Poultry

Various ways of calculating costs and benefits indicate that for a very modest investment, payoffs for village women and their families have been large. One economic analysis of the poultry program (Ahmad, 1991) shows that for a total investment during the year 1990 by BRAC and the government amounting to $471,494, net returns, including interest on loans accruing to BRAC and increases in the income of poultry workers, key rearers, household rearers, feed processors, and egg collectors, have amounted to $2,172,434, a net profit on investment of $1,770,940.

Other benefits not listed above include the vastly improved status of many thousands of women who now have their own sources of income, the nutritional impact in the form of consumption of eggs and chicken by the rearer families and their customers, and the growth of saving, borrowing, and banking habits of the poultry rearers.

Another study (Mallick, 1989) compared the economic profitability of a group of rearers under BRAC's HYV poultry program with the profitability of a control group using traditional breeds and rearing methods. The BRAC intervention group showed mean income almost twice that of the control group.

Livestock

The livestock sector—household goat and cattle rearing (cattle are used as draught animals as well as for milk and meat)—became an emphasis of BRAC in the mid-1980s. Women members in particular asked for credit so that they could rear livestock. This was possible for them on very small plots of household land. Together with poultry, this sector accounts for almost 26 percent of all loans made in the credit programs. BRAC field workers responded to their VO members' demands by taking a hard look at this subsector and seeing how it could be improved. They immediately found that an unacceptably high percentage of the cows or goats died.

A staff study showed that the main obstacles in livestock rearing were the lack of trained veterinarians, a lack of knowledge about rearing methods, shortages of fodder, and the need to improve breeds.

By the end of 1990, RDP had responded by training 636 livestock paravets, more than half female, to give vaccinations, treat simple diseases
and advise on rearing techniques. All of the livestock paravets work on a
fee-for-service basis and by the end of 1990 had vaccinated some 450,000
animals. BRAC also worked with the government's Directorate of
Livestock and Poultry to set up a training program to train artificial inseminators so that breeds could be improved. By the end of 1990, sixty
villagers had been given two weeks of training by the government on insemination, and they now work out of twenty-four newly established or
upgraded artificial insemination centers from which the government
supplies semen and equipment. More inseminators are currently being
trained.

By the end of 1990, over 30,000 livestock rearers had been given three
days of training by BRAC in improved rearing methods and new methods to produce and find fodder.

One important objective of the program is to raise cattle and goats on
fodder from household, embankment, or agriculturally deficient land
and never to utilize land that is otherwise useful for grain production for
grazing livestock. An important part of the training is to teach new methods to produce and find fodder.

Again—Benefits Versus Investment Costs in Livestock

Since the program is relatively new, no rigorous cost/benefit analysis is
yet available; however, it is apparent that for a minimal investment of
$72,000 by the government and BRAC in training and in improved
semen and medicines (the costs of which are retrieved by charges to the
rearers), a relatively large return is being achieved. A study of the output
of milk from traditional breeds of cows, compared with the output of the
improved breed when reared in the same villages, shows the traditional
breed giving 1.25 liters per day compared to 4.00 liters for the new breed,
an increase of 220 percent (Ahmad, 1991). Also, the amount of meat produced by the new breed has increased by 50 percent (Ahmad, 1991).

More than 630 paravets and sixty inseminators are now regularly employed. The income of over 30,000 livestock rearers is growing through
reductions in animal mortality (from 7 percent to 0.3 percent) and improved milk and meat yields. The number of these trained livestock
workers is growing steadily.

In late 1990, VO borrowers (mostly women) were rapidly accelerating
their livestock investments. Figure 4.1 shows the large increase in the
number of borrowers investing in livestock rearing.

Also in 1990, BRAC entered a new cooperative program with the government in which managers in the government's livestock directorate will receive management training in BRAC's Management Development Program (see Chapters 6 and 7).

Sericulture

In the early 1980s, BRAC management decided to attempt to spread sericulture (silk production) from the northern area of the country to villages in much of the rest of the country. The demand for silk was high, yet most silk was imported. Again, using its Manikganj laboratory, managers there, working with the quasi-government Sericulture Board, experimented with this new sector and through experience identified bottlenecks and bottleneck-reduction strategies.

Sericulture, like poultry, is a home-based, labor-intensive activity that can increase the income of women who can work only part-time. It is low investment and low risk. It gives returns in quick succession, yielding income every two and a half to three months for growers and every month for worm rearers. Technologies are simple and by-products are all useful. It is also an industry that feeds textile employment and is still far below domestic demand. (Silk, primarily used for saris, the principal garment worn by women, and men's shirts, is still imported in large quantities from China and India.)

BRAC has established a good relationship with the Sericulture Board, which is supposed to make available improved-variety silkworm eggs to all those who require them. Supply is sometimes a problem. To control quality, no silkworm eggs can be sold in the country except through the board. RDP sericulture specialists train the silk producers in rearing and spinning and in mulberry tree cultivation, while the board supplies eggs to the rearers and buys cocoons in return.

The main constraint to the rapid spread of sericulture has been the lack of mulberry trees, the leaves of which are essential to feed the silkworms for production of high-quality silk. Each rearer needs access to about 100 mulberry trees, two to three years old, to make a good income. And, the mulberry trees must be close to the silkworm producers because mulberry leaves have a "shelf life" of only a few hours after picking; nutritional content decreases markedly after this point. In a land-poor country like Bangladesh the silk industry must rely on scattered, small mulberry plots and scattered, small worm-rearing and cocoon-producing operations.

Starting from almost no mulberry trees in central and southern Bangladesh in the early 1980s, several million trees had been planted by

1990, primarily through BRAC's efforts. RDP has used many kinds of programs to overcome the mulberry tree problem and achieve the spread of mulberry trees. BRAC works with the Sericulture Board to obtain mulberry tree saplings. The Sericulture Board has now set up a special NGO committee through which allocations of mulberry saplings are made. The NGO committee, in turn, stimulates the Sericulture Board to increase supply. BRAC, active in the NGO sericulture committee, receives over half of the allocated saplings and supplies the saplings to its village growers for planting around their homesteads, along roadsides, on pond embankments, and on any unused land that can be found through the cooperation of farmers and local governments.

To further increase mulberry tree supply, several important tree-growing projects have been set up. In conjunction with CARE and the World Food Program's Food-for-Work Program, mulberry tree planting is being done under sixty-five of the RDP area offices, through which some 750,000 trees were planted on roadsides in 1990. Women are paid through the Food-for-Work Program in wheat grants for watering, tending, and guarding the trees until they become productive in the third year. After that time, women silk producers who use the leaves care for the trees.

Because these kinds of tree-production efforts, while substantial, have not been sufficient to supply the ever-increasing demand, some of BRAC's village organizations are now leasing land to set up mulberry tree plantations. On some of these plantations the VOs are again working with CARE, which manages the Food-for-Work Program, to pay the initial labor investment to bring the trees up to the production stage where costs can be recouped.

To make up for government shortfalls in the supply of mulberry saplings, RDP is also encouraging the development of a network of small nurseries to supply additional mulberry saplings to growers. Credit is extended to individuals who want to start homestead tree nurseries. The loans pay for fencing, fertilizers, seeds, bags, tools, and land leasing when necessary.

Through these and other methods nearly 2 million trees are now being planted annually. This year's allocation of mulberry saplings to BRAC from the Sericulture Board was 1,800,000.

Marketing is not a serious problem at this stage of the sericulture sector development because BRAC has been consistently gearing up other sections of its operations to buy all the surplus cocoons or silk thread produced. The Sericulture Board is supposed to purchase all cocoons available, but the cocoon sellers have had some problems with the board about price and delayed payments. The Ayesha Abed Foundation, a sister group to BRAC (briefly described in Chapter 3), has established several textile centers and has invested in sufficient reeling machines to utilize all cocoons not sold to the government. Just over 100 women were employed in 1990 by the Foundation Women's Association as reelers to turn the cocoons into silk thread. Also, many of the village producers have learned to do their own spinning so that they can sell thread rather than cocoons. BRAC supplies credit to the women to purchase spinning wheels and other needed equipment. The foundation's textile centers purchase all available thread, and the *Aarong* shops, BRAC's market outlets, can sell all the silk cloth available from BRAC-related producers as well as from many other sources.

BRAC VO members are major raw silk producers and jointly were expected to be the largest producers in the country (except for the Sericulture Board) by 1992. In mid-1991, the country's entire silk production was thirty metric tons. In 1989, BRAC members produced one metric ton, and the projection for 1991 was seven metric tons. The target for 1992, when the mulberry trees planted over the last two years come of age, is 15 metric tons. The goal is to have 250,000 women involved in sericulture.

Total credit made available in this sector since loans began in 1988 has been only about $15,000, but BRAC has also invested in training and intermediation with the government. So far, some 2,000 women are rearing worms and cocoons with the only serious constraint to growth being the supply of mulberry trees. The 25 percent of these women who have access to 100 or more mulberry trees are earning about Tk 9,000 per year (about $257); the 50 percent who have access to only fifty trees are earning Tk 5,000 per year; and the other 25 percent, with twenty-five or fewer mulberry trees are earning Tk 2,000 per year. (The average annual income in Bangladesh is Tk 3,500.) And, subsidiary businesses have been or are being developed: tree nurseries and plantations; a sizable silk textile production operation; and retail stores.

Benefits Versus Investment Costs in Sericulture

The largest investment, which is being shared by the World Food Program, CARE, the government, BRAC, the Ayesha Abed Foundation, and village women, is in the purchase, planting, and growing of mulberry trees, an investment in future expected payoffs. RDP invests in the training of producers and in the salaries and support costs of technical advisers and program organizers who organize women and introduce them to sericulture. The Ayesha Abed Foundation has invested in reeling machinery, the costs of which will be retrieved by profit on the sale of silk.

Although no formal cost/benefit analysis has yet been done, a simple calculation of costs and benefits is available. Let us assume conservatively that women who become cocoon rearers make an income of Tk 8,000 ($228) per year (this figure assumes an adequate supply of mulberry trees). The costs of mulberry trees amortized over thirty years and BRAC's costs of organizing and training and government facilitation work add up to a total of approximately Tk 2,000 ($57) per new rearer per year. This rough calculation suggests a return of 400 percent on investment, which will be even larger in the subsequent years, because once organizing and training are done and mulberry trees are introduced, these costs will not be repeated.

In the above calculation the benefits to the status of women are not included but are considered to be substantial. The silk subsector holds enormous promise as a potential engine of income growth for poor village households.

Fishing and Fish Culture

Identifying constraints and problems in fisheries has not been difficult. Several kinds of fishing are done in Bangladesh—in existing ponds, reexcavated ponds, reexcavated and dammed river basins, rivers, and the ocean. Since most of BRAC-organized villages are inland, BRAC has concentrated its development in freshwater fisheries activities.

The problems in fisheries have been found to be (1) inadequate supply of the most useful varieties of fish fry (very young fish that are bought in large numbers to stock rivers or ponds), (2) lack of technical knowledge in fish culture (pisciculture), (3) difficulties in establishing and organizing ownership of ponds (the only difficult constraint to overcome), and (4) inadequate management techniques. The fisheries subsector still has abundant untapped resources both in inland rivers and offshore.

RDP fisheries interventions have been concentrated on increasing the supply of several varieties of fish, primarily carp and Nilotica, on nursery programs for the production of fingerlings, and on technical advice and training of fishermen and nurserymen. Fisheries specialists are attached to most of the RDP regional offices.

Most constraints have been overcome through cooperation with the Directorate of Fisheries. For example, RDP specialists and village groups have helped organize the production of improved varieties of fry to add to the government's supply. VO members have organized fry production in some 160 ponds and now sell the fry to the government to release into open river waters, or to other VOs who are doing pisciculture in ponds. Many pond and river basin management problems have been worked out, and cooperation with the government and international NGOs (primarily the Danish International Development Agency) has resulted in construction of flood-control dams, excavation of derelict ponds and river beds, and construction of roads to reach markets.

Fishing and pisciculture activities, which are extensive but not capital intensive, have accounted for only about 1 percent of all money loaned through BRAC's credit programs. Technical assistance and training have been given to fishermen by RDP fisheries specialists, and Tk 5 million ($147,000) has been loaned to fishermen or pisciculturalists to buy nets, boats, and other equipment, or to buy fingerlings to stock ponds. Over a thousand ponds are now under fish production by VO group members. Fingerling production is being carried out in over 6,000 decimals (6 acres) of waterbodies, Nilotica are being raised in nearly 2,000 decimals (2 acres), and carp in 20,000 decimals (20 acres). During 1990, some 2,500 fishermen and women were employed in these activities.

Cost/Benefits of Fisheries Program

A recent cost/benefit study of BRAC's freshwater fish nursery program shows a very positive aggregate net benefit from the government's and BRAC's investment (Hasan, 1991). And, the analysis did not include the value of nutritional improvements to fishermen's families or to others in the villages.

Irrigation

BRAC VOs entered the irrigation sector in the early 1980s, originally experimenting with shallow tubewells and low lift pumps and later introducing large irrigation schemes with deep tubewells. VO members have undertaken about 9,000 very small to large irrigation schemes. The early shallow tubewells were used primarily to irrigate land leased by members, but shallow tubewells for irrigation were found problematic because of changing water tables and the inability to cover sufficient acres to make them financially profitable.

In the mid-1980s, several NGO groups, in addition to BRAC, began experimenting with deep tubewells, which landless groups would buy, install, operate, and derive income from by selling water to farmers. (For a detailed description and analysis of the experience of one of these NGOs, Proshika, see Wood and Palmer-Jones, 1991.) BRAC village organizations joined in these experiments. Constraints appeared immediately: lack of trained mechanics and operators; lack of knowledge about canal and drain construction; and, most important, lack of the management technologies for delineating the command areas, organizing the farmers, and setting price structures and payment methods. Also, if the irrigation was to be profitable, farmers needed to use HYV crops, fertilizers, and improved cultivation techniques, and they needed technical advice to do so successfully.

After several failures in deep tubewells, BRAC, Proshika, and the Grameen Bank entered into an agreement with CARE by which CARE would provide technical assistance in tubewell operation and management. For several years prior to that time, CARE, working with larger farmers, had been operating a program of some 120 deep tubewells, accumulating extensive experience in deep tubewell operation and management (Haggblade, 1990). After weighing this experience and consulting with several indigenous NGOs, CARE decided that it would be beneficial if landless groups, rather than farmers, could own and manage the tubewells (Haggblade, 1990).

The cooperative effort between BRAC and CARE started in 1985 in a small way, with landless groups investing at first in only two deep tubewells. But the program grew steadily, and by January 1991, BRAC groups had invested in a total of 450 deep tubewells. More are being added each month, and 400 new wells were scheduled through the remainder of 1991. In the pilot stage, CARE trained the first few RDP staff members and VO members in mechanical operations and management methods. Based on this experience, a regularized cooperative training and supervision project was undertaken. RDP now has a great deal of experience with tubewell management and has several tubewell management specialists on its staff. Also, fifty trained tubewell mechanics are on staff with 400 more to be trained this year. The CARE assistance has evolved into primarily the training of trainers and is scheduled to phase out in 1992.

Tubewells are obtained from the government by BRAC at subsidized prices, and the government must approve locations and command areas. The government subsidy on deep tubewells is gradually being withdrawn, and the cost will eventually be the market price.

The government's agriculture extension service should be providing the necessary technical advice to farmers on HYV crop production under irrigation, but that service is less than effective in the field. Consequently, the VO tubewell groups must be prepared to supply technical agricultural services along with the water services.

RDP, together with the VO leadership, has worked out a deep tubewell ownership method in which individual members of VOs (females as well as males) buy shares, then the shareholders form an irrigation group with an elected operations committee whose members receive management training. The committee hires employees from among the VO members who receive technical training. Most importantly, the committee members, with the assistance of RDP irrigation experts and agricultural advisers, sign up the farmers to be part of the irrigation district and organize the supply of technical assistance to farmers as needed. RDP specialists charge the shareholder groups Tk 200 per acre to supply necessary advisory services.

The irrigation shareholder groups take two kinds of loans from RDP or RCP: capital loans to buy the tubewells, and operating loans to pay for fuel and wages.

The farmers usually pay a percentage of their crop, 25 to 33 percent, for the irrigation water. All the shareholders are present at harvest time when the crop division is made, a procedure that ensures equitable division between farmers and the landless tubewell operators. The shareholders are encouraged not to sell their surplus rice at harvest time, when the price is lowest, but instead to store it for later sale when the price has increased.

As of December 1990, shareholders from BRAC VOs owned 450 deep tubewells, 137 of which had been in operation more than a year. Of these, 106 units are operating profitably. The thirty-one units that are not profitable are largely those acquired during the learning period with insufficiently large command areas. Attempts are being made where possible to enlarge those command areas. Experience is showing that where the command area is large enough (at least 70 acres) and management problems are solved, profit on investment is running about 37 percent.

One tubewell share bought by a village VO member costs Tk 1,000. For profitable tubewells the return on the one share investment is Tk 200 to Tk 300 per year, or 20 to 30 percent. Shareholders, both men and women, also often work as wage laborers on the tubewell schemes: cleaning and repairing channels, turning water into different fields, acting as mechanics, doing maintenance, or consulting with farmers. Also, as crops improve or multiply, additional labor on the farms is required, providing additional wage-labor opportunities.

It has been estimated that the overall profits from deep tubewell operations go about 60 percent to farmers, 30 percent to labor, and 10 percent to shareholders. During 1990, the total of direct person-days of employment generated by the BRAC VO deep tubewells was 82,160, plus indirect employment of 40,000 person-days in added farm employment.

By June 1990, 50,300 loans had been made in the irrigation sector by RDP and RCP, and over Tk 37 million ($1,088,235) had been loaned.

Although irrigation loans make up only about 9 percent of all loans disbursed by RDP and RCP, the irrigation share of total credit activity is growing steadily. Irrigation loans are the most capital intensive in the portfolio.

Landless groups are performing an important irrigation and farm advisement service, which brings more acreage into productivity and creates much higher annual yields. This increases profit to the farmers, provides more food for the country, and increases employment for irrigation workers and farm laborers. The irrigation arrangement is also giving the landless more respect and power vis-à-vis landed farmers.

From a national perspective, the tubewell program is especially significant because minor irrigation has been the leading subsector in agriculture since 1980 and will continue to be so (Wood and Palmer-Jones, 1991). An irrigation-led solution to the expansion of agricultural production and the target of food self-sufficiency remains the centerpiece of agricultural policy for the country.

Although BRAC has been very active in tubewell promotion, it has had to invest very little money except to provide credit. The largest investments to date have been made by the government through its subsidy of tubewells—subsidies that before the involvement of the landless groups went to the richer farmers—and by CARE through its training and technical advice services to the NGOs. BRAC is now replacing CARE as the principal trainer and provider of technical services and is retrieving most of the costs of those services through charges to the shareholders. (For a detailed profitability analysis of deep tubewells, see Ahmad, *National Profitability*, 1991.)

Importance of BRAC's Subsector Interventions

Some development experts contend that the investments made by the government and organizations like BRAC and Grameen Bank in small income-generating activities might better be spent in encouraging the establishment of large new industries or improving others, actions intended to employ large numbers of people in factories and related supply and marketing operations. The counterargument is that BRAC's interventions are improving the income-generating potential for more of the target people in rural areas than could big-scale factory development. And, employing people in rural areas prevents dysfunctional over-urbanization.

Because BRAC is continually scaling up, by mid-1991 it had in place over 7,000 village organizations and more than 550,000 members. BRAC is therefore in a particularly fortunate position to reach thousands of the village poor quickly and cheaply with any desired intervention. Interventions are quickly tested in BRAC's laboratory areas, then taken to scale as soon as proven successful. In this way, BRAC leverages its interventions rapidly, targeting them to the poorest in the villages who have the greatest need and stand to gain the most.

When group members are encouraged to start new businesses (for example, mulberry nurseries, poultry feed preparation and sales, fish nurseries) to solve problems, they benefit directly. These group members not only provide the labor, but they reap the profits. Investments by outside businesses would not achieve the same results and in most cases would not be able to provide services close to where they are needed by the villagers.

Subsectors Where Next Interventions Will Take Place

BRAC started in 1990 to focus on the leather and handloom subsectors, two potentially large loan sectors where productivity and profitability are low and are expected to remain so unless problems can be identified and solved. Markets for leather goods and handloomed fabrics are available, provided the quality is adequate and the price is competitive. Several expert studies have already been commissioned. The rapid increase in livestock rearing by VO members establishes a base for leather availability. The sophisticated design and production capabilities of the Ayesha Abed Foundation and the *Aarong* shops and the availability of the BRAC garment factories all provide a support system for handloom production.

Conclusion

The interventions in the economic subsectors discussed above have been aided by sector specialists at the BRAC head office and in the field. Working out of the RDP regional offices, their job has been to help identify and then to work on breaking sectoral bottlenecks. As problems are solved and subsectors begin operating profitably, the specialists are employed by the landless investors to provide training and consulting services. Without the developmental infrastructural activities, and the services of these technical consultants and trainers, opportunities in most of the sectors would have remained limited and borrower activities would have limped along at constrained levels.

The discussion of the five different economic subsectors, although brief, demonstrates why BRAC feels that in the infrastructure-starved Bangladesh context, institutional intermediation as well as financial intermediation is needed. In some development circles, particularly in the United States, support for minimalist credit programs has gained ascendancy, primarily because they are easier to take to scale. BRAC's experience shows that combining institutional intermediation with financial intermediation need not prevent scaling up and can vastly improve the prospects of borrowers.

Think for a moment what the subsector interventions have meant to the women VO members. Formerly they derived income from low-yield investments in, for example, traditional manual paddy husking, a low-paid, difficult, time-consuming task. Women are now owning tubewell shares and deriving 20 to 30 percent profits; they are deriving income from taking care of improved breeds of chickens with much lowered mortality rates; they are gaining income from vaccinating chickens for their neighbors in their spare time; they have gained expertise and income from being paravets for livestock; they are becoming shareholders in pisciculture projects. They have their own incomes and their families are better fed. They are not rich, but they have gained status. They have climbed above the bare subsistence level and are taking charge of their own lives. Opportunities for men from the subsector interventions have been equally positive.

BRAC's experience suggests that if real development is to take place in Bangladesh, if people are to be helped to move beyond bare subsistence in highly constrained traditional occupations, more than credit alone is required. The BRAC team are strong believers in the efficacy of the market model and entrepreneurship. Had resources and services necessary to improvements in the various economic subsectors become available through responses to market demands without outside intervention, BRAC would not have found it necessary or desirable to intervene.

The Bangladesh context may be special. In many other countries, government and business infrastructure are at a stage where market opportunities will elicit effective response, and supply from both government and businesses will respond to demand. In those cases, the market can itself identify and solve problems. But experience has not found this to be the case in many economic subsectors relevant to small rural investors in Bangladesh. BRAC's interventions have been necessary and beneficial.

BRAC
at
Work

Clockwise, from upper left:

Mahera Rahman, Senior Manager, Logistics (left): daily planning activities

NFPE organizer and a teacher: "together for education"

Kaniz Fatema, NFPE Program Coordinator: a smile of confidence as more and more schools open

BRAC's training program: a model of the participatory approach

Mahera Rahman, taking charge: the bigger the program, the more the pressure on support activities

Clockwise, from upper left:

Trainers join in the process of self-evaluation

Monitoring: a persistent and tenacious responsibility

BRAC's Computer Center: creating a database for loan operations

F. H. Abed, Executive Director: visiting a school in Manikganj

Clockwise, from upper left:

Aminul Alam, Director of the Rural Development Program: a steersman in organizing the landless into effective cooperatives

In the classroom: a day of supervision by the NFPE program organizer while the teacher watches

F. H. Abed, Executive Director, talking to the management committee members of an irrigation project: planning for the future

A. M. R. Chowdury, Director of Reserarch and Evaluation at work: research is crucial for development

At the brickyard: involving the landless in a bigger economic scheme

Clockwise, from upper left:

Construction department: designing for future area offices and training centers

A. Q. Siddiqui, Director, Commercial: working on BRAC's own income-earning projects

S. K. Sarkar (left): "an old head on young shoulders," discusses credit with a regional manager

Human development training: learning to plan and manage

Layout: Laura Augustine
Photo credits: BRAC-Shehzad Noorani

PART II

How BRAC Does What It Does

CHAPTER 6

The Management of BRAC

THE EFFECTIVENESS OF programs depends on the capacity of the organization to make them work, that is, on the effectiveness of the organization's management. As the previous chapters have shown, BRAC is a large undertaking by any standards. It is not only large but it is also an extraordinarily complex operation combining various kinds of multifaceted field programs, large support systems, and several commercial enterprises. Effective management has been identified as the key to BRAC's success. BRAC employs no expatriate staff members and only occasionally uses short-term expatriate consultants for special tasks. It has been able to undertake substantial and varied programs and scale up rapidly while at the same time maintaining both effectiveness and efficiency.

A Dutch evaluation team recently stated, "BRAC has demonstrated that in the execution of its objectives, management techniques have been applied of a quality level comparable with international standards. . . . BRAC has managed to build up a kind of organization and management style that is widely and justly admired for its smooth running and efficiency" (Wils, Passtoors, and Van Leeuwin, 1988). The team further pointed out that BRAC seldom sacrifices quality for quantity and operates by using modern management techniques along with a continuous training process for its staff.

Unfortunately, management has often been a neglected dimension in explorations of development programs in the Third World. As one World Bank observer suggested in the early 1980s, the focus of discussion has for the most part been on the economic, financial, and political factors relevant to these programs, not on the role of management (Paul, 1982). Although this neglect has been partially overcome in the last decade, primarily in studies of the administration of governmental development projects (see, for example, Bryant and White, 1982; Leonard, 1977; Leonard and Marshall, 1983; Israel, 1989; Paul, 1982), almost no in-depth studies of NGO management have been undertaken. (There are a few noteworthy exceptions: see especially the works of David C. Korten listed in the Bibliography; Mann, Grindle, Shipton, 1989; Edgcomb and Cawley, 1990; Manitoba Institute of Management, 1989; Vincent, 1989.)

This chapter focuses on the current status of the management of BRAC. Management philosophy, structures, and processes are examined in order to explain the organizational dynamics—both internal and interactive with the environment—that have enabled BRAC to work effectively and scale up so dramatically. It should be read in conjunction with Chapter 7, which describes BRAC's management and program support systems, which have been so essential to the performance of its programs and management success. The support programs cover the areas of training and resources, research and evaluation, management development, monitoring, materials development and publications, personnel, logistics, construction, computers, and accounting.

Growth of Personnel

At the end of 1990, BRAC had 4,222 full-time employees, plus some 4,000 part-time teachers. During the first half of 1991, the full-time staff grew to 4,700 and the number of teachers to over 6,000. Figure 6.1 depicts the annual growth showing the particularly rapid scaleup between 1986 and 1990.

BRAC's View of Management

BRAC's managers consider "development management" to be different from other kinds of "management." F. H. Abed, BRAC's founder and executive director, recently explained this premise:

> Development, quintessentially, is action by people. It is something that the people themselves do, or it does not take place at all. Capital, physical resources and infra-structure are obviously necessary for development, but these are secondary. The predominant factor is the people. This is particularly true for rural development. Rural development is basically an issue of individual and societal change—change in the attitudes, values, skills, perceptions, institutions and ways of life of the rural poor. These changes are complex and time consuming. To expedite this change through action by the people we need what we call an "enabling environment." Such an environment enables the people to participate in planning, implementation, monitoring, and evaluation of their own actions. Creating this enabling environment is the responsibil-

Figure 6.1   BRAC 1980–90: Growth of Full-Time Staff*

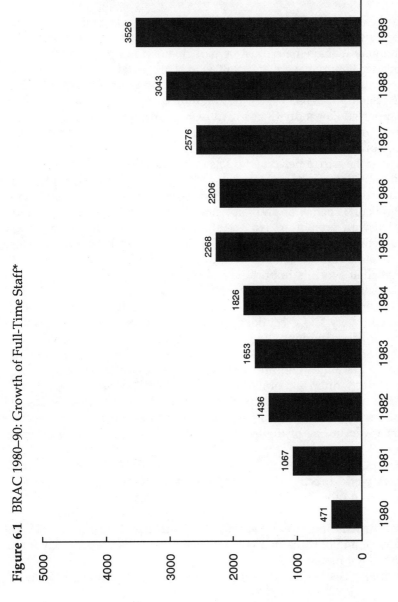

*These figures do not include the more than 4,000 teachers in the Non-Formal Primary Education Program in 1990.

Source: BRAC personnel records

ity of a development manager. His/her prime concern is how to elicit and ensure participation. Commercial management, on the other hand, has somewhat a different role. . . . Development is a complicated job, and its management is much more complex than is usually conceived. Rural development is no longer a job for an amateur. (Abed, *Commencement*, 1990)

Abed expanded on his vision of development management in a series of interviews with the author in 1990 and 1991. He said that successful development management must be participatory and decentralized and is dependent on managers and staff who share certain values. Creation and sustenance of development values is a continuous process in the BRAC system. Managers must be committed to the poor, a value that must supersede an individual's own desire for money. Managers must be able to transmit their values to other staff and to galvanize and motivate others to a "cause" larger than the project.

Further, he said, a person who acts only on instructions cannot do development. Successful development work requires a cadre of people who think for themselves, apply their own values, and act on their own. Entrepreneurial behavior and experimentation is to be encouraged and rewarded with promotion. No one should be penalized for taking risks and sometimes failing. BRAC promotes a strong work ethic, and managers must be role models for this ethic. Staff members are expected to feel that their work is important and that through hard work each of them is contributing something of benefit to the people.

In order to develop and encourage the kind of manager described, BRAC, with very few exceptions, chooses managers from the field after they have had experience and demonstrated their values. New BRAC program organizers (POs), the entry-level position in the field, are all university graduates and are selected after a careful screening process that includes written and oral examinations. All BRAC workers (with the exception of some technical specialists or head office clerical workers) start out as POs in the field after basic induction training on rural development given in one of the training and resource centers (TARCs) (see Chapter 7).

New POs serve a year of probation. In the field camps, new staff members work directly with villagers, participate in regular group discussions with other field workers in the same area office, and regularly lead issue discussions at meetings of the villagers. The field work is difficult and demanding, usually starting at 6 a.m. and ending after dark or after an evening meeting in a village. The following is a typical day for a PO named Rahman.

Rahman rises before six, washes and prays, eats a quick breakfast, then goes to a village a half hour away on a bicycle or motorcycle. In the village, he meets one of his village assistants and attends one of the before-work morning meetings of a village group where savings are collected and loan payments are made. This particular group has some special questions that require answers from the PO.

At 9 a.m. Rahman meets with several of his other village assistants for two hours, during which time they discuss some of the village group problems. He goes back to his camp via the *union* council office where he needs to discuss a problem with the chairman. He arrives back at camp at 2 p.m., eats lunch, talks with the area manager about the problem, and then rests for an hour. But since he needs to be back in another village (an hour away) by 7 p.m. to lead a discussion on issues in the VO meeting, he spends an hour rereading his notes in preparation for the meeting. He eats with some of his fellow staff members at 5:30, then takes off for the village. He returns from the village a little after 10 p.m., chats a while with his friends, and falls into bed.

All days are not the same. On perhaps one day a week the PO spends most of his time at the base camp where his village assistants come to see him, where villagers come to collect loans, and where staff meetings take place. Fridays are normally days of rest and dialogue and perhaps games at the camp.

About half of new recruits resign during their first probationary year. BRAC estimates that of those who come to work for the organization, about one-third are not good for rural development work (unmotivated, unable to adjust to a stiff work ethic, or unsuited to rural life), another third are acceptable and will do adequate work, and the last third are very good, talented, and dedicated. Only after several years in the field as a PO (usually a minimum of three years) can a person be promoted to area manager, the first rung of management.

Women as Managers

Although BRAC's emphasis on programming for women is considered one of its outstanding features, BRAC has so far had few women managers. Until two years ago, women were not appointed as POs (see Chapter 1), where experience to qualify as a manager must be obtained. Now, women are being hired as POs and are being assigned to area offices, where they perform the same functions as the male POs. Since women's groups make up more than half of all village organizations, the addition of female POs is especially useful.

Over the last two years, BRAC has been experimenting with ways to recruit more qualified women as POs and to cut down their turnover rate, which has been running about 10 percent higher than that of men. All interviews for male PO candidates are conducted in Dhaka, the location of the head office. Interviews for female candidates are now being conducted in several regional centers so that women do not have to travel long distances to Dhaka. Also, while men are not allowed to work in villages near their homes, women are assigned nearer their homes so that they can more easily visit their families and their families can keep an eye on them. Women are assigned in pairs or threesomes to area offices, never as one woman alone with otherwise male staff. These measures, learned from field experience, seem to be improving the recruitment and turnover rates for women. In three or four years it is expected that a number of women will have had enough field experience so that some will become area managers and then be eligible for further promotions.

An advisory committee on women was set up in early 1991. It is chaired by the only woman program coordinator in BRAC, head of the Non-Formal Primary Education program. One female PO each from the Rural Development Program (RDP), the Rural Credit Project (RCP), the Income Generation for Vulnerable Group Development (IGVGD), and the sericulture program, and one female each from the research and personnel departments and the paralegal program make up the rest of the committee. The purpose of the committee is to monitor BRAC's progress in incorporating more women into the BRAC staff and to help develop ways to do it. In 1990, a woman attorney, the person who developed the paralegal program, was added to the BRAC board, where two women, out of a total of seven board members, now serve.

The Organizational Structure

The overall organogram of BRAC's structure appears in Chapter 3 as Figure 3.1. BRAC is registered under the Societies Registration Act and the Foreign Donations Act. Ultimate authority rests in the General Body, composed of nine members; the external auditors report to this body. From among the nine members of the General Body, seven are elected to make up the Governing Body. The Governing Body appoints the executive director and generally serves the functions of an executive board.

The basic structure of BRAC remains fairly constant, yet the details of the structure of BRAC programs are always experimental, with changes often made after trial in the field. Although program structuring is flexible, some general principles always govern decisions about it: structure must encourage and enable participation, minimize hierarchy, enable accountability, decentralize decisionmaking, maximize feedback opportunities, and maximize flexibility.

Flat Structure

As discussed briefly in Chapter 3, BRAC's structure is very flat, with few intermediate levels between top management and field implementation. Figures 3.1 through 3.5 show the overall structure of BRAC, and the organization of BRAC's four main programs: RDP, RCP, the Non-Formal Primary Education (NFPE) program, and the Women's Health and Development Program (WHDP).

In all of the programs, the field management units have deliberately been kept small. These units must make operational decisions on a daily basis and every staff member, regardless of his or her seniority, must take part in decisionmaking processes. It is the small field unit that continuously faces new challenges and must adapt to changing circumstances.

Although BRAC is a big organization, it is essentially a management system composed of small units. Bureaucracy is minimized by the decentralization of decisionmaking to small units. The small units also serve a risk-protection purpose. Experimentation in units is encouraged. If something goes wrong in one unit, the negative effects are restricted to a small area. If some new adaptation or initiative goes right in one unit, it can be tried in other units.

Keeping the Head Office Staff Small

All of the functional programs maintain very small head office staffs. RDP, which has organized and works with more than 7,000 VOs and is growing at the rate of 2,000 new VOs each year, operates with fewer than twenty-five head office staff members, including the technical advisers in the various economic subsector programs and clerical staff. The NFPE program runs 4,000 schools with a headquarters staff of eight people, including the program coordinator, a secretary, two statistical monitors, an educational specialist, and two materials developers. The WHDP, which now works with some 2.4 million people in 1,500 villages, operates with only five head office staff, including the program coordinator.

The small size of headquarters program staff is intentional. The most important work is done in the field; responsibility and authority is delegated to the field. To know what is going on and to manage effectively, the program coordinator must spend time in the field, and his or her regional managers must be there most of the time.

The quality of managers in the area offices, branches, or field teams is the key to the success or failure of BRAC programs. The area offices are placed in remote villages, they have no telephones, and mail delivery is slow and not always reliable. Communication must be maintained by personal visits to or from regional offices or headquarters. This isolation means that many decisions have to be made at the field level. Although regular regional meetings take place among area managers with their regional managers, much of the time the area offices are on their own and must manage on their own.

The existence of the strong support systems (research, training, logistics, materials development, and so on, described in Chapter 7), which back up and are shared by all the programs, help make it possible to keep the head office program staffs small.

Staff Development

BRAC's executive director has always operated on his belief that BRAC managers should be promoted from within. In order to be a good manager, the individual must have had field experience in the villages. This belief is one of the main reasons why a key criteria for new POs, the entry-level field worker, is a university degree. Since these people are expected to be promoted and make up the management cadre as the organization grows, they must have the basic educational qualifications. (In Bangladesh, formal educational qualifications are very important, automatically carrying significant levels of respect and deference.) BRAC employees come from many different academic disciplines, very few have had management training, and only a handful will have had previous development experience or technical training in the programs in which BRAC is working. Consequently, the development of management skills, along with program-relevant technical skills, is an important part of the BRAC staff development program.

Management and technical skills for staff are developed in several ways. The first is through field experience and participation in decision-making processes, which are a crucial part of that experience. BRAC's flat and decentralized structure and numerous feedback processes enable participation and learning on a day-to-day basis.

Management and technical skills are also developed through more formal training. BRAC now spends 7 percent of its total salary budget on staff development. Every proposal to donors earmarks this 7 percent. All managers are provided management training in the TARCs and through courses in the new Management Development Program (MDP). They are also given opportunities to take courses from RDP specialists in the various relevant economic subsectors. Additionally, many are sent on field trips to other Asian countries to observe successful development projects, and a number each year are chosen to take various kinds of training abroad, including advanced degrees in management, economics, health, education, financial management, research, and other relevant fields. Most go to the Philippines, India, Canada, Europe, or the United States. By the end of 1990, thirty-seven staff members had been sent for higher degrees abroad. At the beginning of 1991, nine people were studying abroad in various countries.

Some of the external training and other institutional development efforts have been paid for by special grants from donors. Before BRAC began to set aside a percentage of each budget for staff development, the executive director obtained for BRAC two institutional development grants (1977–80 and 1982–86) from the Ford Foundation. These grants were used for short-term staff training programs, both inside and outside the country, for advanced degree programs, for study tours, for short-term consultants' salaries, and for building a small library of books and journals in the management and development fields. Consultancies paid for by these grants were important in establishing and upgrading the Research and Evaluation Division and the computer center.

The British Council, the Dutch and Canadian governments, the Asian Development Bank, the Swiss Development Agency, and others have also provided scholarships for advanced degrees in various countries.

Hierarchy and Participation—
Control Versus Empowerment

The Bangladeshi culture is basically hierarchical. Hierarchy is a fundamental part of family life, village life, and political life. In Bangladesh, superiors, both inside the family and outside, are given respect, and it is considered impolite to challenge a superior. Hierarchy also is a dominant characteristic of all organizations in Bangladesh. BRAC is no exception since all employees bring hierarchical values with them when they join the organization. BRAC tries to minimize the negative aspects of hierarchical behavior by the flatness of its structure, by its participatory training methods, by an emphasis on participation in the workplace, and by redundant feedback systems. A key mechanism for overcoming hierarchy is a continuous round of work-or issue-centered staff meetings that incorporate all levels and in which everyone is asked to participate.

Hierarchical values also play a positive role in BRAC. They reinforce stability by enhancing respect for leadership and by providing the basis for acceptance of structure and rules. An organization as large and complex as BRAC, operating in a turbulent and often corrupt environment, requires a clearly delineated controlling structure and firm rules for some aspects of the work.

Organizational theorists have distinguished between "mechanistic" and "organic" organizational structures. The mechanistic is characterized by a stable specialization of tasks, a precise definition of role obligations and techniques, and a tendency for most operations to be governed by a hierarchical structure of authority and communications. The organic structure is characterized by a continual reallocation of tasks, a flexible definition of role responsibilities and methods, and a propensity for most work behavior to be directed by a purely collegial network of advice and communication (Burns and Stalker, 1961). The mechanistic organization has been considered most appropriate for routine conditions and the organic as best for changing conditions.

BRAC exhibits elements of each type. We have stressed in earlier chapters BRAC's reputation as a "learning process organization," which is a key attribute of the "organic" organization. BRAC is, however, also a carefully structured organization with certain "mechanistic" elements, firm rules that provide coherence and structure in the face of complexity. BRAC's top managers seem to understand the difference between "flexibility" and "control" and the important uses of each. They recognize that there are situations in which control is appropriate (financial transactions, parameters of client targeting, personnel rules, logistics, etc.) and that refusing to control where necessary could lead to organizational collapse. BRAC, therefore, has many carefully delineated control systems.

BRAC managers also appear to understand that they cannot and should not emphasize control in inappropriate circumstances, that they must encourage their staff to take independent action, and that they must enable capacity building and flexibility in the field so that empowered staff can better empower villagers. (For a thoughtful discussion of the need for both flexibility and control in managing rural development, see Bryant and White, 1982, especially pages 286–89.)

The management of BRAC must continuously walk a difficult line between emphasis on accountability and control mechanisms and emphasis on enabling and empowering. Errors occur in one direction or the other, but pervasive and active feedback processes appear to sustain an ability to recognize problems and make creative adjustments if errors go too far either way.

Feedback and Coordination Processes

BRAC managers operationalize numerous informal as well as formal feedback systems both upward and downward. Feedback takes place through the numerous meetings and constant dialogue that are held regularly at all levels. Feedback from and to villagers provides a foundation for learning. The POs meet regularly with village groups discussing issues and problems. Regional managers and head office people visit village meetings or visit with individual villagers when they are in the field. These meetings, together with informal discussions, form the basis for village feedback.

Even though dialogue among the staff is constantly taking place in the living situation in the field offices, formal staff meetings are held weekly. These meetings, to discuss what is happening in the villages and to formulate work plans for the coming weeks, provide an opportunity for upward, downward, and lateral communication among field staff. Every month small groups of area managers meet with their regional manager. A regional manager holds ten or twelve such meetings monthly in order to dialogue with all the area managers. These meetings provide an opportunity for lateral communication—the sharing of experience and problems among the area office managers—and also serve as upward and downward feedback between the head office and the field.

At the head office, the regional managers, together with their program coordinator, meet with the executive director each month to review experience in the field, to problem-solve, and to make decisions about program changes. Many other impromptu meetings are held when some issue comes up. The executive director's leadership style encourages open discussion of difficult issues and acceptance and analysis of apparent errors, yet provides firm decisions when needed.

Another form of informal feedback takes place through the trainers who pick up in training sessions programmatic and attitudinal information from the field, from both villagers and staff members. The managers of each of the TARCs sit in at the regional manager–area managers' meetings in the area covered by that TARC and are able to raise issues that may not come to the attention of the regional managers and area managers through other channels. The trainers are able to discuss what they see and hear from perspectives that are different than those of line staff. The trainers also raise field observations in their own management meetings to feed back data to the appropriate program managers or to the head office.

Field researchers from the Research and Evaluation Division who spend a great deal of time in the field on various research projects also pick up information and report back informally what they have observed.

The executive director (familiarly called E.D. or Abed Bhai—a term of respect that means older brother) has intentionally designed several other opportunities for informal feedback. One rule is that all credit over a certain amount must be sanctioned by him personally. He feels that this procedure gives an important opportunity (which he might not otherwise have) to talk personally with the RDP area managers or RCP branch managers who are asked to bring the sanctioning form to him personally. E.D. also insists that any staff member who wishes may see him by appointment or directly. If no earlier time is available, the staff member may wait to the end of the day and will definitely be seen before E.D. leaves. E.D.'s secretary is instructed never to say no. E.D. also conducts exit interviews with any management-level person who requests a clearance to leave the organization.

Head office personnel, including the executive director, make field trips often. These are usually unannounced because there is no way to inform the field offices or village groups. Although plans exist to locate one telephone in each region, it will not be possible for some time to have telephones at the field offices.

Village organization members also communicate directly with the executive director. He receives one or two letters each day from villagers. These are referred to the appropriate program head, who investigates and reports back to him for necessary action or reply. Also, villagers, if they have a pressing concern, sometimes visit the head office in groups or individually.

More formal feedback is provided by the research reports of the Research and Evaluation Division, by the accounting and reporting systems designed for each program, and by the regular reports of the recently constituted Monitoring Department. For many years BRAC has had a financial and activity reporting system, or management information system (MIS), based on various types of information regularly compiled from village records at the area office level. Reports are reviewed by the regional manager and forwarded to the head office for consolidation. These data include various kinds of general and specific activity information such as number of village organizations, number and gender of members, amount of savings generated, number and amount of loans, loan realization statistics, number of chickens vaccinated by poultry workers, amount and kinds of veterinary medicines sold by the livestock paravets, number of training sessions and attendees, among many others. Detailed financial records are also compiled.

In 1988, finding that the existing MIS was not in itself sufficient, BRAC established the Monitoring Department to simplify and streamline the MIS and to collect data on more qualitative indicators. The new monitoring system added more refined weekly credit recovery reports to the financial and activity data collected. Also, the collection of output data related to institution building and social change was introduced. The purpose of the new indicators is to help distinguish weak VOs from stronger ones and to better target interventions and corrective action where required.

In consultation with field workers and villagers, thirty village indicators covering organizational, social, and health aspects, as well as savings and credit, were created. These indicators are monitored by field workers from the Monitoring Department. Each of the indicators has been grouped as either input or output data and weighted to reveal the quality of the village organizations. Indicators include such items as number of weekly and monthly meetings held by the village organizations; attendance rates at those meetings; whether savings and pass books are up to date; whether the group's Resolution Book is adequately used; whether elections of the management group are properly held; number of households with sanitary latrines; percentage of eligible children attending school; percentage of eligible children completely immunized; number of divorce and polygamy cases recorded among group members during the last year; number of NFPE graduates enrolled in government primary schools; number of pregnant mothers immunized against tetanus during the last year; number of mothers having a second baby in less than three years; and number of VO decisions implemented during the last year. The Monitoring Department translates the numbers into meaningful percentages or other measures.

The Monitoring Department now deploys a program organizer in each region to monitor field implementation and to assist with both quantitative and qualitative reporting by the RDP area offices and the RCP branches. In addition, these monitors work on more detailed special reports. Their first studies, on the implementation of revised credit procedures, have been useful as feedback to management to suggest even further rule changes.

According to the November 1990 *Annual Donor Review Team Report*, some problems of overlap between the Monitoring Department and the Accounting Department remain to be solved. Also identified were some gaps in the MIS, most notably a gap between the budget structure and some of the financial reporting, and a lack of integration in the reporting system between activities and spending. The team noted that because the BRAC approach to programming is a dynamic one, based to a certain extent on natural growth and evolution rather than on rigid blueprints, there is currently a problem in relating some program activities to program expenditures, as well as to earlier plans and budget.

As reality in program implementation moves further from an original plan, and where activity and financial reports go their independent ways, closing the loop between what has been learned and the development of the next plan and budget becomes more difficult. This problem is a complex one in an organization like BRAC because of the flexible nature of the organization in which managers are constantly taking advantage of opportunities and answering needs and do not feel constrained by budget lines or blueprint planning. The review team suggested a reporting system that does not constrain but that can give managers as well as outside reviewers a historical picture of performance (what activities have taken place) in relation to budget plans. New budgets can then be more carefully built on the lessons of the previous period. When BRAC was smaller, such information was known on a day-to-day basis by managers and was easily observable by reviewers; now that BRAC is much larger, more formal reporting is apparently necessary.

The team also urged RDP and RCP to develop ways for their MIS to report more explicitly on the relationship between credit and the activity for which the credit was used so that the quality and effect of loans in particular economic subsectors (i.e., small trading, rural transport, livestock) can be more easily understood.

Supervision and Work Planning

BRAC utilizes various methods of work planning. Most departments at the head office and area offices have established activity and output targets related to time frames. Gantt charts showing planned activities related to time frames for various stages can often be seen posted in area offices. Each PO in the field is required to prepare a weekly workplan, broken down into a daily itinerary and targets. These are usually discussed each morning with the area manager, and progress and problems are reviewed in the weekly meetings. RDP area offices and RCP branches have an array of annual and monthly targets on such variables as number of borrowers, amounts of money loaned, savings, number of new village organizations, number of members, number of graduates of functional education courses, number of poultry rearers trained, etc. Performance against the targets is monitored and the results are published quarterly.

Where feasible, the head office departments have also developed output standards. The Logistics Department, for example, which is responsible for purchasing, among other activities, works to a specific standard in that activity. All purchases of items available on the market in Dhaka must be completed within three working days of the time an order is placed by the program department. Time limits are also placed on the purchase of items that must be ordered from outside.

Supervision is accomplished primarily through workplans and targeting systems, freeing up managers to work on more strategic questions and problem solving.

Coordination Mechanisms in BRAC

Coordination is an essential ingredient in organizations. It is necessary to ensure that the various organizational parts work together to achieve organizational purposes. Since organizations are composed of interdependent parts, each organizational design must incorporate its own coordinative mechanisms. In BRAC, coordination is required within the programs, among the different programs, and between the programs and the supporting systems.

Coordination in organizations takes place in at least three main ways: (1) hierarchically, that is, by "overhead coordination" in which decisionmakers adapt to one another on instructions from a central decisionmaker; (2) through the use of rules, procedures, and the presetting of schedules, outcomes, and targets—which serve to coordinate activities by programming behaviors and providing feedback to decisionmakers about performance; and (3) through "self-coordination," mutual adjustment among decisionmakers characterized by a variety of bargaining, information sharing, and other relationships in which not every program is perfectly adjusted to every other program, yet which results in decisions that are intelligently related. (For further discussion of these types of coordination methods, see Lindblom, 1965; Dahl and Lindblom, 1953; McCann and Galbraith, 1981; Gerwin, 1981.)

Coordination in BRAC shows characteristics of all three methods but appears to rely most heavily on the third method—self-coordination. Through various formal and informal mechanisms, program managers and support system managers share information with one another and negotiate their relationships. In Chapter 7 we note how training plans are developed in negotiation between program managers and training managers, how program managers negotiate directly with logistics managers for various services, and how research plans are coordinated with program needs through mutual adjustment. The same type of self-coordination takes place among the programs at the head office as well as in the field. Where different programs are serving the same village families, coordinating mechanisms are worked out between the programs. In the RDP-NFPE case, the NFPE POs work out of the RDP area offices and are able to coordinate informally their work with that of the other POs who work in the same villages. The NFPE regional managers self-coordinate with the RDP area office managers since they both have a stake in seeing that the NFPE POs operate effectively.

Reliance on self-coordination, rather than overhead coordination, is necessary in flat structures and works best within a framework of shared values and strategies, clear output goals, both short- and long-term, and mutually accepted rules and procedures. In BRAC, all the programs contribute to meeting the long-term goal of advancing the status of villagers. Each program also has its own short-term targets and must coordinate with other programs and the support systems to achieve them.

Overhead coordination is brought into play primarily when self-coordination methods fail, when there is too much conflict, or when rules, procedures, and plans appear to be inadequate to provide a coordinational framework. Because BRAC is so complex and multifaceted, with a very flat structure, overhead coordination can be applied only in these special cases. Without further hierarchy and increased control mechanisms, more extensive overhead coordination could not be applied.

Self-coordination is sometimes considered expensive because much middle-management time is required in meetings, negotiating sessions, and informal discussions. BRAC managers feel that the wider and longer-term benefits are worth the cost in time. The management also feels that because BRAC is essentially an organization of small units working simultaneously on similar problems, yet each with more or less independent subproblems, coordination costs can to some extent be minimized. Furthermore, through the use of self-coordination, problem solving is facilitated and organizational adaptation fostered because the various subsystems have the freedom to adjust to their quasi-unique contextual demands.

Financial Management, the Market Model, and Entrepreneurial Behavior

Throughout all of its activities, including management policies, BRAC maintains a market perspective and encourages entrepreneurial behavior. In its village work the policy is noninterference in normal market operations except to overcome bottlenecks or to prevent obvious exploitation. Villagers pay market rates for credit, pay for forms and minute books, pay for all inputs for their economic schemes, and so on. Inside the organization, cost centering and cost recovery are the norm for most of the supporting units and contribute to the efficiency of those departments. The training centers, for example, must break even or make a profit from the training supplied to the programs and to outside groups and from their farm operations. The computer center charges each program for its services, and by operating three shifts around the clock, it also sells its services to outside businesses and the government so that it can be largely self-supporting. The printing company is profitable, and its profits more than cover the cost of all BRAC printing.

Transportation arrangements in field offices provide another example. Travel and travel costs are kept simple by a basic, uniform system. *Gram sheboks*, the lowest grade of field workers, travel by bicycles furnished by BRAC, as do POs during their probationary year. After confirmation as a regular BRAC employee, POs travel by motorcycle. In order to motivate responsible care and use of the motorcycles, POs are provided with a motorcycle on a hire-purchase basis and are paid a flat rate for operational and maintenance costs. The cost of the motorcycle is deducted from the salary of the PO in sixty monthly installments. To cover the expenses of the use of the motorcycle for work, Tk 2 per kilometer is paid to the PO for the first 500 kilometers in a month and Tk 1.5 for each subsequent kilometer. This system, recently replacing a system where BRAC owned the motorcycles, has effectively removed the costs of the regulation of motorcycle use and maintenance from program costs. Motorcycles are now very well maintained.

These few examples serve to illustrate the market perspective, a guiding principle wherever relevant to efficiency or better service. This perspective has fostered self-reliance and businesslike thinking in both staff and villagers and has enabled BRAC to do far more than the sum of its donor funds would seem to allow.

Can Management Systems Sustain Continued Rapid Growth and Diversity?

In reviewing an accumulation of appraisal and evaluation reports done over the years since the mid-1970s by BRAC's donors and other outside evaluators, a reader will find a constant caution, which may be paraphrased as follows: BRAC is doing very well now, but if it continues to scale up so rapidly we are not sure it can manage. These cautions were raised when BRAC had two main programs and a few hundred employees, continuing to the present with four major programs, all expanding rapidly, several commercial enterprises, over 4,500 regular employees, and another 6,000 teachers.

In spite of the cautions, BRAC has continued to scale up more and more rapidly and continues to have the capacity to manage; and, according to the most recent evaluations, it has the capacity to manage effectively. Does this mean that there is no point related to size, complexity, or diversity at which BRAC should stop scaling up or should limit diversity? The question, in fact, is unanswerable. Perhaps there is a break point, but just where that point might be is impossible to anticipate.

Top managers in BRAC feel that if the organization continues to build support services (research, training, logistics, etc.) at the same rates that it scales up programs, or faster, continued growth is possible. They recognize that staff and villager training capacity, and management development capacity, are among the most important constraining variables. In the past there have been temporary lags in these capacities but not sufficiently serious or long-lasting to harm programs. They recognize that the number of available effective managers must keep up with growth demands. At the same time, they see highly qualified young men and women university graduates coming into BRAC in a steady stream; when a recruitment takes place for 200 new POs, more than a thousand applicants apply for the jobs.

Most worrisome for some observers is the capacity of top management to handle increasingly diversified activities. RDP and RCP (the bank project) are growing very rapidly, while at the same time BRAC is undertaking more extensive health and education programming and adding more commercial enterprises. Does BRAC have the top management depth to handle such diversity? Again, no outside observer can answer.

Availability of donor money is always a constraint to growth and diversity. Although profits from its commercial enterprises now support more than 15 percent of the budget, BRAC is still largely dependent on outside funding. There are limits to donor capacities, but as Chapter 8 shows, BRAC has not yet tapped many potential sources. It is always possible, but not probable, that existing donors could become overcautious and put a stop to growth.

Based on past performance it would appear that BRAC managers, themselves, know best what the organization's potential management capacities are as they relate to both size and diversity. When the General Body, the board, the executive director, and program coordinators feel no longer capable of handling the size, complexity, and diversity, ways will be devised to spin off some of its activities. The executive director, for example, is already talking about spinning off a health research institute or possibly an educational foundation. In the meantime, evaluators will continue to repeat their cautions and BRAC will continue to make its own decisions.

CHAPTER 7

Program and Management Support Systems

IN PREVIOUS CHAPTERS we have described BRAC as a "learning organization." Those discussions emphasized the program learning that takes place in the interaction among the landless villagers, BRAC staff in the field, and central management. In addition to program learning, BRAC has been self-conscious about requirements for its own systemic learning and development. Because of its learning mode, BRAC has been able to respond effectively to early cues indicating the need for certain kinds of program supports as well as management systems. Early in its history it recognized an imperative to build the kinds of structures and systems that would support the work in the field and enable rapid program scaleup. BRAC has invested regularly in its own institutional development.

The following pages describe ten of these support systems. The first two, the training and resource centers and the Research and Evaluation Division, might be considered important programs in themselves, but the two are discussed here rather than in Chapter 3 (which overviews BRAC's programs) because they perform such important supporting roles. These two activities are described rather fully. The remaining eight, vital management and field support systems in any large, geographically dispersed organization, are briefly described.

Training and Resource Centers

Training and technical assistance of various sorts is an essential part of all BRAC programs. BRAC's training and resource centers (TARCs) are responsible for providing most of the training for BRAC staff and a large part of training for village organization (VO) members. The TARCs also provide some technical assistance for various income-generating projects.

The TARCs, however, do not do all BRAC training. A large part of the basic occupational skills training for landless group members—for example, basic poultry rearing training, tubewell and power tiller maintenance training, some aspects of fish culture, sericulture, and livestock training—was turned over in 1988 to the field offices of the Rural Development Program (RDP). RDP specialists now conduct occupational skills training at field sites, close to the villages and close to where the income-generating activities will take place. Only about a third of all training of the landless is now done in TARC's residential centers; the remainder is provided in RDP field offices either by RDP specialists or by TARC trainers who travel to those offices to meet the participants. The TARCs and RDP also share the work of providing technical assistance to landless borrowers.

As of December 1990, BRAC had six residential training centers, located in different parts of the country and staffed by seventy-three full-time trainers. The largest of the centers accommodates 100 participants at a time in residential quarters and training rooms. The other centers vary from the smallest, which can handle fifty participants, to the largest, which accommodates ninety. Facilities at each center include classrooms, an auditorium, offices, hostels for participants, a cafeteria, storerooms, a library, and a small cooperative store where trainees can purchase essentials. Also, living quarters for training staff are attached to each center. One of the six centers, newly opened in early 1991, is designed to concentrate entirely on management development for BRAC staff, for field managers in government ministries whose mandate it is to provide services to the rural population, and for officers of other nongovernmental organizations (NGO)s. A seventh new center was planned for 1991.

Each of the centers is surrounded by from three to thirty acres of land used as experimental and demonstration plots for fish culture, livestock and poultry rearing, and vegetable and fruit raising. These plots serve as laboratories for the practical training of villagers, as laboratories for developing and testing workable ideas and models, and in some cases as sources of the improved varieties of vegetable seeds, tree saplings, and fish seedlings or fry that will be used in income-generating projects by villagers. Also, all of the plots are used to supply food for the center kitchens (vegetables, fruits, milk, eggs, fish, etc.).

Who Is Trained and in What Numbers?

The clients for the TARCs fall into four main groups: BRAC staff (22 percent of training done in 1990), landless group members (65 percent in

1990), staff of other development organizations (6 percent in 1990), and government managers (7 percent in 1990). Sixty percent of the 1990 trainees were women and 40 percent men (BRAC, *1990 Annual Review*, 1990).

The courses offered by the TARCs are grouped into two broad categories: (1) human development and management and (2) occupational skills development.

During 1990, the TARCs conducted a total of 925 courses for 21,366 participants amounting to 158,558 participant-days of training. About 90 percent of the training given at the TARCs was in the human development and management category. Only fifty-four of the courses were in the occupational skills category, since most of that kind of training for the villagers is now done by RDP in its area offices or by TARC trainers who teach at those locations.

Landless group members have always received the largest proportion of all TARC training, averaging over 70 percent in the last decade. Now, 65 percent of all TARC training is provided to group members, and this added to the training provided for them by RDP means that more than 75 percent of all training done by BRAC is for VO members.

The biggest change over the last few years in the types of courses offered by the TARCs has occurred in the occupational skills area as evidenced in the recent increased emphasis on training of trainers and training of paraprofessionals, with a corresponding decline in training for occupational skills at the TARCs. Since RDP is now doing its own basic occupational skills training in such economic sectors as poultry, technical aspects of tubewells, livestock, horticulture, sericulture, fisheries, and so on, the TARCs are concentrating on training of trainers and training of a newly developing group of paraprofessionals who can serve other villagers. Examples include teachers for the primary schools (over 6,000 trained), teachers for the paralegal program (over 200 trained), and specialized training in health for staff and villagers (over 1,000 trained). Training for officials of government agencies who are cooperating with BRAC in rural economic and health activities has also become an increasingly important part of the TARC mission.

Of particular note is the change in the gender composition of training participants over the last decade. In 1981, the number of women receiving training in human development and management was only 20 percent of the total. By 1990, women trainees in those courses accounted for 60 percent of all trainees, a total of 12,255 female participants, almost all from the female VOs. The 1990 number represents an increase of 59 percent in female participant training days over the previous year. In the occupational skills courses in 1981, women made up only a third of the participants. By 1988, when such training was turned over to RDP to do in the field, women made up 48 percent. The occupational skills training provided in the field by RDP specialists since 1988 maintains at least a 50 percent ratio of women to men.

One other significant trend worth noting is an increased emphasis on occupational skills training for the VO members. In the first years of BRAC's village organization activities, human development training (leadership, group skills, etc.) was heavily emphasized, with an average of 65 percent of all training being given to the landless group members in these subjects. In 1985, the ratio began to change, with about 50 percent being human development training and the rest occupational skills. Since then, only about 40 percent of all the training of the landless done by the TARCs and RDP combined has been in human development and management, with the remainder in occupational skills.

The growing importance of occupational skills training reflects BRAC's progression from an emphasis on organization and mobilization of the village poor to an equal emphasis on economic factors—income and employment generation supported by credit. Training in occupational skills to enable more effective implementation and better management of economic projects has become essential. Today, occupational skills training provided by the TARCs and RDP combined amounts to about 65 percent of all training of the landless.

Types of Courses and Technical Support Supplied by TARCs

The objectives of the TARCs are not only to design and implement appropriate training to meet the needs of BRAC's various programs, but also to develop and disseminate ideas, methods, and technologies for landless economic activities, to provide follow-up and technical guidance to those who have attended training, and to develop, test, and implement innovative approaches and strategies to accomplish BRAC's goals.

To make its training effective, TARC trainers follow certain guiding principles. All TARC training is designed to be

- learner centered
- problem based
- life oriented
- needs oriented
- experience based
- flexible

- participative
- action/result oriented

Trainers are expected to conduct training sessions in an atmosphere of friendship, openness of mind, and mutual trust and respect, and to think of themselves as facilitators of learning rather than "teachers."

Several months before the end of each year, annual training plans for the following year are developed by the TARCs in close collaboration with BRAC's program managers (called program coordinators in BRAC). Each year, each program coordinator, in consultation with his or her staff, is required to prepare a training needs analysis for the coming year, which must include projections of the number and types of courses needed and recommendations for locations and schedules, based on the needs of their staff and village group members. In several cross-program sessions among the various program managers and the TARC managers, the following year's overall annual training plan is hammered out, along with the role of each of the TARCs. Training plans can be altered during the year if special opportunities or needs arise.

Table 7.1 lists the titles of the courses provided in 1990 and the types of trainees who attended them. The types of courses provided gives an indication of the priorities of the different programs in 1990.

Follow-up and Extension By Trainers

An important task of TARC trainers is to ensure that the positive effects of training of both the landless and BRAC staff members are backed up by posttraining follow-up. In the early days of the TARCs, most follow-up was done by the trainers themselves but that is no longer possible. Because of the increasingly heavy loads on trainers and the geographic spread of organized villages, additional methods for follow-up had to be developed. Sometimes, trainers are able to visit field projects and meet group members and field staff as a part of follow-up activity, but much of the needed follow-up to landless group members must now be done by the RDP program organizers (POs) who are on the spot. Under the present TARC system, when a batch of landless group members takes a training course, the PO who works most closely and regularly with them in their villages attends the training with the group. In the project planning classes, for example, where actual income-generating projects are planned, the PO takes notes on the strategies recommended for meeting the problems discussed and other training findings. These notes serve as the basis for the design of posttraining follow-up.

Table 7.1   Courses Offered by the TARCs, 1990

Clients	Courses *Human Development & Management*	*Occupational Skills**

Landless Group Members	Consciousness Raising
	Leadership Development
	Project Planning and Management
	Groups Dynamics and Leadership
	
	Functional Education Teachers Training
	Special Training
	Workshop
	Paralegal Training
	Paralegal Teachers Training
	
	Paralegal Refreshers Course
	
	Rural Primary Health Care
		Agriculture:
		• Vegetable paraprofessional
		• Social forestry
		• Workshop on horticulture
		  nursery
		Pisciculture:
		• Fish culture and
		  management
		• Fish nursery preparation
		Poultry and Animal Husbandry:
		• Advanced poultry rearing
		  and management
		• Livestock rearing and
		  veterinary treatment
		• Workshop on poultry
		• Refreshers on rural veterinary
		  workers
		• Workshop on livestock
		• Chick rearing and management
		Appropriate Technology:
		• Bee culture and management

BRAC Staff and Other Organizational Workers	Approach to Development
	FE Teachers Training
	FE Refreshers
	Preservice Foundation
	Development Communication
	Approach to Rural Development
	Social Orientation
	Social Issues
	Management Development
	Training of Trainers
	Credit Management
	Interproject Workshop
	Trainers Workshop
	Program Workshop
	NFPE Shebok Training
	NFPE Staff Training
	NFPE Refreshers Course
	Training of Trainers (NFPE)
	Leadership Development
	Development and Change
	Inservice Training (WHDP)
	Integrated Pest Management
	Follow-up Workshop
	Human Development
	Refreshers on Human Development
	Training Needs Assessment
	Research Methodology
		Agriculture Courses:
		• Irrigation Management
		• Irrigation and Paddy
		  Cultivation
		Pisciculture Courses:
		• Fish, Culture and
		  Management

*Occupational Skills courses provided by TARCs only. Many others offered by RDP.
FE = Functional Education

Source: TARC Annual Report, 1990

TARC trainers continue to serve as consultants and as a support network for BRAC staff members as problems are encountered in the field. TARC trainers also serve an important feedback function for management by identifying problems that emerge in training sessions as well as in the field; they then discuss these problems with head office or field managers.

Who Are the BRAC Trainers? How Are They Developed?

TARC trainers, with very few exceptions, are recruited from BRAC's field staff. To establish credibility the trainers must have served for some years as a PO in a field office working daily with villagers. The exceptions are technical experts in such fields as poultry, fisheries, livestock, or other occupational skills, employed for their technical rather than field knowledge. Problems have sometimes arisen with the specialists because of their lack of village knowledge and experience. These specialists, as a consequence, have been used more and more to provide consultant-cum-training services to the field as well as for technical upgrading of the RDP trainers, the ones who actually work with the villagers in their home areas and tailor the training to field conditions. A large part of the technical skills training was transferred from the TARCs to RDP in 1988, primarily to make it more locally relevant and closer to home for the villagers.

In the early stages of the TARCs, outside consultants were utilized to help develop training methodologies and strategies and to provide training-of-trainers to those who made up the initial core group. Now, new TARC trainers take a series of training-of-trainers courses and workshops given by the more experienced trainers. Each year, five or six of the leading trainers are sent to courses outside the country (many are degree programs in human relations development or management) or to shorter courses at local universities or institutes. Consequently, the training staff is continually being upgraded. Each of the two training divisions (human relations and management and occupational skills) holds regular inter-TARC workshops and refreshers, and all the trainers meet together for self-development activities.

Most of TARCs' seventy-five trainers are still male, although in the past several years more women have been added. The paucity of women trainers has been attributed to two factors. First, women had been precluded from training roles as well as other management positions because of their exclusion from the PO entry posts and required field experiences, a general policy at BRAC during the early years for reasons explained in earlier chapters. Second, to offer training courses in the field and to do the field follow-up work on TARC courses, trainers must undertake grueling travel by public transportation, primarily buses, sometimes over long distances. Women do not normally travel alone on buses over long distances in Bangladesh nor find accommodations with nonrelatives.

The field offices of RDP are now successfully introducing women POs, and that will facilitate their gaining the necessary experience to become trainers. Also, overnight accommodations for women trainers can now usually be found at RDP field offices where other BRAC women staff are resident and that therefore have accommodations for women. These factors are expected to make it possible for the TARCs to develop more women trainers.

TARCs as Self-supporting Entities

In keeping with BRAC's overall dedication to the market model and to entrepreneurial behavior, the TARCs, operating as separate cost centers, are expected to be self-supporting. The six TARCs have a combined annual income of about $700,000. The TARCs charge the various BRAC programs for all training provided for program staff or for villagers covered by those programs. Participants from outside NGOs pay regular training fees. In another market-oriented feature, BRAC's programs may buy training outside the organizations if they can find equally good or better training elsewhere.

Each BRAC program includes a budget for its training needs. The fees charged by the TARCs to the programs or outside groups must cover all expenses, including salaries, living and travel costs of trainers, support staff such as cooks, facilities maintenance and depreciation, food and accommodations for participants, and so on. Expenses are kept as low as possible. All trainees take care of their own rooms and are expected to put in an hour's work each morning before class, cleaning classrooms and grounds or working on the demonstration plots. The food provided in the training centers is modest (intended not to be much above the usual fare of villagers) and is served cafeteria style, with participants returning their dishes to the kitchen and generally cleaning up their tables.

The produce raised on the demonstration plots that surround the centers is sold to the TARCs' kitchens or to the outside public; fish fry or seedlings, HYV chicks, or other needed resources are sold to village groups at market prices. At most of the TARCs, the plots are making incomes just slightly below or at the break-even point. A few make a profit.

Future Plans for TARCs

BRAC's goal is to have one TARC for every five *upazilas* in which BRAC is working, a goal that targets twenty centers in all by the year 2000.

Training Done by Programs
in Addition to That Done by TARCs and RDP

As mentioned above, much BRAC training is done by the RDP and various other programs as well as by the TARCs. RDP now provides about two-thirds of the skills training for landless groups. BRAC's health programs also do a great deal of training as a key part of their activities. TARC trainers serve as consultants to help the programs set up their own training courses. The health programs have been training government health workers who work at *upazila, union,* and village levels, and also training members of village health committees. By early 1990, for example, BRAC's health programs had provided immunization training and efficiency training to more than 3,000 of the government health department's family welfare assistants, who work with villagers on family planning and other health-related issues. Hundreds of members of village health committees were given several days of training on basic health and sanitation issues, and several thousand traditional birth attendants were trained on hygienic birth procedures and pre- and postnatal care. In addition, more than 200 government health managers from the *upazilas* received management training by BRAC's special Management Development Program.

The Management Development Program

The Management Development Program (MDP) was established in 1990. The purpose of the MDP, which though related to the TARCs is a separate entity, is to strengthen management capability in BRAC as well as in government and other agencies. It provides management training to BRAC and non-BRAC workers through six basic program elements:

- management research, documentation, and learning
- materials development
- experimental field laboratories
- in-service education
- field follow-up and experience sharing
- consultative services to other organizations

Initially, the MDP is concentrating on upgrading BRAC's midlevel and senior managers, although it will provide some courses for government managers from departments working most closely with BRAC programs such as the Ministry of Health and the Livestock and Poultry Directorate.

A training center for the MDP, about twenty miles outside Dhaka, opened in early 1991. The faculty is still small. In addition to the program coordinator, two permanent faculty members have been appointed (both are currently abroad for higher degrees, one at Harvard and one at the Asian Institute of Management). Faculty development plans, which are slightly behind schedule, called for three new faculty in 1990, two more in 1991, and three more in 1992. To partially offset this shortfall, the MDP has appointed four research assistants rather than the planned two. Also, in order to develop a professional audiovisual unit for both the MDP and the TARCs, an arrangement has been made with Queen's University in Canada for the training of an additional three trainers who will receive master's degrees there.

Training modules have been developed and tested for government health and family planning managers, for BRAC's new Women's Health and Development Program (WHDP) managers; and for BRAC's *upazila* POs in the Income Generation for Vulnerable Group Development (IGVGD) program. By the end of 1990, some fourteen courses had been given for BRAC staff and six for government health managers. Courses have ranged from two to four weeks each. The courses emphasize an interactive, nonlecture approach and give equal attention to areas of technical, behavioral, and conceptual competency. Follow-up to the courses to help managers practice what they have learned is done, in part, through the assignment of specific exercises that are checked at postcourse intervals.

In the absence of regular faculty, the course trainers have been drawn from the most experienced TARC trainers and existing BRAC managers as well as from external bodies such as the Institute of Business Administration, Dhaka University, and the Bangladesh Management Development Centre. Representatives of these organizations, plus others such as the International Centre for Diarrhoeal Diseases Research and the National Institute of Preventive and Social Medicine, also serve on an MDP consultative committee.

Research and Evaluation Division

The Research and Evaluation Division (RED) plays an essential role in the design, implementation, and evaluation of BRAC programs. RED started in 1975 with a single employee; at the end of 1990 it had a staff of ninety people. RED now produces between thirty and forty research reports and papers each year. Outside organizations (such as international NGOs and the government) sometimes commission RED to conduct special studies, although BRAC, because it is so busy with research essential to its own efforts, does not yet encourage outside work.

Staff of RED

Of the ninety staff members of RED, eighteen are considered professional. One has a Ph.D. from the University of London; seven have master's degrees from universities in the United States, Great Britain, and the Netherlands; the remaining professionals, except for two who have bachelor's degrees only, have master's degrees from Bangladeshi universities—primarily Dhaka University. The most recently recruited staff member of RED (not counted in the eighteen above) has a PH.D. in operations research from the Massachusetts Institute of Technology (MIT) in the United States, but he has gone to work as a PO in a village for six months to provide a rural grounding for his later research work.

RED currently has a professional staff development program under which one or two persons per year are being sent overseas for more advanced degrees. Of the eighteen professionals, four are women. Of the remaining staff, fifteen work as coders in the head office (all have master's or bachelor's degrees), and the rest work as assistants in the field as data gatherers under the direction of the professional staff. Many of these do not have higher college degrees but have been given research training by RED senior staff.

From the beginning, BRAC saw research as a powerful tool for program improvement. Very early participatory research techniques were introduced—for example, asking a panel of villagers to discuss a designated topic and recording their observations. By 1980, as Korten documented, research had become integral to program operations, and the line between researcher, field worker, and even villager was no longer well defined, with each participating in agenda setting, data collection, and interpretation (Korten, 1980). Korten gives an example of the participative research technique:

> Villagers concerned about the misappropriation of "food for work" grains by corrupt officials inspired a study on corruption. When they asked BRAC's help it was decided that nothing could be done without more information. BRAC staff members started recording more reports from villagers. This stimulated still more reports. Adding data gathering from official records, BRAC workers and the villagers determined

exactly how much each individual was taking and how. When Union Councils and Thana officials were presented with these facts, "food for work" grains suddenly became available to the poor for their projects. (Korten, 1980, p. 490)

RED has maintained a healthy skepticism about more conventional research methods and researcher role relationships. The mission of the researchers is to assist the program people by rapid collection and interpretation of social data directly relevant to action. In 1980, Korten noted that BRAC researchers stressed disciplined observation, guided interviews, and informant panels over formal surveys; timeliness over rigor; oral over written communication; informed interpretation over statistical analysis; narrative over numerical presentation; and attention to process and intermediate outcomes as a basis for rapid adaptation over detailed assessment of "final" outcomes (Korten, 1980, p. 501). This remains the norm. Summative or other formal evaluations of the program are not the top priority for RED; such evaluations are usually done by outside teams engaged by the donors.

The research conducted by RED today can be classified in five broad categories:

1. baseline or benchmark studies
2. monitoring studies
3. diagnostic studies
4. impact evaluation studies
5. policy-oriented studies

The five kinds of studies are divided into (1) health studies (of which five volumes have been compiled), (2) economic studies (five volumes), and (3) social studies (three volumes).

Most studies are short-term, requiring from one to several months to complete, although a new, long-term, village studies program (described below) has been started. Decisions about what studies to undertake are made by RED staff in consultation with program managers and the executive director. Research priorities are established each year.

Most studies are carried out by multidisciplinary teams, and according to some outside observers (for example, Vaughan, 1988), there seems to be a good and pragmatic balance between rapid and in-depth evaluation studies and between quantitative and qualitative research approaches.

Of the large number of papers and reports being produced by RED, many are primarily useful to BRAC program staff and management for planning and program design or as feedback on performance and stimulus for changes in programs. A smaller number of papers and reports contain information of more general interest to other agencies and re- search centers working in Bangladesh and other Asian countries. A still smaller number are important scientific contributions. Several papers, all in the health field, have been published in recognized international jour- nals in the past two years.

The valuable Rural Studies series has produced four publications. The most widely known is the two-volume Peasant Perceptions Series. The first volume, *Famine, Credit Needs and Sanitation,* was published in the early 1980s, and the second volume, *Villagers' Perceptions on Law,* was published in 1990.

The Village Study Project

The ambitious, long-term Village Study Project (VSP) was started in 1989. The purposes are (1) to learn more about the processes of change and (2) to operate a laboratory area for testing new project inputs. Ten villages in two different social, cultural, and ecological areas of the coun- try have been selected for ongoing study (using both quantitative and qualitative methods) of ecology, demography, economy, politics, tech- nology, and ideology. One village in each of the two study areas covered by BRAC, and a control village outside BRAC's project area, are being studied intensively, and three villages in each of the two areas are being covered less intensively. These latter serve as laboratories to test new in- puts and to provide additional data when a larger sample is needed.

The study is meeting a long-felt need in BRAC for obtaining in-depth information about the impact of its programs and strategies. Also, by having built-in controls in the same areas, far greater credibility can be attached to the results obtained than to the more normal time-bound studies. The Village Studies Project is designed to overcome the problem of not knowing what would have happened without the project inputs. It is hoped that the VSP will be able to observe and describe the processes of change in order to answer "why" questions, as well as to document the results of interventions that provide answers to the "what" question.

RED is aware that a tremendous amount of multivariable data will be produced by the studies and will create a data bank that should make it possible to carry out many types of analysis. The problem RED faces is to have sufficient qualified researchers to analyze regularly and effectively the large amount of data being generated. The 1990 Annual Donors' Review team recommended that RED might attract external assistance for the analytical work by offering access to the data to other Bangladeshi and foreign scholars who want to study problems of rural development in Bangladesh. The team also urged the RDP-RCP donor consortium to explore the possibility of cosponsoring exchange programs in education and research with institutions in their own countries to help improve research capacity within BRAC and creating more possibilities for further education abroad for RED staff. The team pointed out the advantages of such exchanges with programs in development studies in donor countries.

Uses of RED Studies

As a consequence of the very rapid scaleup of BRAC programs and growth in the numbers of studies RED is now producing, some problems about the uses of RED's studies have developed. Program managers and field staff work extremely hard, and as is often true of busy program people, have little time to read and study research reports. To compound the problem, all research studies have been written in English, and although all managers are able to read English, some managers and many POs in the field cannot read and understand it quickly and easily.

Two methods have now been introduced to facilitate transfer of findings from RED to those who most need to know them—program managers and field workers. The first method has been used for many years: seminars in which the researchers explain their findings to program managers. If the manager thinks his field people would benefit from knowing the research results, further seminars, led by the researchers, are arranged in field offices. A second method, recently introduced to facilitate transfer of research findings to BRAC field staff, is the translation of summaries of all research reports into Bangla, accompanied by wider dissemination to the field.

BRAC has recently added a research administrator to the staff of RED, which continues to be headed by one of the professional researchers. The new administrator's job is to help facilitate improved organization of research studies, improved attention to deadlines, better editing of reports, and more prompt and targeted dissemination of findings.

Monitoring Department

In 1988, BRAC established a monitoring cell. Until that time, BRAC's management had relied on its own field knowledge, extensive program reporting systems, and the studies conducted by the Research and Evaluation Division to keep them apprised of what was happening in the field. By 1988, BRAC was growing so rapidly that the managers felt that even more formal systems for continuous assessment of program performance were needed. In 1990, the monitoring cell was upgraded to department status, making it a major unit in the organization.

The aim of the Monitoring Department has been to upgrade, streamline, and manage BRAC's management information systems, which supply data on output as well as performance on financial, institution-building, and social change variables. In addition to the field data regularly collected by the programs themselves, field monitors from the Monitoring Department also collect data and publish quarterly reports. These reports are useful for all levels of management, as they provide progress data against goals on a series of performance indicators. The reports are also widely circulated among the field workers to show how they are doing in comparison to others.

Logistics Department

Since the 1970s, BRAC has had a logistics department. The department, consisting of some twenty-two inside staff members plus twenty-six drivers, is responsible for all purchasing (everything from automobiles, motorcycles, and bicycles to office supplies and furniture); for storekeeping; for the scheduling of all the BRAC vehicles jointly used (the buses that pick up and return the head office employees, cars that take staff or visitors to the field, and trucks that deliver supplies); for the maintenance of all facilities and vehicles; for the operation of the staff cafeteria, which serves some 200 persons each day; and for all other normal or unexpected logistical problems. This department is organized to serve the programs while at the same time maximizing use of limited resources (such as vehicles) and maintaining cost controls on purchasing. The logistical function is essential where field sites are widely scattered and where infrastructure is limited.

Libraries

BRAC has two small libraries: the main one, located at the Dhaka head office, and a branch at the largest TARC. The libraries provide an information circulation system on development issues for BRAC staff members and interested others and house a small but useful collection of journals, books, and periodicals.

Materials Development and Publications Unit

The Materials Development and Publications Unit has a staff of nine persons and several responsibilities. First, it is responsible for the development of all educational materials needed by BRAC's programs, such as maps, posters, books, and fliers, and for other materials that need to be specially produced, such as savings and credit booklets, charts, and so on. It has developed all the books and other teaching materials for BRAC's nonformal primary schools, all the teaching materials for the adult functional education classes offered for some 300,000 villagers to date, and all BRAC's health training materials. The unit performs a necessary service to the programs, which bring all of their materials development problems to the staff of this unit.

The unit is also responsible for the publication of *Gonokendro*, a monthly magazine that has gone through several metamorphoses over the past decade or so, evolving from a general development journal to a popular monthly magazine focusing on social issues. It is now designed primarily for children and emphasizes stories and articles related to health and other social issues. Thirty thousand copies of each issue are printed. It provides ongoing education and pleasure for the children who have attended the BRAC schools, including those who are continuing in the government schools. Interesting and socially relevant reading materials are otherwise almost totally unavailable in the villages.

BRAC's commercial printing company (briefly described in Chapter 3) works closely with the materials development unit to print materials needed in large numbers.

Personnel Department

Until 1989, the personnel functions of BRAC were maintained as the direct responsibility of the executive director. In 1989, the personnel functions were amalgamated into a personnel department with its own manager. For many years BRAC has had a detailed and comprehensive personnel policy manual that covers conditions of service, discontinuance of service, leave and holidays, service benefits, disciplinary procedures, performance review, and benefits.

The Personnel Department serves all the programs by handling their recruiting and recordkeeping needs. The department arranges for the advertising, examination, and interviewing logistics for recruiting several hundred new employees each year and maintains individual files on each of the more than 4,500 regular employees employed as of mid-1991.

Construction Department

BRAC is continuously building new field offices, training centers, and other specialized structures, and enlarging or repairing existing structures. The Construction Department, staffed by eighteen construction engineers, supervises all construction, hires and oversees contractors or craftspeople, and oversees repairs and maintenance of existing buildings. For large new training centers, or other larger construction projects, the department works with design architects, but it performs the design as well as construction functions for the smaller field offices. Because of the existence of this department, BRAC is able to scale-up where needed without delays. The most recently constructed large management training center, with a capacity to handle seventy-five resident trainees and including staff quarters, was completed in eight months, design through construction.

Computer Department

The Computer Department, established in 1985 with two full-time people, is now staffed by thirty-four men and women and is in operation round the clock in three shifts. The department, with its twenty-seven computers, serves all the recordkeeping, statistical, and word-processing needs of the various BRAC programs as well as for the Research and Evaluation Division and the Monitoring Department. Accounting processes have not yet been fully computerized, but that is in progress.

The Computer Department operates at a profit because it not only does BRAC's own work but it sells its services to outside organizations—other NGOs, businesses, and the government. The profit from outside work covers 50 percent of the cost of BRAC's internal work.

Management and Financial Accounting Department

The Management and Financial Accounting Department is responsible for all financial accounting functions, including budgeting. There are twenty-two accountants located at the head office in Dhaka; in addition, each field office of RCP, RDP, and many other BRAC programs have accountants. Although the field accountants report to their branch managers, the Accounting Department at the head office is responsible to see that these staff are adequately trained, follow the required systems, and file necessary reports on time. Financial control systems are tight.

Internal Auditing Department

BRAC recognized early in its existence that a strict auditing function was required. The internal auditing function is separated from the accounting function and is staffed by eighteen auditors who audit all systems and accounts at the head office as well as in the field offices and in BRAC's commercial enterprises. They are directly responsible to the executive director.

External auditors are appointed by the Governing Body and report to the annual general meeting.

Support Departments Essential to BRAC's Performance

The supporting systems described above have generally kept up with the growth in programs and have played an indispensable supporting and facilitative role in program performance as well as providing the foundations on which rapid scaleup could be mounted. Without the Personnel Department for recruiting, the TARCs for training, the Logistics Department for purchasing and warehousing, and the Construction Department for building new field offices, rapid scaleup would be impossible.

How has BRAC been able to build its own infrastructure capable of supporting program development? *First,* BRAC has paid attention to its own institutional development. Self-conscious about its own institution-building needs, BRAC has sought advice from outside management consultants and donor appraisal teams about its institutional development (advice has always been filtered through "resident" common sense). *Second,* BRAC learned early in its history to include in all program grant proposals an overhead charge for its own organizational systems costs. Sufficient money has therefore been available to pay for these activities. *Third,* BRAC has occasionally requested and obtained direct institution-building grants. The initial costs for the establishment of the TARCs, for the Research and Evaluation Division, and for the establishment of the computer department were covered by special grants.

A Matrix Form

Figure 7.1 shows the BRAC head office organizational structure in a matrix format. The figure illustrates the relationship between the functional programs described in previous chapters and the support systems described in this chapter.

This matrix structure, in which line organizations (programs) relate directly to the program support systems in a negotiating relationship, contributes to the coordination of activities and enhances participatory decisionmaking in an organization that is both functionally and struc-

Figure 7.1   Matrix Diagram Illustrating Relationship of
Support Services and Programs

(Numbers indicate examples of negotiated relationships)

| *Support Service* | *Programs* | | | | |
	RDP	*RCP*	*Health*	*NFPE*	*Paralegal*
RED			Example 1		
TARCs					
Management Development Program	Example 2				
Logistics				Example 3	
Accounting					
Materials Development Unit					Example 4
Monitoring					
Computer					
Construction		Example 5			
Personnel					

Examples

1. The health program requests the RED to undertake a study of the efficacy of the training program for the traditional birth attendants. Negotiated: time, sample, logistics, etc.

2. RDP asks the MDP to design and offer a special management program for its new area managers. Negotiated: scheduling and content.

3. The NFPE Program asks Logistics to obtain 2,000 new blackboards for its new schools. Negotiated: price, delivery, dates.

4. The Paralegal Program asks the Materials Department Unit to prepare a simple illustrated booklet on legal rights. Negotiated: cost parameters, timing, audience relevance, style.

5. The Rural Credit Project urgently needs reconstruction of two branch offices that were destroyed by a recent cyclone. Negotiated: size, plan, cost, timing.

Source: Interviews with program and support system managers

turally decentralized. (For a discussion of the theory and practice of "matrix management," see Davis and Lawrence, 1977.) The matrix relationship tends to push decisionmaking downward. The managers of the primary support departments are on the same hierarchical level as the functional department (program) managers. The program managers must negotiate with the support service managers for the services they need. The managers of the respective units must plan together within a common framework of shared values and goals. No one of the support or program departments can direct the work of the others, nor does the executive director attempt to command their day-to-day activities. The relationships between the programs and the supporting departments and the services supplied are mutually decided.

Examples of one or two more complex matrix relationships may be given. Trainers from the TARCs, for example, do all of the teacher training for the Non-Formal Primary Education program. This has meant over the last few years training several thousand new teachers a year, plus providing the annual refresher training. In effect, many TARC trainers are seconded to the education program. Their line relationship is still to the TARCs, but they are working nearly full-time in the education program training teachers. Another example is in the health programming. All of the staff training for the health program is done by TARC trainers. When the Child Survival Program was gearing up, more than ten TARC trainers were needed for six months to provide training for the new field staff. The TARC trainers were again seconded to the health program but maintained their home and line relationship with their home TARC and returned there when the health training was finished. In the meantime, they worked closely with the health program on content and timing of training.

Matrix management, this kind of flexible, negotiated working relationship between the program and the support departments, although it requires constant interdepartmental negotiations, facilitates program development and efficient delivery of services by the support groups to the programs.

CHAPTER 8

The Financing of BRAC

BRAC's 1991 ANNUAL budget for all of its programs was $20 million, about 15 percent of which was financed by profits from BRAC's own commercial activities (briefly described in Chapter 3).

Between its inception in 1972 and mid-1990, BRAC had received close to $34 million dollars from international donors. At the end of 1989, a consortium of donors pledged another $50 million dollars over three years beginning in 1990 for the Rural Development Program (RDP) and over four years for the Rural Credit Project (RCP). Another group of donors at the beginning of 1991 pledged $8.6 for health programming over a three-year period. Figure 8.1 shows the growth in BRAC's income between 1980 and 1990. The portion indicated as BRAC's own income is not profit but gross income.

Donor grants are based on program proposals initiated by BRAC and refined in close collaboration with donor teams. BRAC initiates all proposals based on its own development strategies and long-term plans, rather than on the development preferences of donors. It has not designed programs to respond to funding opportunities, but rather has made it a policy to control its own strategies and program development. It works closely with a group of donors who trust BRAC as an institution and who do not attempt to impose their priorities.

Who Are the Donors?

Through 1990, ninety percent of donor grants have come from European donors, with the next largest amount from Canada. The few contributions from the United States have come from nongovernmental groups, primarily the Ford Foundation and Oxfam. Of the thirty-one donor groups that made grants to BRAC prior to the formation of the nine-

Figure 8.1 Income 1980–90

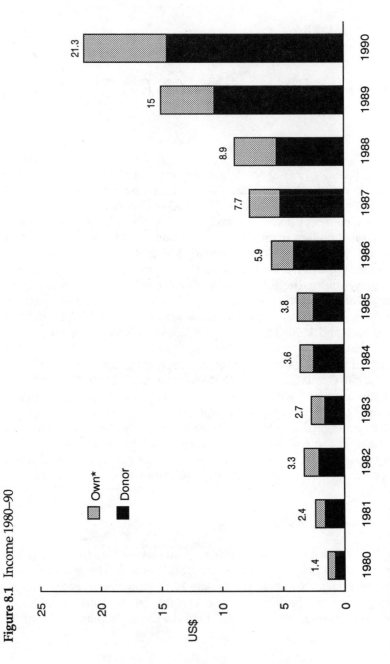

*"Own" income is gross income, not net income.
Source: BRAC accounts

member donor consortium in 1990, the largest contributor was the Netherlands Organization for International Development Cooperation (NOVIB), which has given nearly $11 million since it first began contributing in 1978. NOVIB continues now as an important member of the current donor consortium. The Swiss Development Cooperation (SDC), the second largest donor, did not join the 1990 donor consortium but continues to finance health programming. It began contributing in 1980, providing nearly $4.5 million up to 1990. The third largest has been Germany's Evangelische Zentralstelle für Entwicklungshilfe (EZE) which began giving in 1984. So far EZE has contributed over $3.5 million and continues to give through the donor consortium.

The fourth largest contributor is UNICEF, which as one of the original donors to BRAC provided a small contribution in BRAC's first year of operation in 1972. UNICEF has been a consistent donor ever since. It is not a member of the new donor consortium for RDP and RCP but continues to underwrite health and primary education programs. The fifth largest donor has been the Swedish International Development Agency (SIDA), which has given nearly $3 million since 1986 and is now a member of the consortium.

Through its British, Canadian and U.S. branches, Oxfam has been a consistent donor since 1972. The three groups combined have given over $1 million to various BRAC programs, with a particular focus on women and institutional development.

Other contributors include Swedish Free Church Aid (SFCA), which also serves as a conduit for SIDA funding; The Ford Foundation, concentrating its grants primarily on BRAC's own institutional development; the United Nations Capital Development Fund (UNCDF),which provided $1.4 million for the BRAC cold storage plant; Interpares (Canada); NORAD, the Norwegian aid agency; the German *Brot für die Welt* (Bread for the World); and some eighteen other smaller donors.

Major new donors were added through the 1990 consortium, an innovation, that represents a new kind of relationship between the donors and BRAC. Joining long-time donors—NOVIB, EZE, the Ford Foundation, SIDA, and NORAD—are these new donors: the Aga Khan Foundation, which also serves as a channel for the money from the Canadian International Development Agency (CIDA); the Danish International Development Agency (DANIDA); the British Overseas Development Agency (ODA); and the Japanese government.

In response to BRAC's plans to scale up very rapidly in the next few years, the donor consortium was formed to obviate a large amount of proposal writing to individual donors, and as a vehicle for the donors to combine their efforts to appraise and evaluate programs. The consortium maintains an office in Dhaka, which serves all the donors by providing field reporting, logistical aid to visiting donor teams, office backup to donor teams, and other assistance. Its purpose is to reduce some of the burden to BRAC of donor-related proposal and reporting responsibilities, which are time consuming and often redundant when BRAC must deal with a large number of independent donor groups. It also facilitates donor cooperation and cuts their own evaluation and communications costs.

The consortium arrangement, which incorporates all but two of BRAC's larger donors, was constituted at the end of 1989. The chair revolves among the donors each year. During its first year, the consortium arrangement appears to have worked well from the point of view of both the donors and BRAC. The first major annual review, in November 1990, was conducted by a consortium-nominated team, and the review was accepted by all the donors. Without the consortium BRAC would have had to provide the logistics and management time for nine different donors, and each donor would have had to field a team of its own.

Most funding from donors is provided in the form of grants, but occasionally a donor will loan money on soft terms. Soft loans have been used almost entirely to assist in establishing BRAC's commercial enterprises, primarily BRAC Printers.

Grant Categories

Table 8.1 shows that by far the largest category of donor grants, 39 percent, has been given for BRAC's core Rural Development Program, which includes basic village organization, social development, credit, and economic subsector interventions. The second largest category, 25 percent, has been health programming, including the nationwide oral rehydration program and assistance to the government in immunization and various other primary health care activities. The Rural Credit Project, BRAC's new bank, has utilized 10 percent of funding, and the Non-Formal Primary Education program, 6 percent. BRAC's own institutional development has taken about 3 percent of donor funding, while miscellaneous activities, particularly disasters, has utilized 17 percent.

In the next three years the proportions will tilt even more to the basic RDP and to the RCP. Although real dollar spending on health and primary education will grow rapidly, the spending on RDP and RCP will grow even more rapidly. (Actually, primary education may grow more rapidly than any other sector if current fund-raising plans are successful.)

Table 8.1 Donor Contributions in Taka (millions) by Program Categories, 1972–90

Years Progress	RDP	RCP	Health	Primary Education	Institutional Development*	Miscellaneous**	Total
1972–89	392.2	0.0	340.1	37.7	45.1	271.6	1,086.6
1990	226.8	169.5	58.4	56.6	0.0	5.0	516.3
Total	619.0	169.5	398.5	94.3	45.1	276.6	1,602.9
Percentage of Total	39.0	10.0	25.0	6.0	3.0	17.0	100.0

* Includes TARCs and Research and Evaluation Division
** Includes disasters and small projects.

Source: BRAC accounts

The Bangladesh Government and NGO Grants

The government maintains rather close control over nongovernmental organizations (NGOs) in Bangladesh. An NGO cannot receive a grant from a foreign donor without going through a government approval process managed by a government NGO office. This office was established in 1988 as NGOs proliferated and concerns about corruption in some NGOs surfaced. A program proposal is written by the NGO, and an informal agreement, in the form of a letter of intent on the part of a donor to finance the program, is obtained. The full proposal and the letter of intent are then submitted to the government's NGO office. That office sends the proposal for approval or clearance to the ministries most closely related to the work to be done; for example, the health programs must be signed off by the Ministry of Health, nonformal primary education by the Ministry of Education, and the rural development program by the Ministry of Agriculture. Representatives of the NGO are usually called for various meetings with the ministries and the NGO office before the approval is obtained.

BRAC has maintained good relationships with the ministries, usually keeping them informed and consulting with them during the planning process for any new program. Relations with the government NGO office have been relatively smooth because BRAC has a reputation for effective development work, professional management, and careful control of money. As a consequence, it has had little difficulty in getting its programs approved. The donors, who give to many NGOs as well as to the government of Bangladesh, are usually able to influence the government's actions if serious problems arise. The approval process is time consuming, and maintaining close working relationships with the ministries is an important part of the job of the executive director, as well as of the program coordinators of the principal programs.

Funding the Organization, Not the Program

During informal conversations with various donors, one often hears the comment, "We really fund BRAC as an organization, not so much the individual programs." They go on to say that they have confidence in BRAC as an organization—in its integrity and strategic wisdom as well as its implementation ability. Each of the donors has built a substantial documentation of BRAC's outlook and operations based on the reports of appraisal and review teams and many personal visits by donor leaders to BRAC activities in the field. Confidence on the part of donors is borne out by examining donor histories, shown in Table 8.2.

As Table 8.2 indicates, almost all donors, once they had made a first contribution, became consistent contributors. Only twelve of some thirty-one donors confined their grants to four or fewer years; these twelve were the donors of very small amounts. The large donors have been consistent in their giving and have generally supported more than one kind of programming.

Donor Dependency

BRAC still depends on external donor grants for 85 percent of its total budget each year. The government of Bangladesh depends on donor grants for 100 percent of its annual development budget and for some 15 percent of its recurrent budget. All NGOs, because they do not have the power to tax, and in most cases do not engage in profit-making commercial activities, depend on membership fees, endowment income, or external grants for the support of programs they undertake.

BRAC is attempting to reduce external dependency by building up its commercial enterprise income and by designing development programs to become self-supporting. The Rural Credit Project (which will become the BRAC Bank) is expected to be fully self-supporting through interest income and investments after four years. Because of the transfer of RDP area offices to the RCP at the point of maturity and four years experience, BRAC will be able to greatly expand its coverage in the RDP program without increasing the amount of money invested by donors. The savings generated by village people themselves and invested in income-generating programs continues to grow. To the middle of 1990, the poorest villagers had saved over $3 million, a larger amount than that given by many of the donors. The villagers are, in effect, investing those savings in their own development programs.

Bangladesh remains one of the poorest countries in the world and one continually beset by natural disasters, like the 1991 cyclone. For a long time to come, NGOs working with transfers of resources from more fortunate countries will continue to be needed. BRAC will continue to design programs that lead to self-sufficiency but complete independence from external donors is not realistic for the short-term future of BRAC, other NGOs, or the government itself.

PART III

The Future

CHAPTER 9

Measurement, Strategies, and Sustainability

THE PRECEDING CHAPTERS have described the programs of BRAC, the rationale behind those programs, and how and why BRAC works as it does. The premise on which this book's examination of BRAC began was that BRAC represents a success story in the development field. As demonstrated in the analysis, the premise appears well founded. An underlying assumption, and the rationale for describing BRAC in such detail, has been that an examination of how BRAC has operated and the reasons why BRAC has succeeded might be helpful to other nongovernmental organizations (NGOs), donors, and students of development. Although BRAC works in the unique Bangladeshi economic, political, and social environment, much of BRAC's successful experience, particularly in management and attitude, may have relevance for NGOs in other countries.

The book has also attempted to illustrate how BRAC has answered one of the most basic questions in development management:

> . . . whether desired social outcomes can be achieved through central technocratic allocation of resources to provide services intended to benefit the poor, or whether the real problem of poverty is rooted in basic social structures which relegate the poor to conditions of dependency? If the former, then the central problem may be one of increasing the effectiveness of service delivery. If the latter, then the central problem may be to reduce dependency by measures which increase the potential of the poor to take independent and instrumental political action on their own behalf. (Korten, 1979)

BRAC management has recognized that both approaches have a place. The two approaches, in fact, are demonstrated in different BRAC programs. The core program, the Rural Development Program (RDP), is based on the second assumption, that the problem of poverty is rooted in basic social structures and conditions of dependency. On the other hand, BRAC's Non-Formal Primary Education (NFPE) program demonstrates a highly effective service delivery approach consistent with the first assumption. A third model, BRAC's health programs, which combines attempts to change the attitudes and behaviors of the village poor about sanitation, nutrition, family planning, and other health issues with direct health service delivery and efforts to improve government health services, is a hybrid of both approaches.

The success of BRAC's varied programs is based largely on having achieved a high degree of fit among beneficiary needs, program design, and the organization's ability to adapt to the requirements of program purposes and the needs of the rural poor. One of the characteristics often ascribed to successful organizations, and illustrated so well in BRAC, is the process by which program and organizational capacities are developed concurrently. Chapters 6 and 7, on BRAC's well-developed management and program support systems, illustrated how organizational capacities are developed and adapted to program needs.

Measuring Success

Measuring the impacts of development efforts is usually problematic, particularly when such intangible concepts as self-reliance, conscientization, changes in self-concept, the breaking of vertical dependencies, and improved status of women are among the goals. Such changes, however, can be measured using a primarily anthropological approach to case histories. (For some useful discussions of measurement and evaluation, see Pfohl, 1986; Rugh, 1986; Pietro, 1983; Bowman et al., 1989; Otero, 1989; and Clark and McCaffery, 1979.)

Other goals, such as increased income, improved nutritional and overall health status, reductions in family size, and lower infant mortality rates, are more easily measurable, provided baseline studies have been done and control groups (where the interventions have not been made) are set up for comparison. Also, the extent of "success" of one organization's set of interventions compared to that of others can be measured, provided the goals and criteria for success used in the comparison analysis of the organizations are the same.

Unfortunately, few long-term, observational studies and few rigorous, large-scale studies of the impact of NGO and government programs in Bangladesh, including those of BRAC, have been done. Notable exceptions of high quality are: (1) the careful documentation by Martha Chen of the profound changes in attitudes and the improvements in the status of women organized by BRAC (Chen, 1983); (2) a rigorous, high-quality study of the impacts of the credit program of the quasi-governmental Grameen Bank (Hossain, February 1988); (3) a comparison of the results of the development approach of BRAC in the early 1980s (before the credit program was introduced) with the Grameen Bank's credit program (Streefland, et al., 1986); and (4) a comparison of the BRAC groups receiving credit with a control group of similar villagers not receiving credit (Chowdhury, et al., 1991).

The 1986 Streefland study, comparing the impact of BRAC and Grameen Bank programs in village groups where *BRAC had not yet introduced its credit program,* found results that could have been expected: the rural poor organized by BRAC were more conscientized and self-reliant, were more active in mobilizing local resources, had made profound attitudinal and behavioral changes, and were more socially active than the Grameen Bank borrowers; but the Grameen Bank borrowers had made more economic progress.

The 1991 Chowdhury study compared 100 randomly selected BRAC village organization (VO) members (fifty male and fifty female) who had been associated with an RDP-organized group for at least seven years, had come from separate households, and to whom credit had been made available (the target group) with a control group of 100 randomly selected male and female village organization members who were only very recently organized and to whom no credit had yet been extended.

The findings indicated that the per capita annual income in the target households was Tk 3,502, 26 percent higher than that of the control group. The study also showed that a significantly larger number of the target households had more than one source of income. Among the target households, 60.5 percent had second and 26 percent had third sources of income, whereas in the control households only 47.5 percent and 16 percent, respectively, had second and third sources of income.

Another interesting finding was the extent to which female employment differed between the target and control households. Among males, the number of person-days of employment was 9 percent higher in the target group than in the control group; but for females, employment was 34 percent higher in the target sample.

A final finding was that the target group households owned considerably more cattle, goats, chickens, rickshaws, bicycles, agricultural implements, and weaving machines. Ducks were the only asset the control households owned in larger numbers.

If the number of rigorous studies is as yet so small, on what basis then do most observers of BRAC, both inside Bangladesh and from all parts of the world, base their belief that BRAC is highly successful? The first measure, subjective to be sure, is from personal observation based on accounts described by concerned visitors, government officials, and others who have direct experience in the villages where BRAC has organized the poor, including conversations with BRAC village organization members and others in the villages. A part of BRAC's reputation for effectiveness and honesty has come from these secondary personal observations. A second measure of success has been BRAC's extraordinary ability to manage the vicissitudes of the Bangladeshi political milieu, both formal and informal. Gaining the respect and cooperation of many different government ministries, BRAC has been able to undertake programs in different sectors and to scale up rapidly in those sectors. Without the formal and informal support of important urban as well as rural leaders—an implicit measure of trust and respect—the variety and scale of BRAC's endeavors would be impossible.

Turning to more objective studies, BRAC's own Research and Evaluation Division (RED) is an important source of useful data and analysis of BRAC's operations. RED has conducted hundreds of studies on various pieces of BRAC programs and has published more than ten volumes of these research reports over the last decade. The RED studies have become more rigorous and useful as the research staff has been upgraded and enlarged in the last few years. Rigor is also being improved through a developing collaboration with universities and research centers, primarily in European countries, as described in Chapter 7.

A second group of studies, and perhaps the most influential in documenting the successes of BRAC, are the numerous reports prepared by donors' appraisal and evaluation teams who spend time at BRAC field locations every year. The generally strong positive results found by hundreds of members of these teams over the last decade is documented in their reports. Of significance also is the fact that a large number of donors have consistently supported BRAC's work year after year, thus demonstrating their belief in the efficacy of BRAC's interventions and in the organization's promise for the future.

An additional measure of BRAC's "success" is the number of persons who visit BRAC and the extent to which BRAC's approaches and methods serve as examples both inside Bangladesh and for other developing countries. At least two delegations per month, sent primarily by NGOs and government ministries from developing countries and by international organizations, visit BRAC. The burden on BRAC staff is great, but they have attempted to accommodate these visitors with field trips and staff time.

Finally, other studies, conducted by international organizations such as the World Bank and the United Nations Development Programme (UNDP), have reviewed and generally documented the success of BRAC. One recent example is found in a section of a UNDP study (Rahman, 1988) that compares the performance of selected NGOs and quasi-governmental and governmental credit programs on a series of credit activities and documents their impact. The tables in this study compare BRAC credit recipients with those of Proshika, the second largest NGO in Bangladesh; Swanivar and Grameen Bank, quasi-governmental programs; and the Bangladesh Rural Development Board (BRBD), a government program for the rural poor. According to the data reported, BRAC borrowers had received, applied, and benefitted from the following advice significantly more than did the borrowers of the four other organizations: (1) advice on agricultural practices, (2) advice on livestock and poultry culture, (3) advice on setting up cottage industries, and (4) advice on kitchen gardening. Furthermore BRAC borrowers had gained significantly more person-days of work after joining BRAC than had those from the other organizations.

Criticisms of NGOs

In Bangladesh, as in the rest of the world, there are critics of NGO activities in general. BRAC, particularly because it is so large and active and "successful," is included in many of these general criticisms. The critics fall into two main categories: the first group represents the viewpoint of the political left, while the second group see NGOs as diverting resources and attention from the main job of improving government. An interesting and extensive debate on NGOs and their contribution to development in Bangladesh was carried for twelve weeks in 1989 in the Dhaka Courier, in which more than thirty NGO leaders as well as critics presented their views (*Dhaka Courier*, 1989). Many spokespersons on the political left view all Western donor–supported NGOs as "agents of Western capitalism and tools of imperialism." Although admitting that NGOs have been very successful at reaching the grassroots, they say that too much of the attention of NGOs, including that of BRAC, has been addressed more to the symptoms of poverty than to its underlying causes; and that the NGO approach has been too localized, thus obscuring the national context and the urgent task of radical change for the whole society. This point of view further suggests that NGOs encourage the landless to think that the way out of their poverty is through income-generating, capitalist activity rather than through revolutionary transformation of the exploitative economic and social relationships in the country. NGOs are seen as palliative and income-generating activities as only having assisted petty capitalism without having had any real impact in increasing the productive capacity of the economy. They also contend that NGOs, even though active for twenty years or more, have made no real impact on economic conditions or literacy rates or other measures of life quality, which in general have become worse in Bangladesh over that period.

Critics in the second group, spanning the political spectrum and advancing a mixed bag of criticisms, admit for the most part that their criticisms do not apply equally to all NGOs. Some of these critics specifically exempt BRAC and one or two other NGOs. These critics suggest that NGOs are too small and too limited in their coverage or too inefficient to make much countrywide impact. They see many NGOs as corrupt and in business only to garner resources, very few of which actually reach the grassroots. Others say that NGOs are too broad in their coverage and should stick to organizing and consciousness raising and should not involve themselves with service delivery, which is the job of the government. To the extent that foreign donors channel a great deal of money directly to NGOs, thereby bypassing government, and setting NGOs up as alternative sources of what should be government services, they claim government is weakened or not helped to strengthen itself, or is in fact undermined. Some of these critics see many NGOs as much too critical of government and much too radical because they interfere with "normal" social relationships and economic relationships.

BRAC itself indulges in self-criticism as it carefully tracks external criticism. A self-examination by top staff as reported by Korten (*BRAC Strategy*, 1989) acknowledged that perhaps too little attention has been given to achieving a basic realignment of the resource management systems responsible for the unjust distribution and unproductive use of available resources in the country. These staff discussions recognized that basic institutional changes to achieve long-term correction of current deficiencies need additional reinforcement in BRAC programs.

Regardless of criticisms of NGOs, the number, scope, and scale of NGO activity in Bangladesh continue to grow. In spite of the corruption and inefficiency in some of them, NGOs have become generally well respected for their work, and increasing amounts of resources are flowing to them. Government, albeit often reluctantly, has recognized the benefits from NGO work and in many cases, as previous chapters have demonstrated, ministries and *upazila* leaders are welcoming cooperative programs at least so far as BRAC is concerned.

Distinguishing Features of BRAC's Approach and Expertise

Many development NGOs, both indigenous and international, subscribe to goals similar to those of BRAC as described in Chapter 2. It is not BRAC's goals that make it different from, and perhaps more successful than, many other NGOs in the world. The following ten points summarize those features of BRAC identified in this study as having contributed to its success.

Propensity to Risk

BRAC has shown exceptional propensity to risk, recognizing that programs, activities, and investments will sometimes fail. It has been willing to take the consequences, feeling that "nothing ventured, nothing gained." But BRAC managers have also been willing to involve their landless clients in risk, often under strong criticism from donors or outside observers, with attendant hardship when experiments fail. Risk is accepted with staff appointments, where nearly one-third of all newly hired staff fail in the field; with program strategies; with new kinds of technologies and economic activities such as the early failures with some tubewells and power tiller ownership by village groups; and with many kinds of credit financing options. Overall, successes have far outweighed failures, and high-risk experimentation has paid off for most in the long run. Yet, it is apparent that had BRAC been in less wise management hands and had early warning systems not been in place, such a high-risk strategy might have led to more problems and more people getting hurt.

Investment in Organizational Development

BRAC early recognized the importance of investment in the development of its own staff and in the building of in-house expertise and systems required to support field activities. BRAC sought and received grants specifically designed to continually upgrade staff through training, higher education, and on-site exposure to the work of NGOs in other developing countries. Now, all program grants from donors must include a fixed percentage allocation for staff development. Special grants were sought and received to build the necessary support systems described in Chapter 7. Without these well-designed and effective support systems, program activities in the field would be hampered and scaleup would be impossible. Other NGOs have suffered from failure to invest in their own staff and in their own management and systems development.

Many examples of these failures can be given from Bangladesh.

Strong Fiscal Accountability and Control

Perhaps because the executive director of BRAC was a chartered accountant with years of experience in large-scale business, BRAC from its inception set up rigorous financial control systems. A large accounting department, subject to and enforcing the control systems, an internal auditing department (under separate reporting lines), and annual external auditing have been the norm since the beginning.

Setting Its Own Agenda

BRAC has always set its own agenda, decided on its own programs, and then approached donors for funding, rather than allowing itself to respond to donor-designed strategies or programs in order to take advantage of available money. This does not mean that BRAC does not avail itself of donor expertise or listen to donor advice. Programs are often redesigned for the better as a result of the cooperative interactions between donor appraisal or evaluation teams and BRAC staff. BRAC program designers utilize the insights and expertise of the team members to sharpen their own thinking. The results of these interactions are often improvements in program design. A number of cases in point have been discussed in the previous chapters—in the bank project, the extension of time from three to four years before RDP could sell branches to the bank project, and a slower phaseout than originally proposed of institution-building services to village organizations were two changes urged by the donor team and accepted by BRAC after careful thought.

By controlling its own agenda and not allowing donor strategies or fund availabilities to alter its course, BRAC has been able to stick to its own strategic plans while maintaining its ability to respond to community demands. It has been adept at utilizing resource availabilities (often unexpected) if they fit into program needs, but it has been effective at avoiding resource offers that would divert or dilute its own programs and their fit with overall strategy and directions.

Market Perspective and Entrepreneurial Spirit

Throughout all of its activities, BRAC has maintained a market perspective and encouraged entrepreneurial behavior. It has a policy of not interfering in normal market operations except to overcome obstacles or constraints or to prevent obvious exploitation. Many examples of how

BRAC has incorporated cost recovery and other market-based thinking into its operations were given in Chapter 8. Also, as discussed in Chapter 4, credit has never been subsidized; interest rates have been based on market rates.

This market perspective has fostered self-reliance and businesslike thinking for staff and clients and has contributed both to the efficiency and the effectiveness of the organization. It has enabled BRAC to do far more than the sum of its donor funds would seem to allow. The entrepreneurial spirit has encouraged villagers to invest in new types of businesses, from fish fry production to poultry feed.

Responding to the Field

Rather than decide in advance on a limited number and type of programs, BRAC has remained responsive to demands from the field. The Non-Formal Primary Education program is a case in point. Parents in village groups who had attended the required adult functional education classes kept asking, "Why can't you do something about literacy for our children? The government schools do not meet our children's needs." Although primary education was outside of BRAC's previous experience and seemed to some observers as a diversion of BRAC's main efforts, BRAC did respond. Now, primary education is one of its most successful programs, with plans under way for much more rapid scaleup over the next few years. The program is obviously meeting one of the highest priority needs as defined by the villagers themselves. And, as suggested earlier in this chapter, BRAC is not limited to any one form of program modality. Its planning and management system is flexible enough to utilize different and appropriate modalities for different kinds of programs.

Responding to Opportunities and Resources

Being flexible and constantly in touch with its environment, BRAC has been adept at identifying and cooperating with other NGOs and government agencies that have goals and resources compatible with BRAC's. By this type of collaboration BRAC has been able to make its programs more effective. Several examples have been given in the preceding chapters. BRAC's cooperation with CARE and the government in the deep tubewell operations is one case in point; another is cooperation with the government and CARE in the spread of mulberry trees, combining government sapling supply with CARE-supervised food-for-work programs to pay people to guard and water the trees for the first three years until they reach maturity. In many other instances, BRAC has been able, for example, to connect its village groups with the food-for-work programs, to pay for cleaning river basins to set up fisheries, or to plant, water, and guard fruit or fodder trees planted on roadsides or bunds. The cooperative effort with Directorate of Livestock and Poultry described in Chapter 5 is also a case in point.

Commitment to Rapid Scaleup

BRAC has been able to scale up its programs rapidly and effectively, based on its ability to attract, train, and retain a basic cadre of qualified and dedicated staff members committed to the organization's fundamental philosophy, its management styles (both operational and strategic), its competent and well-designed program support systems, and its ability to generate financial support as required. Most important, however, in the successful scaleup is the prevailing attitude throughout the organization that scaleup is necessary because needs are so great. Everyone is stretched to the limit. Small may be beautiful but bigger is absolutely necessary where the needs are so widespread. Although the best aspects of incremental program development are followed, incrementalism does not become an end in itself. The ultimate objective of every program is to scale up where possible. Anything less is considered inadequate performance. This pervasive outlook may be one of the most important transferable aspects of BRAC.

Facilitation Efforts with the Public Sector

Recognizing that NGOs cannot take the place of government, and that the conditions of most rural people will not improve adequately until government is able to supply needed services in response to village needs, BRAC has undertaken to encourage and assist government units to improve their management and service capabilities. In BRAC's view, government should be reoriented from being a controller and patronage dispenser to being an enabler. BRAC has invested heavily in efforts to reorient some government agencies. As detailed in earlier chapters, there are now working agreements with several relevant national ministries such as the Ministry of Health and Family Planning, where BRAC assists in training and management systems development in the government's immunization and other village health services; the Ministry of Education, through a pilot program requested by the ministry to assist community people in 300 public school areas to cooperate with the schools to improve school performance; and with the Ministry of Livestock and Fisheries in the chick rearing, vaccination, and disease control programs, in livestock's paravet and artificial insemination programs, and in various aspects of fisheries development services. BRAC is also cooperating with the Directorate of Livestock and Poultry and the Ministry of Relief and Rehabilitation in the Income Generation for Vulnerable Group Development (IGVGD) program to help get destitute women off relief by teaching them how to be poultry rearers and vaccinators.

BRAC's public systems facilitation work has been designed not only to assist government agencies to improve their management and service capabilities. This work has also helped the landless groups to increase their awareness of what government should be doing and to improve the landless group's ability to make effective demands on government agencies. The facilitation work with the schools and with various health programs depends heavily on connecting community knowledge and demand with the government service providers.

A Learning Organization

A close examination of the various programs and methods of operating demonstrates why BRAC has been identified as one of the few examples of a "learning organization." The introduction, citing Korten (1980), Chen (1983), and Senge (1990), discussed the characteristics of a learning organization, which BRAC appears to exemplify. BRAC experiments with various strategies and modalities (from staffing patterns to program content) in its regular programming, in addition to experimenting in the two field areas designated as its "laboratories." It operates in a learning atmosphere in which a spiral of program design, implementation, change, new implementation, and expansion is the norm. It has educated its own staff as well as its donors to understand the need for constant monitoring, acceptance of error, learning, and change—in short, understanding how their own actions shape the reality in which they act.

The five characteristics of a learning organization outlined by Senge —building shared vision, encouraging personal mastery, examining mental models, fostering team learning, and promoting systems thinking—seem to fit the BRAC mode of operation. These five "disciplines," in Senge's terms, are about a process of enhancing capacity—ways in which individuals and groups (or teams) within organizations operate to generate new ideas and approaches that empower themselves and others to greater achievement. The actions and behavior of organizational participants illustrate a "learning style." While no organization "is" in effect a full learning organization having achieved an ideal state, BRAC's operating style can be identified as the learning process. "Learning is about enhancing capacity," and BRAC's experience demonstrates this fact.

Shared vision. BRAC builds shared vision, a common picture of a desired future, in many ways. One basic policy, for example, is the requirement that all entering professional staff interested in careers and advancement in BRAC begin in the field working with villagers, living in a field camp with other staff members, and going daily to the villages. This experience gives all staff members a common knowledge of what life is really like for the poorest in the villages.

But building shared vision of what alternative futures could be like is more than just living in the village. It is an ongoing process enhanced through the extensive dialogue that takes place daily with villagers and among staff in the field camps. It is the managers at the Dhaka headquarters dialoguing constantly among themselves and with field staff, both in the head office and during frequent field visits. BRAC recognizes that the "vision thing," as a living force in the hearts and minds of people, is their most important work. Constant dialogue with reflection on and talk about what people really want to create is the operating norm. Shared vision is reinforced by dialogue in training sessions at the training and resource centers (TARCs) for villagers and staff members, in the regular issue meetings held monthly with villagers, in staff meetings at all levels, and through discussions in the various research reports, BRAC staff newsletters, and other publications.

Personal mastery. Shared vision, however, is not possible without personal vision and personal mastery—a real sense in the individual of what truly matters and a personal commitment to living this truth. This means clarifying and deepening the personal vision of organizational participants and connecting personal learning and organizational learning. The bottom line with shared vision is that individuals must have their own visions before a shared vision can exist. Without personal vision, people only follow the vision of others.

The BRAC experience has been and is a continuing exploration in supporting both the staff and their village clients in the continuous process of discovering and verifying their personal abilities and commitments to a desired future, and then forging shared visions in an organizational culture devoted to the destitute and disenfranchised of rural Bangladesh. Regular structured training and refresher training, dialogue and discussion in an open and supportive atmosphere as a part of the regular work procedures, and frequent opportunity for interaction with visiting local and foreign development specialists all contribute to the atmosphere in BRAC that encourages examining personal values and sharing visions of desired futures. Through these means BRAC has developed an unusual organizational culture in which individual staff members are strongly united in purpose in a shared commitment to the village poor for change, empowerment, and self-reliance.

BRAC management has given extraordinary attention to enhancing the personal mastery of its own staff. Staff members are given opportunities to visit development projects in other developing countries. For example, a group of staff working in health is sent to Indonesia to explore what is being done there with the *Posyandu* (voluntary rural health stations); some fisheries program organizers (POs) are sent to the Philippines and Thailand to observe various integrated fisheries projects; and *Aarong* shop designers are sent to India to study design methods. Selected individuals are also regularly sent for advanced study in other countries.

But, advancing personal mastery does not make for a more placid organization; it involves not only vision but also holding what for the person is an accurate picture of current reality, thereby generating "creative tension." People with high levels of personal mastery have a great tolerance for living with creative tension, and such tension does exist in BRAC.

Mental models. The process of enhancing personal mastery and then developing shared vision in an organization setting is related to a third attribute of the learning organization, mental models, in which basic, and often deeply ingrained assumptions about reality and generalizations about the factual world are examined and often of necessity changed. The basic core strategy of conscientization with the village poor in Bangladesh is a strategy for examining and revising mental models. BRAC's training programs for staff and for village group members are designed to alter the perceptions of reality that bind so many of the poor in the endless cycle of poverty. One role of the Research and Evaluation Division is to continuously feed back to staff interpretations from grassroots research that influence mental models.

A concrete illustration of the blockages mental models can create occurred at the beginning of BRAC's oral rehydration therapy program (the nationwide program that taught every village woman in the country to mix her own rehydration solution from household ingredients). Hopes for expanding nationwide were delayed because the top managers had a mental model set in place. They could think only in terms of permanent camps where staff would be housed; therefore, they saw the idea of covering the country as expensive, difficult, and maybe impossible. Inquiry solved the problem and changed the mental model. The executive director, and others, serendipitously happened on another NGO that had experimented with movable camps, housing their staff temporarily in a village, then moving on to find new temporary quarters in another village after covering a certain radius from the temporary camp. The previously held mental model was replaced by a whole new way of thinking about staff deployment and rural coverage.

Team learning. The fourth discipline, team learning, which starts with dialogue and members of teams entering into genuine thinking together, is BRAC's modus operandi. Ninety-nine percent of the decisions in the various BRAC programs are made in meetings. Dialogue on every question is the natural order. Most communication in BRAC is verbal; decisions made in meetings are internalized and seldom are minutes of meetings kept or circulated. Agreement is reached and participants understand the reasons and the outcome. The real learning units of the organization are "teams," groups of people who need one another to act and to make things happen.

Systems thinking. Finally, systems thinking has perhaps best been illustrated by recognizing in basic program strategy the interrelatedness of village problems and the inadequacies in dealing with any one problem alone. The cycle of poverty in Bangladesh, embedded in the complex system of cultural, political, and economic constraints, as described in Chapter 1, is the fundamental understanding that underpins the BRAC intervention strategies.

Systems thinking is the basic justification for the institutional intermediation programs described in Chapter 5, which are essential adjuncts to the financial intermediation programs of savings and credit. Promoting the sericulture enterprise has required, in the BRAC approach, an understanding of the interrelationships among the mulberry tree, the worm, and the cocoon rearer, and among the spinner and reeler, credit, the tailor, and the *Aarong* shops that market the silk, all of which form the production marketing system. Also, earlier documented was the poultry example, where the goal of increasing women's incomes and family nutrition by expanding chicken raising required in turn providing new high yield variety chicks, identifying and training chick rearers and providing them with credit, and vaccinating the chicks, which required the training of vaccinators. Expanding the number of chicks being raised required special chicken feed and feed producers to provide it, and, finally, the increase in egg production in the villages required a new occupation of egg sellers who could take the eggs to larger markets.

Perhaps these are simplistic examples of systems thinking in action, but they do suggest how systemic thinking is a critical tool for understanding much more complex policy and strategy issues in rural Bangladesh.

As the histories of the various BRAC programs have illustrated, to be a learning organization requires shared vision, expertise, and flexibility on the part of both staff and donors. Observation of BRAC managers in the field indicates that their actions must be grounded in a basic self-confidence nurtured by a supportive organizational climate. Most important, to be characterized as successful, learning strategies must result in effective activities that bring positive changes in the lives of village participants.

BRAC's Strategy for the 1990s

BRAC has never been a blueprint planning organization bound by rigid plans. Flexibility and an ability to respond to unexpected opportunities has been one of the organization's strengths, yet the BRAC management team has always recognized the importance of strategic planning. Beginning in 1987, BRAC initiated a particularly thorough assessment of its programs and guiding strategy. The purpose was to evaluate the strategic focus and to make sure that future strategy would increase BRAC's impact on Bangladesh's national development in the 1990s. Several development experts and consulting teams were invited to provide critical feedback and recommendations.

Every year since then, BRAC has undertaken a series of meetings and workshops in which the dozen or so senior staff have examined options in light of BRAC's distinctive history and capabilities. In most of the more formalized strategic planning workshops, the assistance of an outside consultant was utilized. (For a description of two of these meetings and their proposals, see Korten, 1987, and Korten, March 1989. Korten served as the consultant at the two workshops that he documents.)

Rereading these two reports in 1991 and comparing them to what BRAC has actually done and currently plans to do reveals that even the general strategic plans outlined in the documents have not served as blueprints. Following the workshops, the plans were discussed in the field and the practicalities of implementing the more specific program ideas were tested. At that point, changes, sometimes major, usually occurred. Because BRAC is flexible and is a learning organization, programs are always changing as a result of inquiry, experience, and what is possible in the field. This observation must serve as a caution to anyone reading written reports on BRAC's strategic plans; they do represent overall directions, but after the passage of some months they may not describe actual program developments.

Following is a summary of the most basic ideas incorporated in BRAC's strategy for the 1990s as drafted by Korten (March 1989, esp. pp.

24–37). The main areas where practicalities have precluded implementation of approaches outlined in the plan, or other rather different approaches have subsequently been taken, are identified and explained.

Target on the Upazila

BRAC's 1990s strategy focuses on the *upazila* as the unit of action. (An *upazila* is a local government jurisdiction of roughly 200,000 to 300,000 people; there are about ten *unions* in each *upazila*, each including 20,000 to 30,000 people.) The *upazila* becomes the primary unit of BRAC planning and action for developing the capacity of the poorest and most marginalized to define, demand, and assume a substantial and meaningful role in a new relationship with the governments of the *upazilas*. The orientation to the *upazila* is based on the belief that effective progress is most likely at the local government level, where possibilities for mobilizing the people for local initiative and demand making has the best chance to succeed.

This strategy means that BRAC will no longer, as it sometimes did in the past, organize only a few villages in an *upazila*. Landless organizations are to be built in as many villages as possible in the *upazilas* that are entered. In each assisted *upazila*, BRAC will serve as a catalyst, bringing to bear, in a phased manner and in cooperation with other NGOs organizing in the same *upazila*, a full range of program activities for the development of self-sustaining local capacities.

This intensified *upazila* strategy means that BRAC will focus its government facilitation efforts at the *upazila* level as well as at the central government level. It also means that economic subsector interventions will focus at the *upazila* level where they are feasible and apt to be effective.

Stressing Collaboration with Other NGOs

BRAC is aware that in spite of vastly scaled-up programs, 80 percent of the rural population currently lacks the benefits of assistance available from either NGOs or the Grameen Bank. Since a basic premise of BRAC's 1990s strategy is that if the people in an *upazila* are to be assisted, sufficient coverage of the landless population must be achieved to create a sustainable change in the economic and political dynamics, careful thought must be given to how to achieve this coverage. The coverage need not be accomplished exclusively by BRAC. Where other NGOs or organizations such as the Grameen Bank or Proshika are in a position to meet a part of the need, BRAC intends to propose the formation of *upazila*-level coordinating mechanisms through which the assisting NGOs may allocate responsibilities among themselves for achieving the targeted *upazila*-wide coverage. Recently, the Association of Development Agencies of Bangladesh (ADAB) introduced the Shared Visions Initiative, which encourages and helps NGOs to work more closely together.

The number of villages assisted directly by BRAC in any one *upazila* will depend on the activities of other NGOs operating in the same *upazila*. The goal is to provide an opportunity to all landless families in the *upazila* to participate in a landless organization and to engage in a variety of self-help activities, irrespective of which NGO assists. BRAC resources will be applied in a way intended to supplement and, where appropriate, support the work of other NGOs.

In *upazilas* in which a number of NGOs are active in organizing the landless, responsibilities for organizing might be divided among them on the basis of the *union*. In a given *upazila* with ten *unions*, the NGOs might agree that BRAC should take a lead in organizing three, Proshika (another large and active NGO) might take another three, Nigera Kori (another NGO) might organize another two, and CCDB (another NGO) the remainder. Other responsibilities might be divided on a functional basis. For example, it might be agreed that BRAC would introduce nonformal primary schools throughout the *upazila*, while RDRS (another large NGO) might assume the responsibility for organizing health committees on an *upazila*-wide basis. BRAC recognizes that there are many NGOs making valuable contributions to Bangladesh's development and wants to encourage and strengthen their efforts wherever possible, including those of the smaller local NGOs.

Renewed Stress on Self-Reliance

A third feature of BRACs 1990s strategy is a renewed stress on BRAC's role as a development catalyst, taking care to avoid creating long-term dependency on BRAC-subsidized services. The centerpiece of the self-reliance strategy is the graduation of landless groups from RDP to the BRAC bank project discussed in some detail in Chapter 4. As outlined there, the bank operates on a self-financing basis, covering the costs of lending and other services through the collection of interest and fees and through returns on the investment of bank money. A village group graduating from RDP to the bank is no longer eligible for most of the free or subsidized services provided by RDP. The village group members must thereafter purchase services, such as training, from BRAC's training and resource centers or other sources of their choice, and buy economic subsector technical services from BRAC or from others as needed. The bank, as a part of its basic service, coordinates training and technical assistance arrangements between the village group members and the training or technical service providers. Also, as bank staff members have the ability and time, they facilitate cooperation with government entities; yet, the main efforts in this direction fall to the village organizations and borrowers themselves.

While designed specifically to serve BRAC-formed groups, the bank's credit facilities may, with time, be made available to landless organizations formed by other NGOs, depending on agreements with those NGOs and their assisted landless organizations.

A second cornerstone of the self-reliance strategy is a focus on the formation of *union-* and *upazila*-level federations of landless groups. The purposes and activities of such federations are still not entirely clear, but they include serving as (1) forums for cooperation among the VOs and for the exchange of information between BRAC or other NGOs and the VOs; (2) mechanisms for social action, including representation of landless interests in local court cases and in negotiations for needed services with local government; and (3) mechanisms for strengthening landless participation in local elections.

The formation of such federations has been a stated goal for some years, and BRAC, having experimented with such federations in two areas, has gained valuable lessons about a number of different approaches. (For details on these experiments and their outcomes, see a consultative report by Holtsberg, 1991.) Federation formation efforts so far have not been highly successful, and in spite of the renewed emphasis on federation articulated in the 1990s strategy plan, there was by the end of 1991 no formally established policy in RDP or the Rural Credit Project (RCP) on the structure and role of federations. In early 1991, BRAC established an internal working group to review previous experience and suggest an implementation strategy for developing the federations at *union* and *upazila* levels.

The absence of formal mechanisms for inter-VO coordination does not mean that there is no interaction among VOs. Intergroup cooperation takes place both spontaneously (attendance by members of one VO at other VO meetings) and in more planned ways—for special activities, using organizational structures left over from earlier programs (see Holtzberg, 1991). The absence of formal federative arrangements has meant that the staff of RDP or the RCP bank project has to carry most of the burden of getting VOs together if cooperation on social action or economic projects is desired. For a number of larger economic projects, special institutional arrangements have been set up for coordination between VOs and production management systems (such as larger deep tubewell projects and brick fields). The Ayesha Abed Foundation (a sister organization to BRAC) coordinates hundreds of women's VOs in handicraft and silk production and textile operations.

To sustain self-reliance after graduation to the bank, some entity such as a federation is required to assume not only the coordination roles for social action and for collective inter-VO economic activities, but also for the continued institutional development and upgrading of the VOs themselves. All these roles are now played primarily by BRAC staff. If effective federations can be established, BRAC would perhaps be able to channel management and technical services to the VOs or members of the VOs through such a federation. This step would certainly fit well into BRAC's "withdrawal" strategy. Initially, the federations would probably need to receive organizational, technical, and other supports to develop into viable institutions. If the federations are to succeed, some staff will probably be required, and to ensure long-term viability they will need to find ways to generate income, either through charging for services or by asking for membership fees. The Task Force on Federation is looking hard at the experience to date on these and other aspects.

BRAC also recognizes that a functioning federative system will provide an instrument for the members of the VOs to influence BRAC's policy formation and can also serve as a forum for consultation between BRAC and the members. No formal mechanisms are now in place to achieve these purposes.

Enlarged Emphasis on Public Systems Facilitation

A fourth emphasis in BRAC's 1990s strategy is intensification of its efforts to cooperate with government in improving various government services. As pointed out in earlier chapters, BRAC has undertaken cooperative efforts with several ministries with service improvement as the goal. The results of these efforts are mixed. BRAC's facilitation program to improve public primary schools through increased community participation and strengthened management systems has had only modest results. (See BRAC, *Facilitation Assistance*, February 1991.) Efforts to improve the government's rural health delivery system had outstanding success in the government's immunization efforts but only mixed success in some of the other health activities. (See BRAC, *Child Survival*, 1990, and BRAC, *Tale of Two Wings*, 1990.) Cooperative efforts with the government on tubewells, sericulture and livestock, poultry, and fisheries have been promising. Further and more intensified cooperative efforts are required so that community demands can be met.

The strategic plan for the 1990s called for establishing a separate division in BRAC for public systems facilitation. The strategy called for assigning field facilitation teams of from one to five persons to the local offices of given ministries in selected *upazilas*. The plan envisions that there might be several such teams in a given *upazila* working with the *upazila*-level officers of the different ministries. The role of these teams would be to help the assisted offices to (1) increase their effectiveness in the delivery of specific priority services and (2) link these services to village committees that could take the lead in defining needs and facilitating effective service use. The teams would begin by working with ministry personnel to carry out assessments of critical barriers to program performance in the *upazila*, and then jointly plan interventions to address these barriers through management systems improvements, training, or other measures.

By mid-1991, the separate division in BRAC for government facilitation suggested in the plan had not been set up. Cooperation with and management development assistance to the local units of several ministries at the *upazila* level continues to be carried out by the relevant RDP economic subsector specialists and by *upazila* program leaders in the various programs (RDP, health, education), in cooperation with the TARCs and BRAC's Management Development Program. Whether BRAC will follow the proposed strategy and set up a separate public systems facilitation division or continue to concentrate this work through the various program leaders remains to be seen.

Whichever system may be used, BRAC continues to play an important role in stimulating and assisting government service improvements. NGOs cannot take the place of government, but they can help improve government services and they can connect government to the underserved people in the villages. Governments in general are expected to assist all elements in a community equally, but in actual practice it often works out in rural Bangladesh that government assistance goes primarily to the most affluent. BRAC attempts to introduce a counterbias toward the poorest elements of the community, who in rural Bangladesh make up a majority.

BRAC's Expansion Strategy

As noted above, BRAC's expansion strategy for the 1990s concentrates resources on a geographical basis, seeking comprehensive coverage of assistance in the selected *upazilas*. First priority for expansion is to be given to completing program coverage in those *upazilas* in which BRAC is already active.

The second priority is given to completing program coverage of *upazilas* in the designated service areas of one or another of BRAC's six existing or three more planned TARCs, each of which will ultimately support up to fifteen RDP area offices or RCP (bank) branches, or roughly five *upazilas*. As coverage of these *upazilas* is completed, new TARCs will be established to support additional clusters of *upazilas* in priority rural poverty areas that are currently underserved by existing programs of NGOs, the Grameen Bank, or others. A total of twenty TARCs will be in operation by the year 2000.

The initial expansion of BRAC moved forward at the rate of twenty area offices, or seven to eight *upazilas*, per year through 1991. From that time, the expansion rate is to be gradually increased each year through 1997, at which point BRAC will be opening forty new area offices per year, serving thirteen to fifteen *upazilas*. It is expected that by the year 2000, 300 area offices will have been established and from 100 to 115 *upazilas* (depending on the portion of the target population covered by other collaborating NGOs) will have "graduated" to the institutionalized credit program. There are a total of 460 *upazilas* in the country. If BRAC achieves its goal, by the year 2000, one-fourth of the poorest people in the country will have been organized and provided credit and other assistance by BRAC.

Issues of Sustainability

Sustainability has many definitions. (For a useful survey see Bryant, 1991.) One definition is related to environmental sustainability, others to economic, social, and political sustainability. In the eyes of most development-oriented NGOs, the term means that benefits flowing from a development program or project will be able to be maintained after external interventions or donor funding has been withdrawn. Sustainability in these terms is dependent on the degree of self-reliance developed in target communities and on the social and political commitment in the wider society to development programs that support the continuance of newly self-reliant communities.

NGO interventions are often seen as temporary measures in which grassroots people themselves become sufficiently empowered and self-reliant to be able to make progress without outside help, or in which self-supporting institutions or the government are able and willing to assume functions that were introduced or modeled by the NGO. NGOs are urged to have "withdrawal strategies" and operational targets for the staging of such withdrawal. (As an example of such urging see Wils,

Passtoors, and Van Leeuwin, 1988.) In other cases, sustainability is taken to mean the sustainability of the NGO itself and its ability to continue to pursue development goals without or with reduced dependence on outside support.

BRAC has always been aware of the sustainability issue, yet it has also recognized that institution building with the poor is a long process requiring both economic and social programs. The hypothesis that the landless poor can fully stand on their own without services being provided by outside organizations or government is unrealistic. (For discussions of this issue, see statements by two BRAC leaders: Abed, June 1990; Ahmed, 1990.) These leaders point out that as the groups and the individual group members take on progressively higher levels of economic and social activities, they require higher levels of management and skills training and considerably larger amounts of credit. Examples of higher-level activity are the more technologically induced economic schemes such as large-scale irrigation projects or power tiller projects.

As development schemes get larger and more profitable, borrowers can pay for many technical services; however, institutions such as BRAC that can supply these services effectively must be available to do so. Total independence by the landless groups depends not only on their own development but on the availability of support institutions and improved government services.

BRAC's sustainability strategy is grounded in the idea of empowerment of the poor learned through effective participation in the planning, implementation, monitoring, and evaluation of their own development actions. Although BRAC has made many organizing, training, and financial services available, it has refused to enter into a patron relationship. The VO itself supplies the most important support systems for economic projects, social action, and the resolution of conflicts. The insistence on group members' own resource mobilization through compulsory weekly savings is an important self-reliance strategy that reduces their dependence on outside agencies. Although the VOs cannot meet all their credit needs from their own savings, they have been able to meet nearly 40 percent from their own funds.

BRAC's second strategy for sustainability has been to create a sustainable dynamic in various economic subsectors. The poultry program provides an example. As described in Chapter 5, BRAC devised a self-sustaining program for vaccination of chicks to cut mortality. Instead of BRAC employees doing the vaccination, a large number of village women were trained for the job, with the cooperation of the government's Directorate of Livestock and Poultry, which supplies free vaccines to the trained vaccinators. The vaccinators provide vaccination services to the poultry raisers for a fee, which gives them a regular income and a motivation to continue. Since BRAC supplies neither the vaccines nor the vaccination services, the developed system is self-sustaining. When BRAC organizers leave an area, the functions continue. Similar examples were given in the fisheries and livestock subsectors. Programs are consciously designed with self-sustaining systems as the goal.

A third sustainability strategy of BRAC has been to build effective linkages among various agencies and organizations associated with rural development, those that form the political and economic environment in which the poor and landless communities exist. VOs have been linked to the USAID Food-for-Work Program so that the members understand how to utilize the resources of the programs to contribute to economic projects of their own choice, such as pond or river basin enlargements and tree planting. BRAC's federation strategy to build *upazila*-wide VO linkages will enhance the VOs' capacity to bargain with and exert pressure on relevant agencies to enhance the availability of required economic and social services.

BRAC's government facilitation efforts represent a fourth and important sustainability strategy. As discussed in various chapters above, BRAC has been intensifying efforts to work with government agencies in improving their services to rural communities, linking such improvements with community demand. In the health field, for example, people can learn to rely on their own behavior and knowledge in areas such as sanitation, nutrition, and the making and administration of oral rehydration therapy for diarrhea. On the other hand, government health agencies must provide immunization, family planning supplies and services, and TB and other disease treatments. Government or some other effective institution is required to support primary education as an essential investment in development. BRAC cannot withdraw until the government or some other institution is available to provide the required services that people cannot be expected to maintain for themselves.

A fifth sustainability strategy has been the establishment of BRAC's self-financing and self-supporting banking institution discussed earlier. After the first four years of operation the bank will no longer be dependent on donor funds. Also, when the VOs graduate to this bank program, BRAC will no longer need to subsidize the costs of many development services related to economic schemes, such as skills training and technical assistance; the borrowers are expected to pay for such services. The emergence of the bank minimizes dependence on BRAC as an intervening organization, even though BRAC or other competent organizations will still be required to provide training and technical services on a fee-for-service basis along with credit.

A sixth strategy in BRAC's vision of sustainability is to develop selected programs on a sufficient scale to convince the government and the NGO community alike that national-level programs can be effectively designed and managed in the interests of the poor. BRAC's nonformal primary education program and its nationwide oral rehydration program provide such models.

Finally, the question of sustainability of the intervening organization itself, in this case BRAC, arises. Since interventions in most of the villages of the country have not yet taken place and most of the rural poor in the country have not yet been organized or aided, the need for new and expanded development interventions will continue for many years. Most intervening organizations, and BRAC is no exception, depend heavily on outside financial support to fund their programs. BRAC has been striving to generate as many of its own funds as possible by establishing its own commercial projects. These enterprises now generate profits sufficient to fund 15 percent of BRAC's $20 million yearly budget. BRAC's goal is to become more and more self-sufficient and less dependent on donor funds; however, the ideal of self-sustaining operations is not yet within the foreseeable future.

A Concluding Comment

As a final comment on the question of sustainability, withdrawal strategies, and self-reliance, readers from the developed countries of the North are urged to examine the experience in their own countries. Although self-reliance on the part of the poorest and most disadvantaged is always a goal, in no country do large segments of the population survive or advance without extensive and continuing government and nongovernmental organization interventions. Some interventions are more successful than others in reaching the poorest in developed countries, and new modalities of intervention are always under experimentation. Nevertheless, the social and economic conditions of the less prosperous in the North are always strongly supported by various government social security, health, and education programs, as well as by private, contributor-financed nongovernmental organizations. Questions of phasing out "community chests," small-business programs, or charitable and educational foundations seldom arise.

Where social and economic development is just beginning for a majority of the people, and where government services remain nonexistent or ineffective for the poorest, with no signs of major change in the near future, NGO interventions will be needed for many years to come. The case of Bangladesh is a dramatic illustration of this conclusion. Evaluation of the effectiveness of individual NGOs must include questions of sustainability, particularly as to whether program interventions are building the kind of sustainable systems that enable NGOs to move on to interventions in other, as yet untouched, communities. Any hope, however, that sustainable, self-reliant development for all sectors or for the whole country can or will take place in the near future is a vain hope. Organizations like BRAC, supported by a sharing of the resources of the North with the South, will be needed far into the foreseeable future. The prime short-term development goal is to make the intervening organizations as effective and efficient as possible.

Bibliography

Abed, F.H. *Commencement Ceremony Address.* Manila: Asian Institute of Management, July 7, 1990.

———. *Towards Sustainable Development: How BRAC Sees It.* Dhaka: BRAC, June 30, 1990.

Ahmad, Zafar. *National Profitability Analysis of Deep Tubewell Irrigation.* Dhaka: BRAC, 1991.

———. *The Price of BRAC's Development Intervention: How Costly Is Too Costly.* Dhaka: BRAC, 1991.

Ahmed, Salehuddin. *Rural Development for the Poor: A BRAC Strategy.* Dhaka: BRAC, 1990.

Bangladesh Bureau of Educational Information and Statistics (BANBEIS). *Bangladesh Educational Statistics 1987.* Dhaka: Ministry of Education, 1987.

Bangladesh Institute of Development Studies. *The Face of Rural Poverty in Bangladesh: Trends and Insights.* Dhaka, May 1990.

———. *A Profile of Rural Industries in Bangladesh.* Research Report No. 87. Dhaka, October 1988.

———. *Sericulture Industry in Bangladesh: A Case Study.* Dhaka, December 1988.

Bhattacharya, Debapruja. *Evaluation of Poverty Alleviation Programmes.* Vols. 1 and 2. Dhaka: Bangladesh Institute of Development Studies, October 1990.

Biggs, Tyler S., Donald R. Snodgrass, and Pradeep Srivastava. *On Minimalist Credit Programs.* Cambridge: Harvard Institute for International Development, March 1990.

Blair, Harry W., ed. *Can Rural Development Be Financed from Below? Local Resource Mobilization in Bangladesh.* Dhaka: University Press Limited, 1989.

Boomgard, James, Stephen P. Davies, Steven J. Haggblade, and Donald C. Mead. *A Subsector Approach to Small Enterprise Promotion and Research.* An unpublished paper, Department of Agricultural and Resource Economics, Colorado State University, Ft. Collins, Colorado, 1990.

Bowman, Margaret, Jorge Baanante, Thomas Dichter, Steven Loudner and Peter Reiling. *Measuring Our Impact: Determining Cost Effectiveness.* Norwalk, Conn.: Technoserve, 1989.

BRAC. *Child Survival Program, Final Evaluation Report.* Dhaka, February 1990.

———. *Credit Programme Manual.* Various versions, 1979–89.

———. *Cyclone Relief Programme, Interim Report, April 30–June 30, 1991.* Dhaka, September 1991.

———. *Facilitation Assistance Programme on Education (FAPE), Annual Report and Update.* Dhaka, December 1990, March 1991.

———. *Facilitation Assistance Programme on Education, Staff Report.* Dhaka, February 1991.

————. *Final Appraisal Report in BRAC's Rural Development Programmes 1990–1992 and the BRAC Bank Project.* Vols. 1 and 2. Dhaka: Donor's Consortium, April 1989.

————. *1990 Annual Review.* Dhaka: Donor Consortium, November 1990.

————. *Peasant Perceptions: Famine, Credit Needs, Sanitation.* Rural Studies Series. Vol. 1. Dhaka, 1984.

————. *Peasant Perceptions: Law.* Rural Studies Series. Vol 2. Dhaka, 1990.

————. *RDP 2 and RCP, Semi-Annual Financial Report to 30.6.90.* Dhaka, 1990.

————. *Research and Evaluation Division, Annual Report.* Dhaka, 1990.

————. *Rural Credit Programme, Project Document.* Dhaka, December 1989.

————. *Rural Credit Programme, Statistical Report.* Dhaka, June 1990.

————. *Rural Credit and Training Program, Project Proposal.* Dhaka, 1979.

————. *Rural Development Programme, 1990–92, Project Document.* Dhaka, December 1989.

————. *Rural Development Programme, Statistical Report.* Dhaka, December 1989, March 1990, June 1990.

————. *Rural Enterprise Project, October 1985 to June 1989.* Dhaka, September 1989.

————. *A Tale of Two Wings: Health and Family Planning Programmes in an Upazila in Northern Bangladesh.* Dhaka: Research and Evaluation Division, July 1990.

————. *Training and Resource Centers, Annual Report.* Dhaka, 1989.

————. *Training and Resource Centers, Annual Report.* Dhaka, 1990.

————. Various reports of the Research and Evaluation Division. Dhaka, 1985–90.

————. Various six-monthly and annual reports of Outreach, RCTP, and RDP. Dhaka, 1979–89.

Briscoe, J. *The Political Economy of the BRAC Health Insurance Scheme: Report to BRAC.* Dhaka: 1978.

Bryant, Coralie. *Sustainability Revisited: States, Institutions and Economic Performance.* Washington, D.C.: American Society for Public Administration, Annual Meeting, March 1991.

Bryant, Coralie, and Louise G. White. *Managing Development in the Third World.* Boulder: Westview Press, 1982.

Burns, Tom, and G. M. Stalker. *The Management of Innovations.* London: Tavistock, 1961.

Chen, Martha Alter. *A Quiet Revolution: Women in Transition in Rural Bangladesh.* Rochester, VT: Shenkman Books, 1983.

Chowdhury, A. M. R. "Empowerment through Health Education: The Approach of an NGO in Bangladesh." In P. Streefland and J. Chabot (eds.), *Implementing Primary Health Care.* Amsterdam: Royal Tropical Institute, 1990.

Chowdhury, A. M. R., N. Ishikawa, A. Alam, R. A. Cash, and F. H. Abed. "Controlling a Forgotten: The Case of Tuberculosis in a Primary Health Care Setting." *Bulletin of the International Union Against Tuberculosis.* In press.

Chowdhury, A. M. R., M. Mahmood, and F. H. Abed. "Credit for the Rural Poor: The Case of BRAC in Bangladesh." *Small Enterprise Development* 2, no. 3 (September 1991):4–13.

Chowdhury, A. M. R., J. P. Waughan, and F. H. Abed. "Use and Safety of ORT: An Epidemiology Evaluation from Bangladesh." *International Journal of Epidemiology* 17 (1988):655.

Clark, Noreen, and James McCaffery. *Demystifying Evaluation: Training Program Staff in Assessment of Community-Based Programs Through a Field-Operational Seminar.* Boston: World Education, 1979.

Dahl, Robert A., and Charles E. Lindblom. *Politics, Economics and Welfare.* New York: Harper and Row, 1953.

Davis, Stanley M., and Paul R. Laurence. *Matrix.* Reading, Pa.: Addison Wesley, 1977.

Dhaka Courier. Weekly issues, July 21–27 to November 17–23, 1989.

Edgcomb, Elaine, and James Cawley. *The Process of Institutional Development: Assisting Small Enterprise Institutions to Become More Effective.* New York: The Small Enterprise Education and Promotion Network, October 1990.

Gerwin, Donald. "Relationships between Structure and Technology." In Paul C. Nystrom and William H. Starbruck (eds.), *Handbook of Organization Design, Volume 2.* Oxfordshire: Oxford University Press, 1981.

Ghosh, Shanti (SDC), Benjt Hojer (SIDA), Mahmuda Islam (UNICEF), and Mustague R. Chowdhury (BRAC, RED). *Child Survival Program Final Evaluation Report.* Dhaka: BRAC, February 1990.

Government of Bangladesh. *Third Five-Year Plan.* Dhaka, 1985.

Grameen Bank. Annual Review Mission reports. Dhaka, 1986–90.

———. *Phase III, Annual Review Mission, Final Report.* Dhaka, November 1990.

Haggblade, Steven. *Equity and Agricultural Growth: An Evaluation of CARE's Landless Owned Tubewell-Users Support (LOTUS) Project for the 1989 Boro Season.* Dhaka: CARE-Bangladesh, May 31, 1990.

Hasan, M. *The Impact of Sweet Water Fisheries on the Lives of the Rural Poor.* Dhaka: BRAC, 1991.

Hashemi, Syed M. *NGO's in Bangladesh: Development Alternative or Alternative Rhetoric.* Dhaka: Bangladesh Institute for Development Studies, April 1990.

Hellinger, Stephen, Douglas Hellinger, and Fred M. O'Regan. *Aid for Just Development.* Boulder and London: Lynne Rienner Publishers, 1988.

Holtsberg, Christer. *Development of Landless Organizations in BRAC's Rural Development Program.* Dhaka: BRAC, March 1991.

Hossain, Mahabub. *Credit for Alleviation of Rural Poverty: The Grameen Bank in Bangladesh.* Dhaka: International Food Policy Research Institute in collaboration with the Bangladesh Institute of Development Studies, February 1988.

———. *Credit for the Rural Poor: The Grameen Bank in Bangladesh.* Research Mimograph #4. Dhaka: Bangladesh Institute of Development Studies, 1984.

———. *Nature and Impact of the Green Revolution in Bangladesh.* Dhaka: International Food Policy Research Institute with the Bangladesh Institute of Development Studies, 1988.

———. "A Note on the Trend of Landlessness in Bangladesh." *The Bangladesh Development Studies* 14 (June 1986): 93–100.

Hossain, Mahabub, Abu A. Abdullah, Richard Nations, and Ann-Lisbet Arn. *Cooperation Movements in Bangladesh.* Dhaka: Bangladesh Institute for Development Studies, 1989.

Imam, Izadin I. *Peasant Perceptions: Famine.* Dhaka: BRAC, July 1979.

Israel, Arturo. *Institutional Development: Incentives to Performance.* Baltimore: Johns Hopkins University Press, 1989.

Korten, David. *BRAC Strategy.* Dhaka: BRAC, 1987.

———. *BRAC Strategy.* Dhaka: BRAC, 1989.

———. *BRAC Strategy for the 1990's.* Review draft. Boston: Institute for Development Research, March, 1989.

———. "Community Organization and Rural Development: A Learning Process Approach." *Public Administration Review* 40 (September-October 1980): 480–512.

————. *Population and Social Development Management.* Caracas: Instituto de Estudios Superiores de Administración, 1979.

————. "Rural Development Planning—the Learning Process Approach." In David C. Korten and Rudi Klaus (eds.), *People-Centered Development.* West Hartford, Conn.: Kumarian Press, 1984.

Korten, David, C., and Rudi Klaus, eds. *People-Centered Development.* West Hartford, Conn.: Kumarian Press, 1984.

Leonard, David K. *Reaching the Peasant Farmer: Organization Theory and Practice in Kenya.* Chicago: University of Chicago Press, 1977.

Leonard, David K., and Dale Rogers Marshall, eds. *Institutions of Rural Development for the Poor: Decentralization and Organizational Linkages.* Berkeley: Institute of International Studies, 1983.

Lindblom, Charles E. *The Intelligence of Democracy.* New York: The Free Press, 1965.

Lovell, Catherine H. "Case 4: BRAC (C). What to Do about Market Outlets." In Charles K. Mann, Merilee S. Grindle, and Parker Shipton, eds. *Seeking Solutions: Framework and Cases for Small Enterprise Development.* West Hartford, Conn.: Kumarian Press, 1989, pp. 151–56.

Lovell, Catherine H., and Kanez Fatema. *The BRAC Non-Formal Primary Education Programme in Bangladesh.* New York: United Nations Children's Fund, Assignment Children Series, December 1989.

Mallick, N. C. "An Assessment of Economic Profitability of Rearing HYV Chicks and Its Comparability with Other Varieties: Seven Brief Case Studies." Dhaka: BRAC, RED, 1989.

Manitoba Institute of Management. *Managing the Non-Profit Organization.* Winnipeg: Manitoba Institute of Management, 1989.

Mann, Charles K., Merilee S. Grindle, and Parker Shipton, eds. *Seeking Solutions: Framework and Cases for Small Enterprise Development Programs.* West Hartford, Conn.: Kumarian Press, 1989.

McCann, Joseph, and Jay R. Galbraith. "Inter-Departmental Relations." In Paul C. Nystrom and William H. Starbruck (eds.), *Handbook of Organization Design.* Vol 2. Oxfordshire: Oxford University Press, 1981.

North-South Institute. *Rural Poverty in Bangladesh: A Report to the Like-Minded Group.* Dhaka, January 1986.

Osmani, S. R. "Notes on Some Recent Estimates of Rural Poverty in Bangladesh." *The Bangladesh Development Studies* 43 (September 1990):75–87. (Special Issue on Poverty in Bangladesh)

————. "Structural Change and Poverty in Bangladesh: The Case of a False Turning Point." *The Bangladesh Development Studies* 43 (September 1990): 55–74. (Special Issue on Poverty in Bangladesh)

Otero, Maria. *A Question of Impact: Solidarity Programs and Their Approach to Evaluation.* New York: PACT, 1989.

Paul, Samuel. *Managing Development Programs: The Lessons of Success.* Boulder: Westview Press, 1982.

Pfohl, Jake. *Participatory Evaluation: A User's Guide.* New York: PACT, 1986.

Pietro, Daniel Santo, ed. *Evaluation Source Book.* New York: InterAction, 1983.

Population Crisis Committee. *Country Rankings of the Status of Women: Poor, Powerless and Pregnant.* Washington D.C., June 1988.

Rahman, Atiur. "Credit for the Rural Poor." *Bangladesh Agricultural Review.* Dhaka: United Nations Development Program, October 1988.

Rahman, Hussain Zillur. *Notes on the Political Economy of Poverty in Bangladesh.*

Dhaka: Bangladesh Institute of Development Studies, October 1990.

Rhyne, Elizabeth, and Maria Otero. *A Financial Systems Approach to Micro-enterprises.* Washington D.C.: The GEMINI Project, United States Agency for International Development, October 1990.

Rugh, Jim. *Self Evaluation: Ideas for Participatory Evaluation of Community Development Projects.* Oklahoma City: World Neighbors, 1986.

Sen, Binayek. "NGO's in Bangladesh Agriculture: An Exploratory Study." *Bangladesh Agriculture Sector Review.* New York: United Nations Development Programme, October 1988.

Senge, Peter M. *The Fifth Discipline: The Art and Practice of the Learning Organization.* New York: Doubleday/Currency, 1990.

Sobhan, Salma, Azmat Hra Ahmad, and Elina Zubaidy. *Peasant Perceptions: Law.* Dhaka: BRAC, 1989.

Streefland, Pieter, and A. M. R. Chowdhury. "The Longterm Role of National NGO's in Primary Health Care: Lessons from Bangladesh." *Health Policy and Planning* 5 (1990):261–66.

Streefland, Pieter, Hasina Ahmed, Marium Nafes, Dhalem Ch. Barman, and H. K. Arifen. *Different Ways to Support the Rural Poor: Effects of Two Development Approaches in Bangladesh.* Dhaka: University Center for Social Studies, 1986.

Swinderen, Anne Marie, Nasrin Shanaz, and Mahmuda Rahman Khan. *Processes and Constraints of Handloom Intervention in Bangladesh, Rural Enterprise Project.* Dhaka: BRAC, April 1990.

Swiss Development Cooperation. *Appraisal Mission, Women's Health and Development Program.* Geneva, January 1991.

Tendler, Judith. "What Ever Happened to Poverty Alleviation?" Prepared for the Mid-decade Review of the Ford Foundation's Programs on Livelihood, Employment, and Income Generation, March 1987. (Mimeo)

UNESCO Statistical Yearbook, 1989. Paris: UNESCO, 1989.

UNICEF. *The State of the World's Children, 1991.* Oxfordshire: Oxford University Press, 1991.

Vaughan, Patrick. *Comments on the Research and Evaluation Division of BRAC.* London: Planning Centre of London School of Hygiene and Tropical Medicine, University of London, April 1988.

Vincent, Fernand. *Manual of Practical Management.* Vols. 1 and 2. Geneva: IRED, 1989.

Williams, Harold S. "Paradigm: Learning vs. Evaluation." In *Innovating* 1 (No. 4, Summer 1991). The Innovation Group, Rensselaerville Institute, N.Y.

Wils, F., W. Passtoors, and R. Van Leeuwin. *Netherlands Multidisciplinary Team, Assessment of BRAC.* Dhaka: BRAC, 1988.

Wood, Geoffrey D., and Richard Palmer-Jones. *The Water Sellers: A Cooperative Venture by the Rural Poor.* West Hartford, Conn.: Kumarian Press, 1991.

World Bank. *Bangladesh, Promoting Higher Growth and Human Development: A World Bank Country Study.* Washington, D.C.: World Bank, 1987.

———. *World Development Report 1991, The Challenge of Development.* Oxford: Oxford University Press, 1991.

History of Donor Grants

Name of Donor	1972	1973	1974	1975
Oxfam (Oxford)	2,931,304	632,572	415,038	1,587,936
FRC	158,600	250,528	16,427	5,000
UNICEF	20,000	0	0	30,000
Save East Bangladesh	20,000	0	0	0
Oxfam (Canada)	0	0	966,945	217,674
Oxfam (America)	0	0	0	0
Interpares (Canada)	0	0	0	0
NOVIB	0	0	0	0
Community Aid Abroad	0	0	0	0
Ford Foundation*	0	0	0	0
Bread for the World	0	0	0	0
CARE	0	0	0	0
United Town Organisation	0	0	0	0
British Executive Service	0	0	0	0
Overseas Book Center (Canada)	0	0	0	0
EZE	0	0	0	0
Sybrand Balkema (Netherlands)	0	0	0	0
World Hunger	0	0	0	0
Swiss-CARITAS	0	0	0	0
SDC	0	0	0	0
Swedish Free Church Aid	0	0	0	0
Rotary (Netherlands)	0	0	0	0
UNCDF	0	0	0	0
SIDA	0	0	0	0
NORAD	0	0	0	0
Christian Aid	0	0	0	0
USCC	0	0	0	0
Private contribution	0	0	0	0
MCC	0	0	0	0
CIDA	0	0	0	0
NCOS	0	0	0	0
Netherlands Embassy	0	0	0	0
Netherlands Com. Voor Kinderpostzegets	0	0	0	0
DANIDA	0	0	0	0
ODA	0	0	0	0
Japan Embassy	0	0	0	0
TOTAL	3,129,904	883,100	1,398,410	1,840,610
Exchange rate US$ 1 = Taka	8	8	8	15

*Member of RDP-RCP Consortium
Source: BRAC accounting records

1976	1977	1978	1979	1980	1981
335,631	1,405,250	2,333,800	2,812,732	1,040,644	0
0	0	0	0	0	0
373,276	618,188	607,035	457,080	27,000	0
0	0	0	0	0	0
267,049	2,624,744	473,545	0	0	0
1,804,121	0	1,179,960	183,349	184,548	0
157,919	0	0	0	794,965	0
1,051,656	247,525	5,266,620	1,402,588	3,929,050	8,676,255
175,912	515,804	0	41,237	0	0
193,321	269,645	1,429,850	543,087	180,910	610,143
1,035,000	2,059,625	2,180,345	1,000,000	2,600,000	2,219,488
104,400	0	0	0	0	0
27,081	25,200	8,026	0	11,190	0
0	13,095	0	0	0	0
0	0	0	71,813	0	0
0	0	0	450,410	668,046	732,137
0	0	0	500	0	0
0	0	0	6,871	0	0
0	0	0	85,114	0	0
0	0	0	0	2,577,414	3,148,555
0	0	0	0	0	5,966,817
0	0	0	0	0	186,901
0	0	0	0	0	7,606,480
0	0	0	0	0	0
0	0	0	0	0	0
0	0	0	0	0	0
0	0	0	0	0	0
0	0	0	0	0	0
0	0	0	0	0	0
0	0	0	0	0	0
0	0	0	0	0	0
0	0	0	0	0	0
0	0	0	0	0	0
0	0	0	0	0	0
0	0	0	0	0	0
5,525,366	7,779,076	13,479,181	7,054,781	12,013,767	29,146,776
15	15	15	15	15	18

(Continued)

Appendix (cont.)

Name of Donor	1982	1983	1984	1985	1986
Oxfam (Oxford)	0	0	0	0	0
FRC	0	0	0	0	0
UNICEF	0	1,577,550	6,127,350	6,256,290	9,284,733
Save East Bangladesh	0	0	0	0	0
Oxfam (Canada)	0	0	0	0	0
Oxfam (America)	495,341	0	339,373	621,309	1,027,765
Interpares (Canada)	0	0	0	10,735,750	0
NOVIB	18,997,499	7,256,883	33,524,443	9,379,998	40,958,661
Community Aid Abroad	0	0	0	0	0
Ford Foundation*	347,864	370,136	621,860	4,241,346	0
Bread for the World	1,900,000	599,700	682,485	699,965	899,950
CARE	0	0	0	0	0
United Town Organisation	0	0	0	0	0
British Executive Service	0	0	0	0	0
Overseas Book Center (Canada)	0	0	0	0	0
EZE	885,767	2,541,715	5,066,266	7,076,945	17,309,198
Sybrand Balkema (Netherlands)	0	0	0	0	0
World Hunger	0	0	0	0	0
Swiss-CARITAS	0	0	0	0	0
SDC	9,085,784	178,545,926	4,705,114	12,786,562	33,328,996
Swedish Free Church Aid	7,600,422	0	0	0	0
Rotary (Netherlands)	0	0	0	0	0
UNCDF	12,707,949	7,254,996	1,071,610	0	0
SIDA	0	0	0	0	15,480,850
NORAD	0	0	0	0	1,000,000
Christian Aid	0	0	0	0	807,870
USCC	0	0	0	0	0
Private contribution	0	0	0	0	0
MCC	0	0	0	0	0
CIDA	0	0	0	0	0
NCOS	0	0	0	0	0
Netherlands Embassy	0	0	0	0	0
Netherlands Com. Voor Kinderpostzegets	0	0	0	0	0
DANIDA	0	0	0	0	0
ODA	0	0	0	0	0
Japan Embassy	0	0	0	0	0
TOTAL	52,020,626	37,146,906	52,138,501	51,798,165	120,098,023
Exchange rate US$ 1 = Taka	25	25	25	25	31

*Member of RDP-RCP Consortium
Source: BRAC accounting records

1987	1988	1989	1990	Total Taka	Total Dollar
0	0	—	13,494,907	449,830	
0	0	—	430,555	14,352	
13,270,667	33,251,919	42,177,872	35,770,256	149,849,216	4,994,974
0	0	0	—	20,000	667
0	0	0	—	4,549,957	151,685
1,511,201	3,635,977	4,000,206	632,691	15,615,841	520,528
7,447,140	3,929,038	1,291,131	2,068,872	26,424,815	880,827
65,567,334	60,766,191	114,898,461	144,083,210	516,006,374	17,200,212
0	0	0	—	732,953	24,432
3,059,046	0	20,825,954	3,559,870	36,253,032	1,208,434
61,400	234,980	0	—	16,172,938	539,098
0	0	0	—	104,400	3,480
0	0	0	—	71,497	2,383
0	0	0	—	13,095	437
0	0	0	—	71,813	2,394
40,661,675	21,306,203	26,415,504	25,232,865	148,346,731	4,994,891
0	0	0	—	500	17
0	0	0	—	6,871	229
0	0	0	—	85,114	2,837
13,234,000	18,200,000	39,000,000	11,942,997	165,555,348	5,518,512
0	0	0	—	46,177,666	1,539,256
0	0	0	—	186,901	6,230
0	0	0	—	28,641,035	954,701
10,791,300	18,681,550	50,726,133	55,072,733	150,752,606	5,025,007
5,060,000	6,597,056	13,043,478	30,000,000	55,700,534	1,856,684
0	0	0	0	807,870	26,929
894,000	2,329,000	1,435,000	1,263,550	5,921,550	197,385
440,000	0	0	0	440,000	14,667
0	0	4,811,050	—	4,811,050	160,368
0	0	2,990,000	—	2,990,000	99,667
0	0	3,767,079	—	3,767,079	125,569
0	0	400,000	—	400,000	13,333
0	0	1,822,055	—	1,822,055	60,735
0	0	0	78,736,140	78,736,140	2,624,538
0	0	0	126,773,638	126,773,6380	4,225,768
0	0	0	1,207,808	1,207,808	40,260
161,997,763	168,931,914	327,603,923	480,574,414	1,602,941,889	53,431,316
31	31	31	36		

Index

About the Author

CATHERINE LOVELL served as a consultant to BRAC during 1984–86, and wrote a number of articles and case studies about BRAC's work, including a UNICEF monograph about nonformal primary education written with Kanez Fatima, before embarking on this book.

In a long career devoted to humanitarian causes and the alleviation of poverty, Catherine's work included organizations such as the Vallejo (California) Public Housing Authority, the international division of the American Friends Service Committee in Philadelphia, and the Friends Committee on Legislation in Sacramento and Pasadena, California. She was vice-president of the Pacifica Foundation and manager for a time of one of its radio stations, early experiments in non-commercial, listener-sponsored radio.

Professor emeritus of the University of California, Riverside, Catherine Lovell graduated from the University of California, Berkeley, and earned a Ph.D. at the School of Public Administration at the University of Southern California. She consulted and did research for the U.S. government, the Brookings Institution, the National Science Foundation, and several state and local governments. She published in the areas of intergovernmental relations, productivity, financial management, and affirmative action, principally in *Public Administration Review, Publius,* and *The Urban Interest.*

IT IS WITH BOTH regret and honor that Kumarian Press publishes *Breaking the Cycle of Poverty: The BRAC Strategy.* Regret, because Catherine did not live to see this book into print; and honor, because she entrusted to us this story about an organization she cared very much about.

Krishna Sondhi, Publisher